BEAUTY
FOR ASHES

The Spirit of the Lord God is upon me;
because the Lord hath anointed me to preach
> *good tidings unto the meek;...*
to proclaim the acceptable year of the Lord,
and the day of vengeance of our God;
to comfort all that mourn;
to appoint unto them that mourn in Zion,
to give unto them beauty for ashes...

—Isaiah 61:1–3

BEAUTY FOR ASHES

Spiritual Reflections on the Attack on America

EDITED BY
JOHN FARINA

A Crossroad Book
The Crossroad Publishing Company
New York

The Crossroad Publishing Company
481 Eighth Avenue, Suite 1550
New York, NY 10001

Printed in the United States of America

ISBN 0-8245-1973-6

Library of Congress Control Number: 2001097402

1 2 3 4 5 6 7 8 9 10   10 09 08 07 08 05 04 03 02 01

To the citizens of the United States of America and victims of September 11

Our Father Who Art in Heaven
The Father is. There is no time for him.
His being is unchanging in heaven,
Beyond the events on earth.

Hallowed Be Thy Name
Where sanctity spreads,
Confusion leaves, and
Order returns. Because
The world that hallows thy name,
Rests in thine hand.

Thy Kingdom Come
It is part of the essence of the kingdom
That it needs to come,
That we cannot make it.
We must from the bottom of our hearts ask for it,
And praying we need to be prepared.

Thy Will Be Done on Earth As It Is in Heaven
If we cannot receive His holy body every day,
We nevertheless daily want to live on the word
That comes from His mouth.

*Forgive Us Our Trespasses As We Forgive Those
    Who Trespass Against Us*
Sin should ignite love and spread love:
This is the meaning of this prayer.

Lead Us Not into Temptation
Only the humility that your son taught us
Can block the power of the one who tempts us.

But Deliver Us from Evil
We want to pray most profoundly
for those whose prayer died in their hearts
under the violence of the moment.

*For Thine Is the Kingdom and the Power and the
    Glory Forever. Amen*
The prayer of the Lord contains the complete image
    of worldly order as a mirror of heavenly order.

Reinhold Schneider (b. 1903), *Meditations on the Our Father.* Schneider's poem
was secretly distributed among German soldiers during World War II. He was
charged with high treason by the Nazis but spared by the end of the war.

Contents

Acknowledgments   x

Sources   xi

Introduction   1

1. Our Father Who Art in Heaven,
   Hallowed Be Thy Name
   Solidarity in Times of Suffering   3

2. Thy Kingdom Come
   God's Kingdom and the Kingdoms of This World
   "Why?" from the Perspective of Politics
   and Religion   49

3. Thy Will Be Done on Earth As It Is in Heaven
   The Providence of God: How Could God
   Allow Such a Thing to Happen?   101

4. Give Us This Day Our Daily Bread
   How Should We Respond? Justice and Peace   152

5. Forgive Us Our Trespasses As We Forgive Those
   Who Trespass Against Us
   Forgiveness and Understanding   198

6. Lead Us Not into Temptation but Deliver Us
   from Evil
   Temptation and the Power of Evil   221

7. For Thine Is the Kingdom and the Power
   and the Glory, Forever. Amen.
   Healing and Hope   242

A Word from the Publisher   287

Index of Contributors   289

Acknowledgments

I would like to thank Gwendolin Herder for her suggestion that we find some way to respond to September 11, both to aid people in reflecting on the events and to provide victims with proceeds from the sale of this book. Many of the writers in this volume contributed their articles in the same spirit of generosity. To each of them I owe a special debt of thanks. Thanks also to John Eagleson, John Tintera, John Jones, Paul McMahon, Matthew Laughlin, Christine Phillips, and Kevin DiCamillo for their extraordinary efforts in producing this book.

Sources

All selections reprinted in this book are either in the public domain or have been used with the permission of their authors or copyright holders. We are most grateful for their gracious cooperation. At the request of individual contributors we are also including the following additional copyright information:

Introduction

After the atrocities of September 11, 2001, places of worship around the world filled with people seeking comfort and trying to find meaning in the face of staggering inhumanity. They were moved by compassion and solidarity to pray for the victims. They asked how God could allow such things. They thought of justice and considered how to respond to aggression. They dwelt on the nature of evil and feared its terror. They considered forgiveness. And they searched for healing and hope to enable them to continue living with dignity.

Religion was their resource. God would be entreated often for mercy and protection or he would be questioned and blamed for neglect. Many would ask whether he was there at all. Others would feel his presence most acutely in the realization of the great distance between God and this world.

In the following pages I have collected a broad range of reflections on September 11. Because this was a tragedy that affected us all, I have included many different voices: Christians, Jews, Muslims, Buddhists, and religious movements. There are statements from official bodies, from famous political leaders and pundits, from well-known theologians, and reactions from ordinary folks, whose names few will recognize.

Some of the responses are published for the first time

here; others have appeared elsewhere. To those responses, I have added a small number of statements from other ages. Throughout I have tried to let the many voices here gathered speak for themselves — in unison on issues such as solidarity and hope, in counterpart in probing why and in discussing how best to respond.

The reflections have been organized as a meditation on the Lord's Prayer. That prayer has been called by many commentators a perfect prayer, encompassing the full range of our needs and concerns.

In 1941 in war-torn France, a young women named Simone Weil wrote an essay on the Lord's Prayer. She noted that the prayer begins with the word "Father" and ends with "evil." In living that prayer, she said, we must move from confidence to fear, fear that humanity might be abandoned to its own resources in the presence of evil.

As sobering as that thought is, the tremendous out-pouring of good will that followed the disaster is reason to hope that such a fear will never come true. This book is a testimony to that hope.

1

Our Father Who Art in Heaven, Hallowed Be Thy Name

Solidarity in Times of Suffering

What Is an American? A Primer

Peter Ferrara, professor, George Mason University School of Law, senior fellow, Hudson Institute, September 25, 2001

You probably missed it in the rush of news last week, but there was actually a report that someone in Pakistan had published in a newspaper there an offer of a reward to anyone who killed an American, any American.

So I just thought I would write to let them know what an American is, so they would know when they found one.

An American is English ... or French, or Italian, Irish, German, Spanish, Polish, Russian, or Greek. An American may also be African, Indian, Chinese, Japanese, Australian, Iranian, Asian, or Arab, or Pakistani, or Afghan.

An American is Christian, or he could be Jewish, or Buddhist, or Muslim. In fact, there are more Muslims in America than in all the major cities of Afghanistan. The only difference is that in America they are free to worship as each of them chooses.

An American is also free to believe in no religion. For that he will answer only to God, not to the government, or to armed thugs claiming to speak for the government and for God.

An American is from the most prosperous land in the history of the world. The root of that prosperity can be found in the Declaration of Independence, which recognizes the God-given right of each man and woman to the pursuit of happiness.

An American is generous. Americans have helped out just about every other nation in the world in their time of need. When Afghanistan was overrun by the Soviet army twenty years ago, Americans came with arms and supplies to enable the people to win back their country. As of the morning of September 11, Americans had given more than any other nation to the poor in Afghanistan.

An American does not have to obey the mad ravings of ignorant, ungodly, cruel old men. American men will not be fooled into giving up their lives to kill innocent people so that these foolish old men may hold on to power. American women are free to show their beautiful faces to the world, as each of them chooses.

An American is free to criticize his government's officials when they are wrong, in his or her own opinion. Then he is free to replace them, by majority vote.

Americans welcome people from all lands, all cultures, all religions, because they are not afraid. They are not afraid that their history, their religion, their beliefs, will be overrun, or forgotten. That is because they know they are free to hold to their religion, their beliefs, their history, as each of them chooses.

And just as Americans welcome all, they enjoy the best

that everyone has to bring, from all over the world. The best science, the best technology, the best products, the best books, the best music, the best food, the best athletes.

Americans welcome the best, but they also welcome the least. The national symbol of America welcomes your tired and your poor, the wretched refuse of your teeming shores, the homeless, tempest tossed. These in fact are the people who built America. Many of them were working in the Twin Towers on the morning of September 11, earning a better life for their families.

So you can try to kill an American if you must. Hitler did. So did General Tojo and Stalin and Mao Tse-Tung, and every bloodthirsty tyrant in the history of the world.

But in doing so you would just be killing yourself. Because Americans are not a particular people from a particular place. They are the embodiment of the human spirit of freedom. Everyone who holds to that spirit, everywhere, is an American.

So look around you. You may find more Americans in your land than you thought were there. One day they will rise up and overthrow the old, ignorant, tired tyrants that trouble too many lands. Then those lands too will join the community of free and prosperous nations.

And America will welcome them.

Nous sommes tous Americains

Jean-Marie Colombani, *Le Monde*, September 12, 2001, translated by Mary-Alice Farina

In this tragic time when words seem unable to describe the shock we are feeling, the first thing that comes to mind is this: we are all Americans! We are all New Yorkers, just as surely as John Kennedy declared himself, in Berlin in 1963, a Berliner. How can we not feel, as in the most grave moments in history, profoundly connected to this people and this country, the United States, to which we are so close and to whom we owe our liberty, therefore our solidarity?

At the same time, how can we not be troubled by the fact that the new century has come? The day of September 11, 2001, marks the entry into a new era, which seems so far away from the promises and the hopes of another historic day, November 9, 1989 [the end of the Berlin Wall], and the somewhat euphoric Year 2000, which we thought could have ended with peace in the Middle East.

A new century is upon us, technologically advanced, as is demonstrated in the sophistication of war operations which struck all of the symbols of America: economic superpower in the heart of Manhattan, military power at the Pentagon, and finally protective power of the Middle East at Camp David. The reasoning behind it all is just as unintelligible. To hastily rally behind the popular cliché — the beginning of a war between the South and the North — is crediting the authors of this insanely murderous act with "good intentions" or with some project for which it was necessary to avenge oppressed people of their only oppressor, America. This is simply permitting them to claim "poverty" in inflicting harm to innocent people! What monstrous hypocrisy. Not one of these people who had a hand in this operation can pretend to act for the greater good of humanity. These people do not want a better, more just world. They simply want to cross our world off the list. . . .

But the reality could also be that of an America caught

up in its own cynicism: if bin Laden is indeed the mind behind the events of September 11, as the American authorities seem to think, how can we not remember that he himself was formed by the CIA, that he was one of the political elements believed to be a saving force against the Soviets? In this case, is it not America who created this monster?

In any case, America is going to change. Profoundly. The U.S. is like an ocean liner, gliding along for ages on the same path. And as soon as this path changes, it stays that way for a long time. The United States is going to suffer from a shock that is entirely without precedent. Not including earlier skirmishes on American soil, like the War of 1812 when the British Army destroyed the first White House, Pearl Harbor comes closest to resembling today. It was in 1941, far from the continent; there air bombers and a military fleet were under attack: the horror of Pearl Harbor is nothing compared to what has just happened. Then, twenty-four hundred servicemen were lost; today many more innocent civilians....

Despite their apparent murderous insanity, those responsible do in fact rely on a certain logic. It's obviously a barbarous one, a new nihilism that disgusts a great majority of those who believe in Islam, for whom their religion, like Christianity, does not authorize suicide — certainly not suicide coupled with the loss of innocent lives. It's about political logic as well. By resorting to extremes, many Muslims are being obligated to "choose their camp," against those who are currently being called "The Great Satan."

In the long run, this attitude is obviously suicidal. It will inevitably attract the wrath of many others. This situation calls our leaders to rise to the occasion, for we can reasonably say, with dread, that modern technology permits the attackers to go even further. Insanity, even in a hopeless setting, has never been a regenerating force. That is why, today, we are Americans.

Islamic World Shares America's Pain and Sorrow
By a staff writer of the *Arab News*, Jeddah, September 13, 2001

The Organization of the Islamic Conference yesterday strongly condemned as "brutal and criminal" the attacks on the United States that killed and wounded thousands of people.

OIC Secretary-General Abdelouhed Belkaziz, in a statement issued here, said he was "shocked and deeply saddened by the news of the attacks, which led to the death and injury of a large number of innocent Americans."

Extending condolences on behalf of Muslims all over the world to the U.S. government and the American people, Belkaziz said the Islamic world as a whole was sharing their "pain and sorrow in this terrible and devastating ordeal." He went on to say that OIC, which groups fifty-seven Muslim states, has always been firm in its condemnation of terrorist acts.

"All human values and norms and all divine religions — the foremost of which is Islam, which values human sanctity and forbids unjustified murder — have prohibited such brutal and criminal acts," Belkaziz said in the statement faxed to *Arab News*.

"Our tolerant Islamic religion highly values the sanctity

of human life and treats the willful killing of a single soul as tantamount to killing humanity," the statement added.

The six-nation Gulf Cooperation Council (GCC) also condemned yesterday Tuesday's attacks that targeted New York and Washington.

Secretary-General Jameel Al-Hujailan said in a statement in Riyadh that the GCC states have reaffirmed their condemnation of terrorism and all forms of extremism and violence, and expressed sympathy with the American people.

But Hujailan called on the U.S. and European media to exercise restraint by not making accusations without proof. "This may incite enmity and provocation against states and peoples who have no relation with such criminal acts, and who have always condemned it," Hujailan said.

Major Muslim groups around the world also condemned the killing of innocent people as against their religion. "To kill innocent men, women, and children is a horrible and hideous act of which no monotheistic religion approves," said the imam of Al-Azhar, Sheikh Muhammad Sayed Tantawi.

"Islam is a religion which rejects violence and bloodletting," Tantawi told Egypt's MENA news agency.

Kuwait Collects Blood. Kuwait yesterday launched a blood donation campaign for the victims of the attacks, the official KUNA news agency said.

The decision was taken at a meeting of Kuwait's National Security Council devoted to examining "all information pertaining to the terrorist attacks" and chaired by Crown Prince and Prime Minister Sheikh Saad Al-Abdallah Al-Sabah, KUNA said.

The campaign is designed to "help victims of these painful events and show sympathy with the friendly American people in this human catastrophe," the agency added.

Kuwait's parliament meanwhile condemned the attacks, calling them a "violation of humanity." Acting Speaker Mubarak Al-Khrainej said the Kuwaiti people were deeply sorry and offered their full sympathy to the families of those killed and injured.

Condolences from the Queen of England

The Queen has the following message to President George Bush of the United States of America after the tragic events of Tuesday, September 11, 2001:

It is with growing disbelief and total shock that I am learning of the terrorist outrages in New York and Washington today. On behalf of the British people, Mr. President, may I express my heartfelt sympathy to the very many bereaved and injured and our admiration for those who are now trying to cope with these unfolding tragedies. Our thoughts and prayers are with you all.

The Queen sent the following message to the memorial service for British victims of the tragedy in New York, held at St. Thomas Church, New York, on September 20, 2001:

You come together today at St. Thomas Church in New York united in sorrow by the terrible events of last week. Each and every one of us has been shocked and numbed by what we have witnessed on these recent days. But none of us should doubt the resilience and determination of this great and much loved city and its people.

Men and women from many nations, many faiths and many backgrounds were working together in downtown Manhattan when this unimaginable outrage overtook them all. At your service today we think especially of the British victims. For some of them, New York was simply a stopover on some busy travel schedule, for others it was a work place of excitement and opportunity, for many it was a familiar second home.

These are dark and harrowing times for families and friends of those who are missing or who suffered in the attack, many of you here today. My thoughts and prayers are with you all now and in the difficult days ahead. But nothing that can be said can begin to take away the anguish and pain of these moments; grief is the price we pay for love.

A Brazen Challenge to the Whole of Humanity

Statement by President Putin of Russia on the terrorist acts
in the U.S., Moscow, September 12, 2001, publication of the
Ministry of Foreign Affairs of the Russian Federation

The United States today faced an unprecedented act of aggression on the part of international terrorism.

First of all, I express sincere and profound condolences to all the victims and the families of the dead.

The event that occurred in the U.S. today goes beyond national borders. It is a brazen challenge to the whole of humanity, at least to civilized humanity. And what happened today is added proof of the relevance of the Russian proposal to pool the efforts of the international community in the struggle against terrorism, that plague of the twenty-first century.

Russia knows at first hand what terrorism is. So, we understand as well as anyone the feelings of the American people. Addressing the people of the United States on behalf of Russia I would like to say that we are with you, we entirely and fully share and experience your pain. We support you.

Palestinian Christians Grieve over U.S. Tragedy

Revd. Dr. Mitri Raheb, pastor of Christmas Lutheran Church – Bethlehem, and Dr. Nuha Khoury, International Center of Bethlehem, September 14, 2001

With deep sorrow and profound grief we write this message to offer our heartfelt condolences to the mothers, fathers, children, friends, and families of the thousands of innocent people who have been the victims of the terrorist attacks yesterday morning on the U.S.A. We would like to reach out to all of our American friends to assure them that we stand by them at this difficult and tragic time. Constantly, for the past eleven months, we have received many messages from our friends from America expressing their solidarity and sharing with us our grief. Never in our worst nightmares did we imagine that we would be witnessing such a horrendous event and human tragedy inflicted on our American friends. We care for every life, and we pray for all those who are mourning the loss of loved ones taken away by this indiscriminate act of organized terror.

Our thoughts and prayers are with you all.

We are aware that the media has shown President Arafat's shocked reaction to this act and his strong condemnation of it. Unfortunately, the media has also shown scenes of a few Palestinians celebrating this tragedy. We want you to know that these few do not speak for or represent the entire Palestinian people. What the media failed to acknowledge was the majority of Palestinians who were shocked, saddened, and mournful. We believe that this media campaign is biased and aims at dehumanizing the Palestinian people. Such a campaign follows the same logic of the terrorists, since it deliberately attempts to punish innocent people indiscriminately. In our grief, we are asking ourselves why did the people immediately associate us Palestinians with the perpetrators rather than the victims.

As Palestinians, we can very well understand the pain of our American friends. We know what it means when political leaders are targeted and are not safe in their own offices. We understand what it means when planes attack security headquarters. We know how it feels when the backbone of the economy is assaulted. We do not want to compare suffering, since every suffering is unique and this particular tragedy has such hideous dimensions. Yet, never before have Americans and Palestinians shared so much.

We express our solidarity with the American people. We invite people all over to:

> Hold vigil prayers for the victims and their families.

> Raise awareness and sensitivity to the brutality that the media perpetrates through the images projected.

> Monitor the way that certain nations and peoples are stereotyped (The Americans, The Palestinians, etc.), thus inciting hatred and legitimizing aggression.

Develop alternative media that will set new ethical standards in reporting.

Actively participate in the WCC's "Decade to Overcome Violence" so that future generations will have compassion, do justice, and value life.

Commit to prophet Micah's vision that "they shall sit every person under his vine and his fig tree and none shall make them afraid." So that no American, Palestinians, Iraqi, Israeli, Japanese, etc. will be afraid to be in his/her office, home, or airplane, no matter what nationality they hold.

May the peace of Christ be with us all.

A Call for International Cooperation
United Nations, condemnation of terrorist attacks in the
United States of America, September 12, 2001

The General Assembly,

Guided by the purposes and principles of the Charter of the United Nations,

1. Strongly condemns the heinous acts of terrorism which have caused enormous loss of human life, destruction and damage in the cities of New York, host city of the United Nations, Washington, D.C., and Pennsylvania;

2. Expresses its condolences and solidarity with the people and Government of the United States of America in these sad and tragic circumstances;

3. Urgently calls for international cooperation to bring to justice the perpetrators, organizers, and sponsors of the outrages of September 11, 2001;

4. Urgently calls for international cooperation to prevent and eradicate acts of terrorism, and stresses that those responsible for aiding, supporting, or harboring the perpetrators, organizers, and sponsors of such acts will be held accountable.

A Terrible Affront to Human Dignity
Pope John Paul II, general audience, September 12, 2001

I cannot begin this audience without expressing my profound sorrow at the terrorist attacks which yesterday brought death and destruction to America, causing thousands of victims and injuring countless people. To the President of the United States and to all American citizens I express my heartfelt sorrow. In the face of such unspeakable horror we cannot but be deeply disturbed. I add my voice to all the voices raised in these hours to express indignant condemnation, and I strongly reiterate that the ways of violence will never lead to genuine solutions to humanity's problems.

Yesterday was a dark day in the history of humanity, a terrible affront to human dignity. After receiving the news, I followed with intense concern the developing situation, with heartfelt prayers to the Lord. How is it possible to commit acts of such savage cruelty? The human heart has depths from which schemes of unheard-of ferocity sometimes emerge, capable of destroying in a moment the normal daily life of a people. But faith comes to our aid at these times when words seem to fail. Christ's word is the only one that can give a response to the questions which trouble our spirit. Even if the forces of darkness appear to prevail, those who believe in God know that evil and death do not have the final say. Christian hope is based on this truth; at this time our prayerful trust draws strength from it.

With deeply felt sympathy I address myself to the beloved people of the United States in this moment of distress and consternation, when the courage of so many men and women of good will is being sorely tested. In a special way I reach out to the families of the dead and the injured, and assure them of my spiritual closeness. I entrust to the mercy of the Most High the helpless victims of this tragedy, for whom I offered Mass this morning, invoking upon them eternal rest. May God give courage to the survivors; may he sustain the rescue-workers and the many volunteers who are presently making an enormous effort to cope with such an immense emergency. I ask you, dear brothers and sisters, to join me in prayer for them. Let us beg the Lord that the spiral of hatred and violence will not prevail. May the Blessed Virgin, Mother of Mercy, fill the hearts of all with wise thoughts and peaceful intentions.

Today, my heartfelt sympathy is with the American people, subjected yesterday to inhuman terrorist attacks which have taken the lives of thousands of innocent human beings and caused unspeakable sorrow in the hearts of all men and women of good will. Yesterday was indeed a dark day in our history, an appalling offense against peace, a terrible assault against human dignity.

I invite you all to join me in commending the victims of

this shocking tragedy to Almighty God's eternal love. Let us implore his comfort upon the injured, the families involved, all who are doing their utmost to rescue survivors and help those affected.

I ask God to grant the American people the strength and courage they need at this time of sorrow and trial.

Profound Participation in Grief

Address of the Holy Father to the new ambassador of the
United States of America to the Holy See, September 13, 2001

Mr. Ambassador,

I am pleased to accept the Letters of Credence appointing you Ambassador Extraordinary and Plenipotentiary of the United States of America to the Holy See. You are beginning your mission at a moment of immense tragedy for your country. At this time of national mourning for the victims of the terrorist attacks on Washington and New York, I wish to assure you personally of my profound participation in the grief of the American people and of my heartfelt prayers for the President and the civil authorities, for all involved in the rescue operations and in helping the survivors, and in a special way for the victims and their families. I pray that this inhuman act will awaken in the hearts of all the world's peoples a firm resolve to reject the ways of violence, to combat everything that sows hatred and division within the human family, and to work for the dawn of a new era of international cooperation inspired by the highest ideals of solidarity, justice, and peace.

In my recent meeting with President Bush I emphasized my deep esteem for the rich patrimony of human, religious, and moral values which have historically shaped the American character. I expressed the conviction that America's continued moral leadership in the world depends on her fidelity to her founding principles. Underlying your nation's commitment to freedom, self-determination, and equal opportunity are universal truths inherited from its religious roots. From these spring respect for the sanctity of life and the dignity of each human person made in the image and likeness of the Creator; shared responsibility for the common good; concern for the education of young people and for the future of society; and the need for wise stewardship of the natural resources so freely bestowed by a bounteous God. In facing the challenges of the future, America is called to cherish and live out the deepest values of her national heritage: solidarity and cooperation between peoples; respect for human rights; the justice that is the indispensable condition for authentic freedom and lasting peace.

In the century now opening before us, humanity has the opportunity to make great strides against some of its traditional enemies: poverty, disease, violence. As I said at the United Nations in 1995, it is within our grasp to see that a century of tears, the twentieth century, is followed in the twenty-first century by a "springtime of the human spirit." The possibilities before the human family are immense, although they are not always apparent in a world in which too many of our brothers and sisters are suffering from hunger, malnutrition, and the lack of access to medical care and to education, or are burdened by unjust government, armed conflict, forced displacement, and new forms of human bondage. In seizing the available opportunities, both vision and generosity are necessary, especially on the part of those who have been blessed with freedom, wealth, and an abundance of resources. The urgent ethical issues raised by the division between those who benefit from the globalization of the world economy and those who are excluded from those benefits call for new and creative responses on the part of the whole international community. Here I would emphasize again what I said in my recent meeting with President Bush, that the revolution of freedom in the world must be completed by a "revolution of opportunity" which will enable all the members of the human family to enjoy a dignified existence and to share in the benefits of a truly global development.

In this context, I cannot but mention, among so many disturbing situations throughout the world, the tragic violence which continues to affect the Middle East and which seriously jeopardizes the peace process begun in Madrid. Thanks also to the commitment of the United States, that process had given rise to hope in the hearts of all those who look to the Holy Land as a unique place of encounter and prayer between peoples. I am certain that your country will not hesitate to promote a realistic dialogue which will enable the parties involved to achieve security, justice, and peace, in full respect for human rights and international law.

Mr. Ambassador, the vision and the moral strength which America is being challenged to exercise at the beginning of a new century and in a rapidly changing world call for an acknowledgment of the spiritual roots of the crisis which the Western democracies are experiencing, a crisis characterized by the advance of a materialistic, utilitarian, and ultimately dehumanized worldview which is tragically detached from the moral foundations of Western civilization. In order to survive and prosper, democracy and its accompanying economic and political structures must be directed by a vision whose core is the God-given dignity and inalienable rights of every human being, from the moment of conception until natural death. When some lives, including those of the unborn, are subjected to the personal choices of others, no other value or right will long be guaranteed, and society will inevitably be governed by special interests and convenience. Freedom cannot be sustained in a cultural climate that measures human dignity in strictly utilitarian terms. Never has it been more urgent to reinvigorate the moral vision and resolve essential to maintaining a just and free society.

In this context my thoughts turn to America's young people, the hope of the nation. In my Pastoral Visits to the United States, and above all in my visit to Denver in 1993 for the celebration of World Youth Day, I was able personally to witness the reserves of generosity and good will present in the youth of your country. Young people are surely your nation's greatest treasure. That is why they urgently need an all-round education which will enable them to reject cynicism and selfishness and to grow into their full stature as informed, wise, and morally responsible members of the community. At the beginning of a new Millennium, young people must be given every opportunity to take up their role as "craftsmen of a new humanity, where brothers and sisters — members all of the same family — are able at last to live in peace" (*Message for the 2001 World Day of Peace*, 22).

Mr. Ambassador, as you begin your mission as your country's representative to the Holy See, I reiterate my hope that in facing the challenges of the present and future the American people will draw upon the deep spiritual and moral resources which have inspired and guided the nation's growth, and which remain the surest pledge of its greatness. I am confident that America's Catholic community, which has historically played a crucial role in the education of a responsible citizenry and in the relief of the poor, the sick, and the needy, will be actively present in the process of discerning the shape of your country's future course. Upon you and your family and all the American people I cordially invoke God's blessings of joy and peace.

We Are Not Afraid
Cardinal Edward Egan, archbishop of New York,
statement issued September 11, 2001

September 11, 2001, has been a day of tragedy here in the City of New York, in our nation's capital, and across the land. We here in New York have been dealing with this tragedy as best we could from 9:00 in the morning until now, when the skies are darkening and we have an opportunity to reflect on what has happened. These are what I hope and trust will be the reflections of the noble, courageous citizenry of New York City. First, we are not afraid. We are a courageous people living and working under the guidance and with the love of Divine Providence. Secondly, we remain at peace in the face of the tragedy that has beset us. Our peace is grounded in that confident trust in providence. Finally, we call for justice. We insist that those who have committed this crime be called before the courts of civilized people. We must not, however, allow our pursuit of justice to descend into sentiments of hate and retaliation.

Today I have witnessed the generosity and heroism of the police officers, firefighters, and health care professionals of the City of New York. They have been an inspiration to me, and I am confident they are that for all of my fellow New Yorkers.

To the families of those who have died we extend our heartfelt sympathy. They and their loved ones are in our thoughts and in our prayers. Likewise, all who are injured may be sure that we hold them in our hearts and look forward to their complete and speedy recovery.

To the President of these United States and his administration, to the Mayor of the City of New York and his administration, and to the Mayor of the City of Washington, D.C., and his administration, we offer our loyalty and promise our support at this difficult time. With the help of our God and united as free men and women under God, we wipe away our tears, roll up our sleeves, do what needs to be done, and look confidently to the future.

The Heavy Burden of Defending the Common Good

U.S. Council of Catholic Bishops to President Bush, September 19, 2001

Dear Mr. President:

In the aftermath of last week's terrorist attacks, I would like to reiterate that we stand in solidarity with you and the American people in prayer for our beloved nation at this time of terrible loss and momentous decisions.

The war-like acts of last Tuesday were appalling attacks not only against our nation but against all humanity. Our nation, in collaboration with others, has a moral right and a grave obligation to defend the common good against such terrorist attacks. Therefore, we support efforts by our nation and the global community to seek out and hold accountable, in accord with national and international law, those individuals, groups, and governments which are responsible. It is incumbent upon all citizens to recognize this common threat, and to be willing to make appropriate sacrifices in support of our nation's multifaceted and long-term effort to respond in a morally responsible way.

Your administration has been clear that a broad range of security, political, diplomatic, legal, and military measures will be necessary to stop this kind of terrorism and bring the perpetrators and their supporters to justice. While we must take into account the unique nature of this new kind of terrorist threat, any military response must be in accord with sound moral principles, notably the norms of the just war tradition such as probability of success, civilian immunity, and proportionality. Our nation must ensure that the grave obligation to protect innocent human life governs our nation's political and military decisions.

As we undertake the heavy burden of defending the common good, in morally appropriate ways, against global terrorism, we must not lose sight of the ultimate goal and responsibility of using our nation's considerable influence and power to contribute to a more just and peaceful world. Among other things, I hope our foreign policy will give new emphasis to deepening our engagement with the Arab and Muslim worlds and, in particular, will continue every effort to press for a just and peaceful resolution of the Israeli-Palestinian conflict.

I want to commend you for calling on Americans to repudiate acts of ethnic and religious intolerance. Arab-Americans and Muslims are not our enemies but are our brothers and sisters, part of our national family. Attacks on them are attacks on all of us. Your continued leadership in this area will be critical in the months ahead.

We pray that you will find just, wise, and effective ways to respond with resolve and restraint to the long-term task of ending terrorism, confident, in the words of Pope John Paul II, that Americans will not "give in to the temptation to hatred and violence, but [will] commit themselves to serving justice and peace."

> *Sincerely yours,*
> *Most Reverend Joseph A. Fiorenza, President,*
> *United States Council of Catholic Bishops*

Confront Every Evil
Canadian Catholic bishops to the bishops of the U.S., September 20, 2001

The Bishops of Canada in Plenary Assembly convey to you and all the Bishops of the United States of America our compassionate prayers and deepest condolences over the recent tragic events that have beset the citizens of your country.

We assure you of our common commitment to the solidarity which binds together the Church in both our nations and throughout our continent as we together search for justice in the face of the "terror of violence."

Terrorism, as the Post-Synodal Apostolic Exhortation *Ecclesia in America* goes on to note, is among those "social sins which cry to heaven because they generate violence [and] disrupt peace and harmony" (no. 56).

Prepared with you and all pastors and faithful to name and confront every evil that degrades human dignity, we reaffirm, as reiterated by *Ecclesia in America* (nn. 56, 57), that profound vision of respect and concern for life which is the only secure foundation for public order and true peace.

United in this difficult but compelling quest for justice and solidarity, we pledge the prayerful hopes and heartfelt collaboration of all the Church in Canada.

> *Gerald Wiesner, O.M.I., president,*
> *Canadian Conference of Catholic Bishops*

Our Nation's Darkest Day Was Their Finest Hour

Carl A. Anderson, supreme knight of the Knights of Columbus, address at St. Mary's Church, New Haven, Conn., September 14, 2001

President George W. Bush has proclaimed today a National Day of Prayer and Remembrance. In that spirit we have joined with our fellow citizens throughout the country to pray and reflect on our national tragedy.

We have prayed for those who have suffered great and disastrous loss. We have prayed for those who still await word of the fate of their loved ones. We have prayed for justice and for peace.

And now we resolve to stand together today and in the days ahead.

Unity, charity, fraternity, and patriotism. These are

the founding principles of the Knights of Columbus. They are the principles by which our founder, Father Michael J. McGivney, called together the first members of our organization in the basement of this church in 1881.

These principles guide us today as Knights and as citizens.

We are honored today by the attendance of His Honor the Mayor and of New Haven's finest and bravest. We thank them for their efforts.

And, through them, we thank their colleagues — the rescuers in New York and Washington.

They continue to bear eloquent witness to the truth that brings us together today — that good will triumph over evil.

The Knights of Columbus has long felt a special bond with our police and firefighters: James T. Mullen, our first supreme knight, was New Haven's fire commissioner during the 1880s — even while he served as supreme knight.

Another of my predecessors, John W. McDevitt, served as a police commissioner in New Haven in the late 1970s and early 1980s.

This tradition continues. Just weeks ago I signed the charter of a newly instituted council — 12911, St. Florian, Patron Saint of Firefighters and Paramedics — comprised entirely of Chicago firemen. Yesterday, on behalf of our 1.6 million members worldwide, I was honored to announce the creation of a $1 million "Knights of Columbus Heroes Fund" for the families of law enforcement officers, firefighters, and emergency medical personnel who lost their lives this week or may yet lose their lives in the days ahead at the World Trade Center.

We cannot but be awed by the knowledge that so many brave men and women gave their lives that others might live. Truly, our nation's darkest day was their finest hour.

Forty years ago, an American president — himself to be the victim of a cowardly act of terror — told the nation that we must bear the burden of a long twilight struggle for freedom.

Now we know that the twilight extends farther than we had come to believe.

Today is called a day of remembrance. We will never forget what we have seen this week. From this memory will come a new resolve. And from this resolve will come a new victory of good over evil.

Violence Knows No Boundaries
The Most Rev. Frank T. Griswold, presiding bishop,
Episcopal Church, USA, September 11, 2001

The events of this morning in New York City and Washington, D.C., make me keenly aware that violence knows no boundaries and that security is an illusion. To witness the collapse of the World Trade Center was to confront not only our vulnerability as a nation in spite of our power, but also the personal vulnerability of each of us to events and circumstances that overtake us. My heart goes out to those who have been killed or injured, and to their stunned and grieving families and friends.

Our President has vowed to hunt down and punish those who are responsible for these depraved and wicked acts. Many are speaking of revenge. Never has it been clearer to me than in this moment that people of faith, in virtue of the Gospel and the mission of the Church, are called to be about peace and the transformation of the human heart, beginning with our own. I am not immune to emotions of rage and revenge, but I know that acting on them only perpetuates the very violence I pray will be dissipated and overcome.

Last week I was in Dublin where I found myself convicted by the photograph of a young girl in Northern Ireland being taken to school amid taunts and expressions of hatred because she was Roman Catholic. I know the situation in Northern Ireland is complex, and that religion is a convenient way of ordering hatred and justifying violence, but the tears running down the little girl's terrified face spoke to me of all the violence we commit in word and deed against one another — sometimes in the name of our God whose passionate desire is for the well-being and flourishing of all.

Expressions of concern and prayer have poured into my office from many parts of the world, in some instances from people who themselves are deeply wounded by continuing violence and bloodshed. I pray that the events of today will invite us to see ourselves as a great nation not in terms of our power and wealth but measured by our ability to be in solidarity with others where violence has made its home and become a way of life.

Yes, those responsible must be found and punished for their evil and disregard for human life, but through the heart of this violence we are called to another way. May our response be to engage with all our hearts and minds and strength in God's project of transforming the world into a garden, a place of peace where swords can become plowshares and spears are changed into pruning hooks.

God Is Not Absent from Human Suffering

Message from Anglican archbishop of Sydney, Australia,
Rt. Rev. Dr. Peter Jensen, September 13, 2001

All the people of Sydney are welcome to pray with us for the United States in its present time of need. We are all stunned and horrified at the violent scenes from the U.S. that we watched on our TV screens through the night and this morning. Our hearts are overflowing with sympathy for the American people, especially those in New York and Washington, and above all for the families who are bereaved, and for those who are suffering and injured. It is a fearful tragedy.

We must pray for them, for President Bush and others in leadership positions in the U.S., and also for leaders of nations throughout the world, including our own. May they seek and find wisdom from the God who is the Creator, and sovereign Lord of the universe.

In such a time as this, when we may all be feeling a measure of fear and uncertainty, we should all turn to our God who is the Rock and the Comforter of those who put their trust in him. This is not the time for any racist attitudes that attribute blame to new communities in our midst, especially the Islamic people who have come to share their lives with us.

The violence that has occurred is an evidence of the evil that resides in this world. May we all turn for comfort to the loving and gracious God, who is not absent from human suffering, but who is present with us, waiting for us to call upon him for forgiveness, mercy, and love.

We may heed and read the words of Psalm 46:

God is our refuge and strength,
an ever present help in trouble.
Therefore we will not fear, though the earth
        give way....
The Lord Almighty is with us.

Look to the Word of God for Wisdom
Statement of National Association of Evangelicals, press release,
September 12, 2001

"We are deeply shocked and saddened by these terrorist attacks and call upon followers of Jesus Christ in this
country and around the world to pray and to reach out
with compassionate help," said Dr. Edward L. Foggs,
NAE's chairman of the board.

"The Scriptures call us to 'pray for those in authority'
so we urge prayer as well for President George W. Bush,
Vice President Richard Cheney, and our government
leaders through this national tragedy," he said.

Many people will look to churches, pastors, and people
of faith for guidance and help. The National Association
of Evangelicals encourages the denominations, churches,
and organizations affiliated with the NAE to look to the
Word of God for wisdom at this time and to be the people
of God in the midst of tragedy.

The National Association of Evangelicals is joining
with National Prayer Committee, National Day of Prayer,
and Mission America Coalition in sponsoring a full-page
advertisement in the newspaper *USA Today* on Friday,
September 14, calling for a "National Day of Mourning
and Prayer" on Sunday, September 16.

Over the next hours and days many are holding prayer

services, seeking to discern the situation, and will have the opportunity to express Christ's love and care to those who grieve or are in despair. We want to encourage all denominations and churches across the country to be sources of light and life.

At the same time, World Evangelical Fellowship, of which NAE is a member internationally, is calling for the prayers of Evangelicals throughout the world and seeking counsel from churches in other nations that have faced similar acts. This is sadly not the first time that churches have had to respond to acts of terrorism.

Hatred and Death Cannot Build the Kingdom of God

Michel Sabbah, Latin patriarch of Jerusalem, homily of the Mass for Peace and Remembrance of the Victims in the U.S.A., September 17, 2001

Brothers and sisters:

We are gathered this morning to pray, to come into the presence of God almighty and merciful, to pray for our brothers and sisters who died in the tragic events of this week, in the U.S.A. We are here with our own pains, with the pains of the American people and American Churches, with whom we are in a constant and fraternal relation in our quest of justice and peace in this land. To all of you, Americans here sharing in this prayer, we present our sincere condolences. With you, and with the people and the Church of America, we mourn the departed, we entrust them to the mercy of God. In the same time, we pray for the survivors, for the relatives and friends, and for the leaders of America, may God give them faith, hope, and strength to go on building their land, with their faith in God and love for their brothers and sisters in America and in the world.

In the first reading of today, from the book of Exodus, we read the following verses: "I shall make a great nation out of you" (Exod. 32:10). For that, Moses had prayed and asked the intercession of the Fathers: "Remember Abraham, Isaac, and Jacob." The greatness of the nation, for the Jewish people as for all peoples of the earth, will depend from the presence of those forefathers and their followers, the prophets and the saints, who had listened to the word of God, who had made it known to the people, and who, through the spirit of God Almighty and merciful, had prepared the peoples of the earth to become great nations. This is to say that the greatness of every nation will always rely upon the word of God, and from the capacity of the nation, leaders, and people, to listen to it and to be faithful to it. The nearer to God, to his greatness, the nearer to the true greatness in this world. Jesus had also said: "Be perfect as your Father in heaven is perfect." All progress and all greatness in this world can only be a sharing in the greatness and the perfection of God.

The question comes naturally to the mind: There are so many interpreters of the Word of God and they are often contradictory. Some find in the Word of God love and mercy, and some find death and hatred. Jesus had said: "Be perfect as Your Father in heaven is perfect." So our guide is God himself. Those interpreters who conform in their interpretation with the love and mercy of God, those we can trust and follow. Those who affirm attributes contrary to the very essence of God, as hatred and death and exclusion of other brothers and sisters, cannot be from God; they cannot work neither for God nor for the children of God; they cannot build the kingdom of God neither in this world nor in the world to come. Those who love, those for whom God is the source of their own love for others, these are the interpreters of the word of God.

This brings back the role of religion in our present world. It happened in history that religion has served to be a cause of wars. Today, too, religion is manipulated and God is prayed to overcome the enemy. In our country here, religion on both sides is having a big role in the conflict and in the cycle of violence. Religion cannot be a cause of wars. God is not the God of hatred and death. God is the God of all his children, whatever be their faith or nationality, and it is the role of all leaders to come out of their conformism to the political system of which they are a part, even to overcome a dominating vision in the crowds, to become the prophets for the building of the future. It is a common responsibility of all religious leaders to free themselves, not to remain obedient parts of the political system, in order to be the voice of God, not of men, the God of mercy, righteousness, and love for all.

World leaders, on their side, should make God more present in their own life and plans. They should know that progress of humankind cannot be done without God, without an education which allows the new generations to know God, as God of mercy, of righteousness and love. The religious vacuum in the present society should be filled with a true religious education, starting from the leaders to all the strata of the people in order to know God, and to know that he is the father of all. God cannot be a source of discrimination among his children. The present developed society should not leave God out of its plans: seeing God the human progress will follow more appropriate, better ways, and God will not remain a weapon in the hands of the poor to take revenge of the strong.

There will be always and everywhere oppositions and differences among religions, and religious views or positions. The same among peoples and nations and persons. But no one should remain enemy: neither seeing himself as enemy, nor seeing the other as enemy, to kill and to hate. Religion should educate all to see in the other a brother and sister to build together this world of God, as true children of God.

For that we pray, this morning, brothers and sisters, may God help us to find in our tragedies seeds of a new life, as was the Cross of our Lord Jesus Christ. The Cross led to the Resurrection because Jesus gave his life out of love for all, and because he forgave to those who were the cause of his death. Therefore, through love and forgiveness, death became the seeds of a new life. Amen.

Caught Up in the Agony
Statement from the Middle East Council of Churches, letter to the church in America, September 15, 2001

Dear friends, our brothers and sisters in Christ in the United States,

The grace of our Lord Jesus Christ, the Father's love and mercy, and solace of the Holy Spirit, the Comforter, surround and bear you up on this morning after the day of tragedy.

The world — we all — stopped, horrified. The massive scale of the violence particularly in New York but also in Washington has been beyond belief. Imagination cannot picture what may be its repercussions as anger yields to cries for vengeance. Almost instantly the images flooded out over the TV networks, horrific descriptions over our radios. Where we were first touched was in our human soul. We were caught up in the agony of individuals amplified manyfold. And words are not enough to describe this even though that is all that we have at the moment.

I wish to express to our friends in the United States our profound condolences for the loss of loved ones. In gathering after gathering in America, Christians will lift up their hearts in prayer. We assure you that we too are gathering, and our prayers join yours. We ask for healing beyond understanding, we pray for courage beyond our outrage and fear. We ask for the grace, the steadfast poise of faith, to stand with integrity and minister in an ever more dangerous world.

We are devastated by the bestiality that can infect ordinary human beings and transform them into mass murderers and deranged suicides. Evil raised its head. Its taunting must be resisted. Evil does not overcome evil; it augments it. Christ taught us that. The democratization of terror and violence on a massive scale points to a profound distortion in the human spirit of our times. And as those who bear the Gospel of Peace, it is this distortion we must overcome. With you we mourn the innocent dead; we bewail our own loss of innocence, our loss of confidence, our loss of a sense of security. And we do so out of a Middle East that has known more than its fair share of death, disillusionment, and fear over all-too-many decades. But with you too we are determined that death shall have no dominion. Your hope and our hope will not be crushed.

In the name of all the member churches of the Middle East Council of Churches, in the name of our presidents and staff, I stretch out to you our love and compassion in Christ's name and for his sake. We break one bread and are one Body. Holding to that reality with a firm grip, you will rise above this tragic moment and, with you, we too will rise. Let us together seek the healing of the nations, and overcome this and all evil with good.

In Christ's name and in his peace that passes understanding,

Rev. Dr. Riad Jarjour, general secretary
The Middle East Council of Churches

Nourish All We Hold in Common
Joint statement by U.K. religious leaders, Lambeth Palace, September 12, 2001

We and all people of good faith and good will — whatever their religious, ethnic, or racial background — are appalled by these terrible attacks on American cities. Such evil deeds have no place in the world we seek to build and share.

Our hearts go out to the people of America and all those who grieve and mourn. We pray for them and with them. We remember the dead, the bereaved, the injured, and the missing, and all those working to save life.

As Christian, Jewish, and Muslim religious leaders, we believe that it is vital amid so much anguish and suffering to nourish all that we hold in common and to resist all that would drive us apart.

We share a belief in God's compassionate love and a commitment to cherish and respect our common humanity.

We pray that at this time of tragedy, we may be worthy of that gift and that challenge.

This joint statement has been issued by:

> *The archbishop of Canterbury, Dr. George Carey*
> *Cardinal Cormac Murphy-O'Connor, Archbishop of*
> *Westminster*
> *Chief rabbi, Dr. Jonathan Sacks*
> *Dr. Zaki Badawi, principal of the Muslim College,*
> *and chairman of the Imams and Mosque Council*
> *of the United Kingdom*

And endorsed by:

> *Revd. Anthony Burnham, the Free Churches moderator*
> *Revd. Joel Edwards, general director of the Evangelical*
> *Alliance*
> *Revd. Christina Le Moignan, president of the Methodist*
> *Conference*

A Shameful Distortion of Justice

American Baptist Churches USA Interim General Secretary
Robert H. Roberts, September 11, 2001

I believe I speak for American Baptists and all people of good will when I express my profound grief and immeasurable sadness over the tragic events that have transpired this morning in New York City, Washington, D.C., and other parts of country. The Bible speaks of lamentations, and I deeply and profoundly lament the tragedy in our country today.

The enormity of these acts of violence is almost incomprehensible, and yet it lays bare the reality of how desperately some people seek to exact something that is a shameful distortion of justice.

We need to pray fervently today for the thousands who have suffered the loss or injury of loved ones. We pray for the caregivers, those who even now work to save those trapped and those who will need to provide ongoing care to those scarred in body and spirit. We pray that the hardened hearts of those responsible for — and supportive of — such acts be softened and reformed by the love that comes only from the God who cherishes and models reconciliation. We pray for swift justice, but a justice tempered by appropriate restraint. We pray for shalom — God's peace — in our broken world.

We pray that as Christians charged with the ministry of reconciliation we continue to work — now with renewed incentive — for the healing of this world. We call upon American Baptists to look to our Savior Jesus Christ as the model for all our thought and action in times of trial, and to work in His name toward that healing.

May the Spirit of Almighty God take this tragic day and set forth in its aftermath the miracle of redemption and renewal.

Reject Violence of Every Kind

U.K. Adventist statement on terrorist attacks,
Pastor Cecil Perry, president of the British Union Conference
of the Seventh-day Adventist Church, September 2001

The deadly attacks on the financial and military symbols of the United States of America, including the civilian population, have left us numb. It is shocking to know that wickedness could have reached such proportions. The British Union Conference of Seventh-day Adventists wishes to give its heartfelt sympathies to the hundreds of families who have lost loved ones in the triple tragedies, and to those others who have been physically and psychologically hurt. We reject violence of every kind and promote respect for human life. Wars and terrorism have no place in a civilized world.

We request our members to pray for America and the people who have become victims of such terrorist activities. Pray that God will let the rescuers find many more alive in the debris. Ask the God who cares to give the leaders wisdom to do what is right in these difficult circumstances. It is the Church's desire that hope in Christ's healing mercies will not elude the people of America. May many find comfort, and answers to the inexplicable, in God's promises to take full control of this world and vanquish the evil.

Incomprehensibly Tragic

Bishop Dr. Christian Krause, president of the Lutheran World Federation (LWF), and Rev. Dr. Ishmael Noko, general secretary, September 12, 2001

Dear brothers in Christ,

The events which occurred yesterday in New York, Washington, D.C., and elsewhere in the United States of America can only be described as catastrophic and incomprehensibly tragic.

Through you, we wish to express our most profound sympathy to the families of the victims and to the whole people of the United States of America in this moment of grief, uncertainty, and anger. Our prayers are with the many grievously injured, that they may recover from their wounds and trauma.

We pray that you and all church and religious leaders of your country will be strengthened for the pastoral responsibility that you must carry for consoling the bereaved, healing the traumatized, guiding the lost and confused, strengthening the faith and restoring the confidence of a shaken nation.

We also pray that God will give political courage and wisdom to the leaders of the United States as they consider their response to this unprecedented outrage. We pray that the traumatic experience of hatred will not lead to the spread of hatred and violence. We pray for peace.

May Jesus Christ, Lord of justice and mercy, comfort and accompany you and all the people of the United States of America in this time of trial.

They Have Twisted the Teachings of Islam
Muhammad Ali, as reported in the *New York Daily News*,
September 16, 2001

These radicals are doing things that God is against. Muslims do not believe in violence. If the culprits are Muslim, they have twisted the teachings of Islam. Whoever performed, or is behind, the terrorist attacks in the United States of America does not represent Islam. As an American Muslim, I want to express my deep sadness and anguish at the tremendous loss of life.

An Extraordinary Discussion

Jean Bethke Elshtain, Laura Spellman Rockefeller Professor of
Social and Political Ethics at the University of Chicago Divinity
School, October 3, 2001, from *Sightings,* a publication of the
Martin Marty Center, University of Chicago Divinity School

On Thursday, September 20, only hours before his speech
before Congress, President George W. Bush spent over an
hour talking and praying with a group of twenty some
leaders of America's diverse religious communities. I was
surprised and honored to be included in the meeting —
this despite the fact that I can by no means be described
as a leader of a particular religious community....

My hunch is that someone on the White House staff
decided that they needed a representative from one of
America's leading divinity schools, and chose me because I have in the past addressed the ethics of war and
war-making. I did not know most of those included. I
recognized Franklin Graham, son of Billy Graham, from
media sightings. I greeted Cardinal Bernard Law of Boston by name because he was, in fact, the one person I had
met in the past.

We gathered, as requested, at 12:15 p.m. at the north-
west appointments gate of the White House. We cleared
security, and were then ushered into the Eisenhower Executive Office Building across from the White House. There
we gathered together, greeted one another, and shared
expressions of peace and concern. I found it rather extraordinary that the single most ecumenical event I have
ever attended had been put together by the White House.
All Christian orientations were represented, as were members from the Orthodox, Jewish, Sikh, Hindu, Buddhist,
and Muslim communities.

We discussed a proposed statement — put together by a member of our group, not by the White House — for around forty minutes. A few of us made proposals for additions and corrections. These were accepted and the statement was signed by all of us. We offered up our prayers for the bereaved. We lifted up those who "selflessly gave their lives in an attempt to rescue others." We expressed our gratitude that "the President has spoken out early and clearly to denounce acts of bigotry and racism directed against Arabs, Muslims, and others in our midst. To yield to hate is to give victory to the terrorists." We called the attacks of September 11 acts against all of humanity — over sixty other countries lost citizens in the attacks — and we argued that there was a "grave obligation to do all we can to protect innocent human life" because "the common good has been threatened by these attacks." We called for a response that was just and peaceful — understanding, as many of us do, that the claims of justice and of peace must guide any reaction.

After our deliberations concluded, we were ushered to the Roosevelt Room of the White House. Chairs were arranged in a circle. There was no table. When the President entered the room, he greeted people he knew by name and asked us to be seated. When he noticed that the chairs on either side of him were empty — people giving the President some room — he gestured and said, "Come on in here. I feel lonely down here." People scooted in. The President then offered twenty to twenty-five minutes of reflection on the situation, indicating the need to steer a careful course between calling for Americans to be attentive but doing so in a way that doesn't instill fear in hearts already bestirred and stunned by what had happened. He indicated that he would oppose anyone who singled out those of the Muslim faith or Arab background for acts of vigilantism and bigotry as Islam, he stated, is a "religion that preaches peace," and those who had hijacked Islam to murder nearly seven thousand people did not represent Islam.

The President discussed the terrible day, going over some of the events as he experienced them, doing what so many Americans are doing in trying to come to grips with what happened. He told us that it is clear the White House was a target; that it was an "old building made of plaster and brick" and that had it been struck it would have been demolished and many people killed, "including my wife." (He paused and choked up at that thought.) The overall sense the President conveyed was that of a man who is horrified, saddened, clear about his Constitutional responsibility to protect the country and her citizens, determined to build an international coalition and not to go it alone, equally determined to respond in a way that is measured and not unlimited.

Following this gripping presentation, the President asked us to share concerns and thoughts. Some among the group lifted up particular Scriptural passages they found apt for our tragic circumstance. Others — the representatives of the Sikh, Hindu, Buddhist, and Muslim communities — brought their support and thanked the President for his words against bigotry.

Deciding this might be my only opportunity to offer advice to a President of the United States face-to-face, I indicated that I taught "political ethics," to which the President responded jocularly (as do most people when I tell them this), "Is there such a thing?" I replied that "I like to think so and I believe you are attempting to exemplify such in operation through this crisis." I then said that a President's role as "civic educator" has never been more important. That he must explain things to the American people; teach patience to an impatient people; the need to sacrifice to a people unused to sacrifice. The President indicated he was aware of this important responsibility, and it was clear that he had already given the civic education role some thought.

The entire meeting was unhurried, casual, thoughtful. As the President's aides began to gather in the room, it was clear the meeting—now well into its second hour—was about to end. One of our group asked, "Mr. President, what can we do for you?" He indicated that we could "pray for me, for our country, for my family." He believes in the efficacy of prayer and needs wisdom and guidance and grace, he said. A Greek orthodox archbishop was invited to lead us in prayer. We all joined hands in a prayer circle, including the President. It was a powerful and moving moment.

As the prayer ended and we began to rise, one among us began, haltingly, to sing "God Bless America," a distinctly unchauvinistic song that Americans have turned to over the past few weeks. We all began to join in, including the President. He then mingled, shook hands, and thanked us as we left.

All of us were aware we had participated in an extraordinary event. People shared addresses and business cards. We departed the White House to face a bank of cameras—always set up on the lawn. It began to rain softly. I stood next to my Sikh colleague and found myself gently patting him on the shoulder. I said, "I hope you don't mind my doing that." He said, "No, of course not. Please. I find it reassuring, very reassuring."

As I got into a taxi for the long ride to Baltimore-Washington International Airport, I realized that I had no desire to "spin" the event; to analyze it to bits; to engage in some sort of tight exegesis. Sometimes events just stand. They are what they are. If the President had simply wanted a public relations event, he would have done a quick photo-op (preferably the prayer circle scene, no doubt); cameras would have been whirring; we would have had a few well-timed and choreographed minutes. None of that happened. It was clear that the President wanted counsel; that he sought prayer; that he also hoped to reassure us that he understood the issues involved.

It was an afternoon I will not soon forget. I am grateful that I was able to join a group of my fellow citizens and members of our diverse religious communities, for an extraordinary discussion with the President of the United States.

Deny Them Their Victory
An interfaith response to terror, September 17, 2001

The signers include a broad spectrum of Protestant, Roman Catholic, and Orthodox Christians as well as Muslim and Jewish leaders. They include heads of denominational, national, and regional religious organizations and parachurch groups; local pastors and rabbis; and theologians and professors from across parts of the nation. The document was developed in consultation with Christian, Jewish, and Muslim clergy and circulated for signature by the Rev. Jim Wallis, Call to Renewal and Sojourners; Dr. Robert W. Edgar, National Council of Churches; the Rev. Wesley Granberg-Michaelson, Reformed Church of Amer-

*ica; Rabbi David Saperstein, Religious Action Center of Reform
Judaism; and Dr. Ron Sider, Evangelicals for Social Action.*

We, American religious leaders, share the broken hearts
of our fellow citizens. The worst terrorist attack in history that assaulted New York City, Washington, D.C.,
and Pennsylvania has been felt in every American community. Each life lost was of unique and sacred value in
the eyes of God, and the connections Americans feel to
those lives run very deep. In the face of such a cruel catastrophe, it is a time to look to God and to each other
for the strength we need and the response we will make.

We must dig deep to the roots of our faith for suste-
nance, solace, and wisdom.

First, we must find a word of consolation for the untold
pain and suffering of our people. Our congregations will
offer their practical and pastoral resources to bind up the
wounds of the nation. We can become safe places to weep
and secure places to begin rebuilding our shattered lives
and communities. Our houses of worship should become
public arenas for common prayer, community discussion,
eventual healing, and forgiveness.

Second, we offer a word of sober restraint as our nation discerns what its response will be. We share the
deep anger toward those who so callously and massively
destroy innocent lives, no matter what the grievances
or injustices invoked. In the name of God, we too demand that those responsible for these utterly evil acts be
found and brought to justice. Those culpable must not
escape accountability. But we must not, out of anger and
vengeance, indiscriminately retaliate in ways that bring
on even more loss of innocent life. We pray that President

Bush and members of Congress will seek the wisdom of God as they decide upon the appropriate response.

Third, we face deep and profound questions of what this attack on America will do to us as a nation. The terrorists have offered us a stark view of the world they would create, where the remedy to every human grievance and injustice is a resort to the random and cowardly violence of revenge — even against the most innocent.

Having taken thousands of our lives, attacked our national symbols, forced our political leaders to flee their chambers of governance, disrupted our work and families, and struck fear into the hearts of our children, the terrorists must feel victorious.

But we can deny them their victory by refusing to submit to a world created in their image. Terrorism inflicts not only death and destruction but also emotional oppression to further its aims. We must not allow this terror to drive us away from being the people God has called us to be. We assert the vision of community, tolerance, compassion, justice, and the sacredness of human life, which lies at the heart of all our religious traditions. America must be a safe place for all our citizens in all their diversity. It is especially important that our citizens who share national origins, ethnicity, or religion with whoever attacked us are, themselves, protected among us.

Our American illusion of invulnerability has been shattered. From now on, we will look at the world in a different way, and this attack on our life as a nation will become a test of our national character. Let us make the right choices in this crisis — to pray, act, and unite against the bitter fruits of division, hatred, and violence. Let us rededicate ourselves to global peace, human dignity, and the eradication of injustice that breeds rage and vengeance.

As we gather in our houses of worship, let us begin a process of seeking the healing and grace of God.

Deny Intolerance
American Jewish Committee, September 13, 2001

The catastrophic terror inflicted on American soil must not become an occasion for stereotyping or scapegoating.

Jewish history makes us painfully aware that, too often, times of crisis provide opportunities for expressions of bigotry.

An entire people or religion should never be implicated because of the heinous crimes committed by some of its members. We call on all Americans of good will to denounce any form of ethnic, racial, or religious intolerance and reaffirm the American spirit of pluralism and openness.

A Prayer for Clarity
Maharaji, Malibu, California, September 14, 2001

> In this hour of need, dear God
> Grant us your grace,
> Guide us from darkness to light
> From confusion to clarity
> From pain to joy
> From hate to love.
> Give us the strength to endure.
> Give us the courage to go on.
> Bless us with your kindness.

2

Thy Kingdom Come

God's Kingdom and the Kingdoms
of This World: "Why?" from the
Perspective of Politics and Religion

Captain Ahab in Pursuit of Moby Dick

Edward Said, *The Observer* (London), © Edward Said,
September 16, 2001

What is most depressing . . . is how little time is spent trying to understand America's role in the world, and its
direct involvement in the complex reality beyond the two
coasts that have for so long kept the rest of the world
extremely distant and virtually out of the average American's mind. You'd think that "America" was a sleeping
giant rather than a superpower almost constantly at war,
or in some sort of conflict, all over the Islamic domains.
Osama bin Laden's name and face have become so numb-
ingly familiar to Americans as in effect to obliterate any
history he and his shadowy followers might have had before they became stock symbols of everything loathsome
and hateful to the collective imagination. Inevitably, then,
collective passions are being funneled into a drive for
war that uncannily resembles Captain Ahab in pursuit

of Moby Dick, rather than what is going on, an imperial power injured at home for the first time, pursuing its interests systematically in what has become a suddenly reconfigured geography of conflict, without clear borders or visible actors. Manichaean symbols and apocalyptic scenarios are bandied about with future consequences and rhetorical restraint thrown to the winds.

Rational understanding of the situation is what is needed now, not more drum-beating. George Bush and his team clearly want the latter, not the former. Yet to most people in the Islamic and Arab worlds the official U.S. is synonymous with arrogant power, known for its sanctimoniously munificent support not only of Israel but of numerous repressive Arab regimes, and its inattentiveness even to the possibility of dialogue with secular movements and people who have real grievances. Anti-Americanism in this context is not based on a hatred of modernity or technology-envy: it is based on a narrative of concrete interventions and depredations, such as the Iraqi people's suffering under U.S.-imposed sanctions and U.S. support for the thirty-four-year-old Israeli occupation of Palestinian territories. Israel is now cynically exploiting the American catastrophe by intensifying its military occupation and oppression of the Palestinians. Political rhetoric in the U.S. has overridden these things by flinging about words like "terrorism" and "freedom" whereas, of course, such large abstractions have mostly hidden sordid material interests, the influence of the oil, defense and Zionist lobbies now consolidating their hold on the entire Middle East, and an age-old religious hostility to (and ignorance of) "Islam" that takes new forms every day.

Intellectual responsibility, however, requires a still more critical sense of the actuality. There has been terror of course, and nearly every struggling modern movement at some stage has relied on terror. This was as true of Mandela's ANC as it was of all the others, Zionism included. And yet bombing defenseless civilians with F-16s and helicopter gunships has the same structure and effect as more conventional nationalist terror. What is bad about all terror is when it is attached to religious and political abstractions and reductive myths that keep veering away from history and sense. This is where the secular consciousness has to try to make itself felt, whether in the U.S. or in the Middle East. No cause, no God, no abstract idea can justify the mass slaughter of innocents, most particularly when only a small group of people are in charge of such actions and feel themselves to represent the cause without having a real mandate to do so.

Besides, much as it has been quarrelled over by Muslims, there isn't a single Islam: there are Islams, just as there are Americas. This diversity is true of all traditions, religions, or nations even though some of their adherents have futilely tried to draw boundaries around themselves and pin their creeds down neatly. Yet history is far more complex and contradictory than to be represented by demagogues who are much less representative than either their followers or opponents claim. The trouble with religious or moral fundamentalists is that today their primitive ideas of revolution and resistance, including a willingness to kill and be killed, seem all too easily attached to technological sophistication and what appear to be gratifying acts of horrifying retaliation. The New York and Washington suicide bombers seem to have been middle-class, educated men, not poor refugees. Instead of getting a wise leadership that stresses education, mass mobilization, and patient organization in the service of a cause, the poor and the desperate are often conned into the magical thinking and quick bloody solutions that such appalling models provide, wrapped in lying religious claptrap.

On the other hand, immense military and economic power are no guarantee of wisdom or moral vision. Skeptical and humane voices have been largely unheard in the present crisis, as "America" girds itself for a long war to be fought somewhere out there, along with allies who have been pressed into service on very uncertain grounds and for imprecise ends. We need to step back from the imaginary thresholds that separate people from each other and reexamine the labels, reconsider the limited resources available, decide to share our fates with each other as cultures mostly have done, despite the bellicose cries and creeds. "Islam" and "the West" are simply inadequate as banners to follow blindly. Some will run behind them, but for future generations to condemn themselves to prolonged war and suffering without so much as a critical pause, without looking at interdependent histories of injustice and oppression, without trying for common emancipation and mutual enlightenment seems far more wilful than necessary. Demonization of the Other is not a sufficient basis for any kind of decent politics, certainly not now when the roots of terror in injustice can be addressed, and the terrorists isolated, deterred, or put out of business. It takes patience and education, but is more worth the investment than still greater levels of large-scale violence and suffering.

Their Violent and Cruel Nature
Ayatollah Khamenei, Iranian spiritual leader, as reported by the
IRNA in terhrantimes.com, October 9, 2001

TEHRAN — Leader of the Islamic Revolution Ayatollah Seyed Ali Khamenei on Monday condemned the U.S. military attacks on Afghanistan and its defenseless people.

In a meeting with Friday prayer leaders from throughout the country, the Leader rejected the U.S. justification for its fighting against terrorism and said that the main goal behind the military action is hegemonism and expansion of domination over other parts of the world.

This is a reality that although other countries might keep silent in the short run, they will not bow to the U.S. policy in the long run, the Leader said.

"The United States is going to set a model in the world by taking military action against one country under the pretext of arresting several suspects. There have been notorious terrorists in different parts of the world, but when had such an action been taken in the past?" the Leader questioned.

They (the U.S. officials) have accused several people of involvement in the terrorist attacks in the U.S., the Leader said, adding that they acted like a judge and have taken military action against a country to carry out the sentence they issued on the suspects. They also have exposed the Afghan people to missile attacks and bombardment, Ayatollah Khamenei said.

"The U.S. officials have unjustified expectations from world peoples and said that whoever is not with us, is with the terrorists. But the public opinion has reacted to these false and illogical words," the Leader said.

"The world community fairly condemned the terrorist attacks against the innocent people in the United States, but the Americans deal with the issue in a way as if no such an event has ever happened elsewhere in the world," Ayatollah Khamenei said.

The Leader recalled a series of terrorist events in Iran including downing of an Iranian passenger plane over the Persian Gulf by the U.S. warship USS *Vincennes* in 1988, explosion of the Islamic Republic Party headquarters in 1981 martyring seventy-two government officials and subsequent bomb blast at the presidential office martyring president Mohammad Rajaie and prime minister Mohammad Javad Bahonar.

"It is for several decades that the Palestinian people have become the target of the Zionist regime's terrorist attacks. In Lebanon too, the Lebanese people have been the target of the terrorist attacks. Why has the U.S. not shown any reaction in the face of the terrorist attacks? Now the question is whether the Muslim world has the right to put a question mark before the U.S. military action against Afghanistan," the Leader said.

The Leader blamed the U.S. and the Zionist regimes for the state of war in Afghanistan and the situation in occupied Palestine and said that the United States should explain to the world peoples under which authority it has waged a war on Afghanistan, targeting the Afghan people with missiles and bombs and forcing the Afghan people to flee their homes.

"Who knows what is happening to the Afghan people right now? Which Muslim can see the plight of the Afghan people and overcome his emotion? Is it possible that the current situation in Afghanistan will not entail any opposition to the American military action?" the Leader questioned.

"The American and British military action against the Afghan people indicate once again their violent and cruel nature. These governments do not regard a right for other nations to protest," he said.

It's Not All America's Fault
Hazem Saghiyeh, columnist for the Arabic newspaper *al Hayat*, London, *Time*, October 15, 2001

Millions of Arabs and Muslims hold U.S. foreign policy responsible for the calamity of September 11. Is it? The answer is: yes, but also no.

The yes has been widely articulated. Yes, there was and is a deep sense of frustration because of the bias shown by the U.S. to Israel and because of America's cruel insistence on continued sanctions against Iraq. Plus, for historical reasons, Muslims and Arabs can always feel bitterness toward America: in the early 1950s, the CIA helped topple the elected government of Iran to reinstall the Shah. In the late 1980s, the U.S. left Afghanistan very messy after using it as a battleground against the Soviets.

But there is a no here as well, which hasn't been voiced much in the Arab world. Certainly the international community has a responsibility to address the political grievances of Muslim societies, especially the Palestinian question, and try to reduce the poverty and inequality endemic in most of the Middle East. But no effort at redress by the West will work unless the Muslim world as a whole rethinks its relation to modernity. Why is it that Africa, though poor and more hurt by the West, did not create a terrorist phenomenon? Why did Latin America export its "purest" terrorist product, Carlos the Jackal, to the Middle East?

The reasons lie in the fact that we in the Muslim world have not been able to overcome the trauma caused by colonialism. We could not open up to the tools that modernity suggested, for the simple reason that they were introduced by way of colonialism. Our oil wealth allowed us to import the most expensive consumer commodities, but we could not overcome our suspicions of outside political and ideological goods: democracy, secularism, the state of law, the principle of rights and, above all, the concept of the nation-state, which was seen as a conspiracy to fragment our old empire.

A certain fixation on the past took hold alongside a deep uneasiness with the present. Religious reform did not take off. The Muhammad Abdu project to renew Islam the way Martin Luther reformed Christianity ended at the turn of the nineteenth century in disarray, opening the way to more extreme versions of religion. Efforts to modernize the Arab language and bridge the gap between the spoken vernaculars and the written classical did not materialize. Public spheres — such as a free press, trade unions, civil societies — for debating matters related to the common good were not established. And most important, Muslims and Arabs never resolved the question of political legitimacy. They failed to develop workable models, which has made every attempt at political change long and dangerous.

The question of legitimacy is flagrant in Iran, where

President Mohammed Khatami and his supporters won all the popular elections but could not win real power, which instead resides with Ayatullah Ali Khamenei. In Syria it seems there is no way out of Hafez Assad's authoritarian legacy. If Saddam Hussein finally falls from power in Iraq, heaven knows who might replace him, so ruthless has he been in suppressing rivals. Yasser Arafat's lack of a mandate has made him unable to make historic decisions in the peace process, so he instead alternates between directions.

The weak legitimacy of local regimes leaves the most essential themes of social and political destiny hanging, creating a vacuum to be filled only by populist politicians and extremist groups, by wars and civil wars. By failing to establish effective polities, we have perpetuated our impotence, making it all the harder to catch up with the West. Lebanon, the only pluralistic example in the Arab world, was destroyed by its own religious sects and its neighbors. Among the states in the area that don't work or barely do so are Iraq, Sudan, Pakistan, Algeria, and Lebanon.

Arab intellectuals, who ought to encourage change, have largely failed in that role. For the most part, they did not detach themselves from the tribal tradition of defending "our" causes in the face of the "enemy." Their priority has not been to criticize the incredible shortcomings that they live with. They tend ceaselessly to highlight their "oneness." Thus they help stereotype themselves before being stereotyped by any enemy. It is in this particular history and this particular culture, and not in any alleged clash of civilizations, that the roots of our wretched present lie.

What Stirred Such Hatred?

Drew Christiansen, S.J., senior fellow, Woodstock
Theological Center, Washington, D.C., September 27, 2001

"Why do they hate us?" What deeply held resentments could have led the nineteen hijackers to work a catastrophic wave of terrorism against the United States September 11? Why is there such bitterness in the Muslim world toward the United States? Why on learning of the collapse of the World Trade Center would refugee children dance in the street?

Ousting the Infidel from Arabia

If the question applies to Osama bin Laden, the alleged mastermind of the assaults on the World Trade Center and Pentagon, he has been quite open about his motives. The Saudi-born millionaire was exiled from his own country for his opposition to its royal government. His complaint? By permitting foreign, that is, U.S., troops on its soil, the government of King Fahd has defiled "the Holy Land" of Arabia, home to the most sacred Muslim shrines, Mecca and Medina. His aim? Departure of American forces from the Arabian peninsula and the Persian Gulf.

Bin Laden's desire to purify Saudi Arabia of the "infidel" presence is only the first step in his attempt to purge Arabia and the Muslim world of impurity. While the Saudi royal family adheres to a strict, traditionalist form of Islam, the Wahhabi sect, their observance is not strict enough for bin Laden. The extravagant lifestyles of the royals and the Saudi elite offends bin Laden's puritanical moral sense. Furthermore, the corruption resulting from the country's oil wealth — corruption which ironically gave bin Laden's family much of its own fortune — violates his sense of justice. He hopes to recapture the oil resources of the Arabian peninsula and the Mideast to serve Muslim interests and the Arab masses.

Behind the hatred of the terrorists lie the resentments of the multitudes. Those resentments have many sources, but what brings them to bear on the United States is the role, over the last half-century or so, of the United States in the Middle East and Central Asia.

The Great Game Today

In the nineteenth century, the European powers, especially the British and the Russians, competed for dominance in Central Asia and the Middle East in a struggle of diplomacy, espionage, and military adventures the "players" called "the Great Game." Since the end of World War II, the United States and before its collapse the Soviet Union carried out a similar struggle. It was hardball politics of the most unsavory kind.

In 1953, the CIA helped overthrow the elected government of Iran and placed the Shah on the Peacock Throne. When the Shah was overthrown in an Islamic revolution, the U.S. was named "the Great Satan." Later when the Islamic Republic of Iran was at war with Iraq, the U.S. supported Iraq, only to make it a pariah state after the Iraqi aggression against Kuwait. In Afghanistan, after a communist coup was defended by the Soviets, the U.S. supported Muslim *mujahidin,* among whom was Osama bin Laden, in a guerilla war to oust the Soviet invaders. In the ensuing civil war, the Taliban, the most ruthless and puritanical of the factions, won out to rule most of Afghanistan.

Religion and Dissent

In a region of autocratic governments where dissent is sel-
dom tolerated, whether by governments friendly to the
U.S. or hostile to it, religion is frequently the source of
moral and political renewal. In Islam, there has never been
the separation between religion and politics found, at various times in various ways, in the West. For both these
reasons, dissent and political opposition are frequently
nourished in the mosque. Religious leaders, like Iran's late
Ayatollah Khomeini or Sheik Ahmad Yassin of Hamas or
Sheik Omar Abdul Rahman of al-Gamaa-i Islamiya, read-
ily become the "spiritual leaders" of militant movements.

These militant movements see the U.S. as the adversary
because in the twenty-first-century version of "the Great
Game," the U.S. government has supported and still supports the autocratic governments they oppose. In the case
of the oil states of Arabia and the Gulf, it is U.S. military
forces which help keep the rulers in power. Then there is
U.S. support of Israel, which in Arab eyes has for three
generations stood in the way of an equitable settlement
of the Palestinian question.

Moral Renewal: Islam and the West

Much of the power of Islam as a political force in countries where neither opposition or dissent is permitted
comes from the feeling that what their countries need
most is moral renewal. That moral revitalization sometimes comes nonviolently, but we do not hear about it,
because it does not make for headlines. What captures
our attention is the more militant forms of political Islam,
like the Taliban, Hezbollah, and Islamic Jihad.

The militants and the masses share another motive for hostility to the U.S. Their societies are largely traditional, and often their conception of moral renewal is concerned with preserving or retrieving traditional Muslim and Arab culture. Devout Muslims are particularly offended by the excesses of Western materialism: the commercialism, sensuality, and hyperindividualism celebrated by Hollywood and broadcast by U.S. media around the world. For such reformers the U.S. represents the epitome of modernity, and so the source of all that threatens their traditional or idealized way of life.

It is overstated to say all these reformers reject the best American values: freedom, human rights, and democracy. The progress of once-revolutionary Iran toward democracy shows that. Muslims are looking for their own modus vivendi with modernity. Given the chance, they elect democratic reformers. In time, they evolve their own ways of being Muslim and modern.

Rejection of the material culture of the West does not amount to a "clash of civilizations," as Sam Huntington styles it. The West has its own internal religious and social critics who lament the abuse of freedom in immoral behavior. Pope John Paul II has repeatedly criticized the immorality of "hyperdevelopment," warned against the temptations of consumerism, and opposed "the culture of death." Evangelical preachers and social conservatives, likewise, inveigh against moral decline in the U.S. For both East and West, the issue is where to draw the line between liberty and license. They may set the balance point differently, but each is struggling with how to establish what the late John Courtney Murray and political philosopher Clinton Rossiter called "ordered liberty," that is, a society that is both free and morally responsible.

Extremists, like the Taliban, of course, are opposed to any balance. Virtue, as they dictate it, is the goal of their version of Islam. No compromise is permitted. Such religious revolutionaries are doomed to failure. In our own time, we have seen their secular counterparts, the Maoists in China and the Khmer Rouge in Cambodia, rise and fall because they had no positive vision to offer, only the harsh discipline of the sword. Such political puritans end up devouring their own people, exactly as the Taliban has done in Afghanistan. If the human price were not so high, the pattern of self-destruction of such puritanical regimes suggests that containment may be a preferable strategy to war or political overthrow. But as we are becoming aware, prescinding from the prospect of war, the Afghan people have already paid a cruel price for Taliban's rule.

Overcoming Resentment

Already the Bush administration seems to have learned that to prevent terrorism in the future the United States must address the resentments others have toward us. Remarkably, they have begun with what one would have thought to be the most intractable problem of them all, the Israeli-Palestinian conflict. They have pressed the two sides to return to the negotiating table and made clear for the first time that the cornerstone of any resolution must be a viable Palestinian state. If it is possible to tackle that century-long dispute head on, who is to say ways will not be found to respond to other grievances too?

This country is already doing a quick course in Islam. At some point, it will not be enough simply to say Islam does not condone terrorism. It will become possible to understand Islam as a vehicle for political expression in autocratic societies, to appreciate and support efforts at moral renewal amid corrupt systems, and to find a people's moral compass in freedom.

Of course, some problems, like the fractiousness of the Afghan tribes, may endure for centuries. All that can be done is contain them. The worst forms of extremism, like bin Laden's al Qaeda movement, will still require tough policing, keen intelligence, and precise military action in the short run. In the long run, however, the best hope for ending terrorism is to drain the swamp of resentment from which terrorism takes its rise. That will require understanding the discontents of the people and assisting them where we can in solving their own problems in their own ways.

They Hate Us for a Reason
Michael Novak, George F. Jewett Scholar at the American Enterprise Institute, September 25, 2001

I was in Bratislava, Slovakia, about to give a lecture when news of the bombing of the Twin Towers was brought to the lectern. In the days that followed, my friends and I were deeply touched by the tears, sympathy, and signs of solidarity we saw all around us. Weekend football (soccer) games were canceled; a three-minute silence was observed Friday morning just before noon; in Prague, vigil lights and flowers were strewn on Wenceslaus Square, as they had been some decades before in honor of the fallen Jan Palluch; ecumenical prayer services were held in St. Vitus

Cathedral, in the presence of President Havel and the U.S. ambassador.

It was a little harder, in Europe, to get the news. Basically, we had CNN and, in the morning, the *International Herald Tribune*. I found myself playing Sherlock Holmes, detail by detail, to try to arrive by inductive logic at a picture of the whole.

I figured two things out soon enough. First, the "root cause" of terrorism is not poverty. The biographies of the perpetrators, like those of the Students [*Taliban*] of Afghanistan, show that they are from middle-class elites, educated, schooled, technically adept.

Second, their governing ideology is a lethal and perverse mixture of political nihilism — *destroy, destroy, destroy* — with a patina of stray snippets of Muslim religiosity. Terror does not spring from the essence of Islam, which it in fact contradicts. Instead, it gathers together, in one lethal poison, every text and historical incident of Muslim history that encourages both death to infidels and military adventurism.

"Islam has never in history taken over a nation by voluntary conversion," reads the terrorists' manual prepared by Osama bin Laden, "but only by war." That manual (which I cite by oral memory, only having heard it read aloud) calls for asymmetrical war — a war not by armies arrayed, but by sneaky acts of terror — against the leading powers of the West.

The impulse of this war, I infer, is not religious, but political. Unlike the wars of the twentieth century, its goal is not even rhetorically "progressive." Its goal is not to correct or improve the West. Its goal is not even to make the Islamic nations more democratic or prosperous or innovative. Its goal is to remove the goad that the existence of the West — proactively democratic, proactively urging nations to economic development — has presented to Muslim elites.

Radical elites cannot stand that goad. It causes them unendurable torment. It places them in a psychologically unbearable position.

Radical elites in the Middle East have given up on the dream of building progressive societies by their own devices. They cannot abide by the demands of democratic living. Their socialist, anti-capitalist tradition blocks them from even considering economic development based upon private property, enterprise, innovation, and discovery. The ideal of the equality of women and men profoundly disturbs their inner peace. The practices of open dissent, loyal opposition, negotiation, compromise, ambiguity in practice, and diversity of religious worship and belief seem to them socially destructive.

Therefore, the ordinary daily practices of the West fill the souls of these radicals both with powerful inner attractions, to which they cannot admit, and with deep feelings of fear, terror, and revulsion. If Western ways triumph, their psyche, which is rooted in an altogether different reality, comes under threat of extinction. If international progress prevails, they will break apart inwardly under its pressure, disintegrate, evaporate into nothingness. There is, they think, no place for them in a world of progress, international style.

The Taliban "government" is not, in fact, building up the infrastructure of Afghanistan, laying out new roads, or even keeping existing roads in repair. It is not building schools, clinics, or economic centers. It has no plans for progress of any kind. The Taliban is not a government at all, but a military-security force rooted in religio-political ideology, not ethnic cohesion. Its leadership and many of its crack cadres are disproportionately Arab, not Afghan.

The Taliban ideal is to enforce an abstract idea — an academic's idea — of the simple life of yesteryear, in an Arab rather than an Afghani style. Its first emphasis is to keep women covered and uneducated and out of the schools — as if they do not exist in public life at all. It imposes the discipline not of the mountains but of the desert, not of history but of abstract ideals. (The Buddhist monumental carvings had endured for centuries, only now to be condemned by a new set of standards.) Born from warlike resistance to atheistic Communist invasion, the Taliban turned to hating the outside world.

If I understand correctly, the Taliban are profoundly hated throughout Afghanistan, nearly as much as the Soviets were hated. That is one reason I suspect that the bombing of the World Trade Center was on a changeable time line, awaiting the assassination of the main political and military threat to the Taliban, the Panther of Panjshir: General Massoud, the Invincible, whose lightly armed but undefeated troops had been forced by the superior Taliban arms to retreat into the mountains of the northeast. Only after the assassins, disguised as Belgian journalists, managed to deceive Massoud and complete their dirty work was the signal given for the operation in New York and Washington — or so I imagine. If the New York bombings went first, Massoud would have been on guard. Without Massoud, domestic opposition to the Taliban is relatively leaderless.

A very large section of the educated middle class in

Middle Eastern countries, unlike the Taliban and the terrorists, has not given up on the dream of economic progress — progress in literacy, schooling, and medical care, among other things — in their region. Many see in Islam resources for empowering economic growth. Of itself, Islam is more powerfully anti-socialist than it is anti-property, anti-market, or anti-innovation. Islam once inspired a great civilization that far outshone the Christian West (then submerged by barbarian invasions) in wealth, commerce, architecture, and the fine arts. This period of Islamic preeminence lasted from about the eleventh through the fourteenth centuries. Its civilizing effects remain still a powerful social memory. That is why the rough barbarism and political nihilism of today's terrorists repulse and embarrass many. Bin Laden's is not the face of Islam that they love and cherish. And they would love to be free from the very real threat of terror in their own midst.

For the truth is that nearly every traditional institution of the Middle East is now under threat from the terrorists. It is quite difficult for Islamic scholars and clergy to condemn the terror outright, or to point out that it is a perfidious perversion of Islam. They do not want to be kneecapped, or to have their children kidnapped on the streets. (This is true even in such cities as London and Paris.) Only when there is a huge social convulsion against the terrorists, a thorough effort by all international and national institutions to make war on terrorism, will more and more middle-class Muslims resolve to join in. They will be grateful for liberation from the daily fear they now experience. But they cannot move to insist upon it until they feel they have a reasonable chance of success.

Many Americans have also been ready to go on "suicide missions" in the name of their country, following the flag, as the boys at Utah Beach did, or as the men of New York's Fire Department did who climbed the Towers floor by floor to their death. So too did the bomber pilots flying into nearly solid walls of flak over German industrial centers in World War II. We Americans, too, are willing to die for our fellows and to call upon God as we fall.

The terrorists' vision of the malevolent role of the United States in the world must have been reinforced, or at least comforted, by the violent anti-globalization rhetoric and actions in Seattle, Prague, and Genoa.

I find it quite easy to sympathize with the equanimity of Muslim terrorists facing certain death. What I do not find quite credible is the view that their motivation is chiefly religious, or that their comfort is a vision of paradise for "martyrs." The evidence seems to show a predominant will to *destroy,* and to *rejoice* in the humiliation of those destroyed. One would not have to be a Muslim to share in this will. Islamic faith has nothing essential to contribute to it, and much with which to redirect it.

Among our journalists (and law professors) we seem to find a disproportionate number who might be described as secular fundamentalists. They never met a religion they didn't dislike; their understanding of religion is practically zero. They take any conviction for which people are willing to die to be a kind of "fanaticism." "Martyrdom" is not on their charts. The prospect of "paradise" after death makes them nervous. Not understanding such terrain, they too easily display their own gullibility, unable to make crucial distinctions.

The motivation of the terrorists was not essentially religious, but only given a religious cover to serve political purposes — to incite a larger Islamic vs. Western war. They were trying to *use* Islam for their own destructive purposes. They were not trying to make Islam become better, greater, more beautiful, an ornament to the human race. Their aim was to destroy the United States and its friends.

The terrorists imagine the United States to be an enemy of their own souls. To give their lives to destroy that enemy is a way of relieving the unbearable inner pressure they feel.

I don't doubt that they in part enjoyed their time in the United States, and in other Western countries, and admired the free society even while they also loathed and plotted to humiliate it. Sitting around a swimming pool in Florida, having a drink in a bar, going easily where they wished, being accepted and respected by colleagues and friends — all this could not have been entirely unpleasant to them, or wholly irksome. Being human, they are not immune to the vision of the natural rights of all human beings. Yet they could easily think of an America they hated.

That very inner division of soul made living in peace with themselves intolerable. In a flaming act of destruction, they brought themselves psychological rest.

To be perfectly clear about this inner division, let me distinguish its two phases. First, America represents an intolerable goad to progress, political and economic, in human rights and in innovation, demanding constant change, the rule of law, equality between the sexes, and pluralism of worship. When elites, or a portion of the elites, give up on the possibility of realizing these goals in national life, they do not cease feeling these restless imperatives in their own hearts. One solution to the inner contradiction is to destroy the source of that unrest — to display before one's astounded soul that the United States is helpless and contemptible.

Second, even for one who begins to believe that the condition of the poor in the Middle East and elsewhere can be improved — and that justice and due process can be brought back to political life, with an end to secret police and repression and rule by political favor — the pressure of modern ideals (lifting up the poor, the protection of human rights) entails so much *psychological change,* such a radical reconstruction of both the existing outer world and the personal inner world, that as far as the eye can see there will be only turmoil and strife, inhuman efforts, and a high probability of failure. Wouldn't it be easier *not* to go forward into the twenty-first century? Wouldn't it be easier to *restore* the calmer, quieter world of the twelfth or thirteenth century?

There was a time when Arab culture was happy and at peace with itself, without invidious comparison with others, without the imperative to become what it is not — when one could eat, drink, and be merry; worship, pray, and know inner peace; and dwell in peace and happiness in home and harem. The soul that is asked to become modern (even postmodern) *suddenly, today,* can recall (or thinks it can recall) a far happier and better world than today's. Certainly, people were far poorer. But poverty is not mutually exclusive with happiness; on the contrary, wealth brings cares and unhappiness. The inner soul longs for the world of the twelfth century. It cannot bear the tensions of the twenty-first.

In a word, the imperative of progress injures the souls of the less-developed world, especially the souls of educated elites. That imperative introduces an at times unbearable tension into the soul.

Worse still, this imperative has a single, symbolic source.

Among its symbols yet to be destroyed are the Statue of Liberty, the U.S. Capitol, the White House, the John Hancock Building in Boston, the Sears Tower in Chicago, the Golden Gate Bridge in San Francisco, and others.

To protect their own egos from dissolution, certain souls today see no choice but to destroy these symbols, and to render what they stand for contemptible. They do not die for Islam, which of itself condemns what they do; they die to save their own humiliated egos.

What Became of Tolerance in Islam?

Khaled Abou El Fadl, professor, UCLA Law School,
Los Angeles Times, September 14, 2001

Extreme acts of violence and evil such as the recent terrorist attacks test the mettle and moral depth of societies — the society that is targeted by the violence and the society that generated it.

The Japanese stealth attack on Pearl Harbor tested both the aggressor and the victim. Pearl Harbor challenged the moral integrity of Japanese normative values, but it also tested us. We responded to an extreme act of aggression with another extreme act: We interned our Japanese citizens in concentration camps, resulting in deep fissures in our constitutional and civil rights fabric.

We do not have a good record when responding to aggression. As a society, we tend to vent our anger and hurt at our own citizens and then spend decades expressing regret and talking about lessons learned. Considering the scale of what has been called the second Pearl Harbor, I fear that there will be an explosion of hate crimes against Muslim and Arab Americans, both by police and by ordinary citizens. Anticipating the backlash, Muslim and Arab organizations have rushed to issue condemnations of terrorism and hate-motivated violence and have gone to pains to explain that terrorists who happen to be Muslim do not represent Muslims at large, Islam, or anyone else.

Nevertheless, the recent terrorist attacks mandate a serious introspective pause. As Americans, we should reflect on our own Middle East policies and the arrogance by which we deal with the dark-skinned people we collectively refer to as Arabs. Muslims, American and otherwise, should reflect on the state of their culture and the state of the Islamic civilization.

As a Muslim, I feel that the horror of recent terrorist attacks demands a serious, conscientious pause. Terrorism is an aberration, but most often it is of a particular type, an extreme manifestation of underlying social and ideological currents prevalent in a particular culture. Terrorism is not a virus that suddenly infects the brain of a person; rather, it is the result of long-standing and cumulative cultural and rhetorical dynamics.

In Islamic law, terrorism (*hirabah*) is considered cowardly, predatory, and a grand sin punishable by death. Classical Islamic law explicitly prohibits the taking or slaying of hostages or diplomats even in retaliation against unlawful acts by the enemy. Furthermore, it prohibits stealth or indiscriminate attacks against enemies, Muslim or non-Muslim. One can even say that classical jurists considered such acts to be contrary to the ethics of Arab chivalry and therefore fundamentally cowardly.

It would be disingenuous, however, to propose that this classical attitude is predominant or even that familiar in modern Arab-Muslim culture. I like many other Muslims grew up with an unhealthy dose of highly opportunistic and belligerent rhetoric, not only in the official media but also at popular cultural venues such as local mosques. Even in the U.S., it is not unusual to hear irresponsible and unethical rhetoric repeated in local Islamic centers or Muslim student organizations at universities. It is disheartening to hear contemporary Arab news agencies, for example, refer to acts of terrorism in neutral terms such as guerrilla attacks (*amal fida'i*) and to suicide bombers as martyrs (*shuhada*).

All of this begs the question: What happened to the civilization that produced such tolerance, knowledge, and beauty throughout its history? A lot has happened. The Islamic civilization has been wiped out by an aggressive and racist European civilization. Colonialism and the expulsion of Palestinians happened. Numerous massacres against and by Muslims happened. Despotic and exploitative regimes have taken power in nearly every Muslim country. Most important, however, a dogmatic, puritanical, and ethically oblivious form of Islam has predominated since the 1970s. This brand of Islamic theology is largely dismissive of the classical juristic tradition and of any notion of universal and innate moral values. This orientation insists that only the mechanics and technicalities of Islamic law define morality. Paradoxically, it also rejects the classical juristic tradition and insists on a literal reinterpretation of all Islamic texts.

Fundamentally, this puritanical theology responds to feelings of powerlessness and defeat with uncompromising symbolic displays of power, not only against non-Muslims but also against Muslim women. It is not accidental that this puritanical orientation is the most virulent in flexing its muscles against women and that it is plagued by erotic fantasies of virgins in heaven submissively catering to the whim and desire of men.

This contemporary orientation is anchored in profound feelings of defeatism, alienation, frustration, and arrogance. It is a theology that is alienated not only from the institutions of power in the modern world but also from its own heritage and tradition.

The extreme form of this puritanical Islam does not represent most Muslims today. But there are two ways in which contemporary Muslim culture, Arab or non-Arab, inadvertently feeds these extreme trends. First, since the fall of the Ottoman Empire and the onslaught of colonialism, Islamic intellectuals have busied themselves with the task of "defending Islam" by rampant apologetics. This produced a culture that eschews self-critical and introspective insight and embraces projection of blame and a fantasy-like level of confidence and arrogance. Second, Muslims got into the habit of paying homage to the presumed superiority of the Islamic tradition but marginalize this idealistic image in everyday life.

Muslim intellectuals justified hijacking airplanes and taking hostages. Terrorist attacks such as the 1976 Entebbe operation or the 1972 killing of Israeli Olympic athletes were justified on purely pragmatic grounds: How else are we to fight Israeli arrogance and belligerence?

The reality of contemporary Muslims is unfortunate.

Easy oil money, easy apologetics, easy puritanism, easy appeals to the logic of necessity have all but obliterated the incentive for introspection and critical insight. Arab and Muslim organizations in the U.S. are right to worry about hate crimes and stereotypical projections of Muslims and the Islamic religion.

The problem, however, is that Muslims themselves responded to the challenge of modernity by stereotyping and then completely ignoring their own tradition. It is not surprising that some extremists have taken this tendency to its logical and heinous extreme.

Fighting the Forces of Invisibility

Salman Rushdie, British novelist and author of *The Satanic Verses*, *Washington Post*, October 2, 2001

NEW YORK — In January 2000 I wrote in a newspaper column that "the defining struggle of the new age would be between Terrorism and Security," and fretted that to live by the security experts' worst-case scenarios might be to surrender too many of our liberties to the invisible shadow-warriors of the secret world. Democracy requires visibility, I argued, and in the struggle between security and freedom we must always err on the side of freedom. On Tuesday, September 11, however, the worst-case scenario came true.

They broke our city. I'm among the newest of New Yorkers, but even people who have never set foot in Manhattan have felt its wounds deeply, because New York is the beating heart of the visible world, tough-talking, spirit-dazzling, Walt Whitman's "city of orgies, walks and joys," his "proud and passionate city — mettlesome, mad, extravagant city!" To this bright capital of the visible, the forces of invisibility have dealt a dreadful blow. No need to say how dreadful; we all saw it, are all changed by it. Now we must ensure that the wound is not mortal, that the world of what is seen triumphs over what is cloaked, what is perceptible only through the effects of its awful deeds.

In making free societies safe — safer — from terrorism, our civil liberties will inevitably be compromised. But in return for freedom's partial erosion, we have a right to expect that our cities, water, planes, and children really will be better protected than they have been. The West's response to the September 11 attacks will be judged in large measure by whether people begin to feel safe once again in their homes, their workplaces, their daily lives. This is the confidence we have lost, and must regain.

Next: the question of the counterattack. Yes, we must send our shadow-warriors against theirs, and hope that ours prevail. But this secret war alone cannot bring victory. We will also need a public, political, and diplomatic offensive whose aim must be the early resolution of some of the world's thorniest problems: above all the battle between Israel and the Palestinian people for space, dignity, recognition, and survival. Better judgment will be required on all sides in the future. No more Sudanese aspirin factories to be bombed, please. And now that wise American heads appear to have understood that it would be wrong to bomb the impoverished, oppressed Afghan people in retaliation for their tyrannous masters' misdeeds, they might apply that wisdom, retrospectively, to what was done to the impoverished, oppressed people of Iraq. It's time to stop making enemies and start making friends.

To say this is in no way to join in the savaging of America by sections of the left that has been among the most unpleasant consequences of the terrorists' attacks on the United States. "The problem with Americans is... " — "What America needs to understand.... " There has been a lot of sanctimonious moral relativism around lately, usually prefaced by such phrases as these. A country which has just suffered the most devastating terrorist attack in history, a country in a state of deep mourning and horrible grief, is being told, heartlessly, that it is to blame for its own citizens' deaths. ("Did we deserve this, sir?" a bewildered worker at "ground zero" asked a visiting British journalist recently. I find the grave courtesy of that "sir" quite astonishing.)

Let's be clear about why this *bien-pensant* anti-American onslaught is such appalling rubbish. Terrorism is the murder of the innocent; this time, it was mass murder. To excuse such an atrocity by blaming U.S. government policies is to deny the basic idea of all morality: that individuals are responsible for their actions. Furthermore, terrorism is not the pursuit of legitimate complaints by illegitimate means. The terrorist wraps himself in the world's grievances to cloak his true motives. Whatever the killers were trying to achieve, it seems improbable that building a better world was part of it.

The fundamentalist seeks to bring down a great deal more than buildings. Such people are against, to offer just a brief list, freedom of speech, a multiparty political system, universal adult suffrage, accountable government, Jews, homosexuals, women's rights, pluralism, secularism, short skirts, dancing, beardlessness, evolution theory, sex. These are tyrants, not Muslims. (Islam is tough on suicides, who are doomed to repeat their deaths through all eternity. However, there needs to be a thorough examination, by Muslims everywhere, of why it is that the faith they love breeds so many violent mutant strains. If the West needs to understand its Unabombers and McVeighs, Islam needs to face up to its bin Ladens.) United Nations Secretary General Kofi Annan has said that we should now define ourselves not only by what we are for but by what we are against. I would reverse that proposition, because in the present instance what we are against is a no-brainer. Suicidist assassins ram wide-bodied aircraft into the World Trade Center and Pentagon and kill thousands of people: um, I'm against that. But what are we for? What will we risk our lives to defend? Can we unanimously concur that all the items in the above list — yes, even the short skirts and dancing — are worth dying for?

The fundamentalist believes that we believe in nothing. In his worldview, he has his absolute certainties, while we are sunk in sybaritic indulgences. To prove him wrong, we must first know that he is wrong. We must agree on what matters: kissing in public places, bacon sandwiches, disagreement, cutting-edge fashion, literature, generosity, water, a more equitable distribution of the world's resources, movies, music, freedom of thought, beauty, love. These will be our weapons. Not by making war but by the unafraid way we choose to live shall we defeat them.

How to defeat terrorism? Don't be terrorized. Don't let fear rule your life. Even if you are scared.

It's Not about Religion
Vincent Carroll, editor, *Rocky Mountain News,* September 26, 2001

"Religious fanatics are the worst fanatics," the critic Garry Wills once declared, and who would want to argue after the events of September 11? Yet is it really true? Are zealots motivated by religious belief more absolutist, intolerant, and, yes, violent than zealots motivated by nonreligious aims?

Is the biologist Richard Dawkins correct when he denounces religion because it "causes wars"? Does it even cause "most wars," as Paul Harvey asserted in a 1998 broadcast?

Such sentiments are virtually conventional wisdom in America, and they will become even more deeply entrenched given the facile pronouncements of the past two weeks. One TV network's expert analyst, a former federal agent, marveled at the hijackers' capacity to live in this country for many months and not be seduced by middle-class materialism. Only a singular sort of indoctrination could produce such automatons, he suggested, the long-term treachery of Communist moles somehow having escaped his attention.

It so happens, of course, that religious enthusiasm probably does cause wars. And it probably also prevents them. Or at least that has been the case with Christianity, which itself is often accused of the same sort of fanaticism that brought down the World Trade Center.

"More people have been killed in the name of Jesus Christ than any other name in the history of the world," maintains Gore Vidal. Such anti-Christian bigots usually have in mind the religious wars of the sixteenth and sev-

enteenth centuries — and of course the Crusades. These
are fat targets, to be sure, although perhaps not quite so
fat as many of those who cite them imagine.

For one thing, even at the height of the post-Reformation
bloodletting between Catholics and Protestants, secular
motives were everywhere at play, and often held the upper
hand. They involved rival rulers contending for power,
local leaders resisting central government or a foreign
state, and one class or region pitting itself against another.
The suppression of the Irish under Oliver Cromwell, for
example, looks a lot like a religious war from one perspective. From another, it looks like nothing so much as
an old-fashioned imperial conquest in which the natives
are dispossessed and massacred while the victors seize the
spoils.

This is not to discount a genuine religious factor even
in some of the worst atrocities. Pope Gregory XIII was
so impressed by the Saint Bartholomew's Day Massacre
of French Huguenots by Catholic mobs in 1572, for example, that he actually commissioned a commemorative
medal. Religious sentiment was perhaps even more promi-
nent in the Crusades — although it is usually forgotten, as
Piers Paul Read has pointed out, that "the Christians' per-
ception was that wars against Islam were waged either
in defense of Christendom or to liberate and reconquer
lands that were rightfully theirs." Still, there is no getting around the fact that Pope Urban II galvanized the
church's first holy war with his speech at Clermont in
1095, that St. Bernard exhorted the faithful to join the
Second Crusade some half century later, and that popes
such as Gregory VIII and Innocent III drummed up combatants for subsequent campaigns. There is equally no

doubt that the ensuing slaughter could be breathtaking —
and that the Crusades involved, in the words of the historian Stephen Neill, "a lowering of the whole moral
temperature of Christendom."

The catalog of Christian aggression includes many
entries besides these highlights, of course. Some are well-
known abominations, such as the Inquisition; others have
been widely forgotten, such as the forced conversion of
the Saxons in the eighth century. Yet there are at least four
reasons why it is nonetheless reckless and misleading to
label Christianity a warmongering faith.

The first is that most of the important opponents of
war, persecution, oppression, and slavery in the history of
the West have also been driven by religious conviction. It
was churchmen, after all, who often restrained the worst
instincts of the converted barbarian kings, counseling
mercy where none had been known. It was mainly church
officials who sought to suppress private violence and im-
pose rules on the conduct of war. And it was church canon
law, reinforced by the code of chivalry, that provided the
basis for a right of immunity for noncombatants.

Even the original Christian ethic of total nonviolence —
"Put your sword back into its place; for all who take the
sword will perish by the sword" (Matt. 26:52) — survived and was carried forward through the centuries: here
by Catholic monks, there by Anabaptists, Mennonites,
Moravians, Quakers, Dukhobors, Brethren, and many
others. It was religious agitation that convinced the British government to grant exemption to military service for
reasons of conscience as early as 1802. And, as secular
governments embarked on imperial adventures that eventually circled the globe, it was men and women expressing

their Christian conscience that decried the often-naked exploitation of these enterprises.

"The Christian acceptance of warfare was always somewhat conditional," observes historian James Turner Johnson. "The use of force was justified only if it was undertaken against evil, and the soldier was enjoined to hate the sin against which he was fighting, not the sinner."

The second reason is one well known to anthropologists: The vast majority of societies everywhere have engaged in warfare, and many have done so on a continual basis. One study of 186 societies found war "rare or absent" in only 9 percent of them. The most common reason for conflict? Not religion, but fear of shortages or impending natural disaster.

The third reason is that other ideologies wedded to state power, including nationalism, seem equally ferocious with or without a religious component. Even the brutality of ethnic rivalry often appears unrelated to religious differences. The worst explosion of violence in modern Africa, for example — in Rwanda — occurred without the goad of religious animosity. And where religious difference does seem to heighten ethnic conflict — in Sudan, for example — it is difficult to believe that the clashing groups would have been holding hands had they shared the same faith. After all, as the British sociologist David Martin has observed: "Turks, Iraqis, and Iranians can slaughter Kurds, and vice versa, with an enthusiasm entirely unaltered by the presence or absence of religious difference. In Turkey Turks are largely Sunni, Kurds often Alawite. In Iraq Kurds are Sunni, like most Iraqis, and in Iran they are Sunni and the Iranians mostly Shia. But the degree of conflict remains fairly constant."

The final reason is as obvious as it is irrefutable: Religious zealots have not in fact been the biggest butchers in Western history, or even close to it. The body count of corpses from the two great secular barbarisms of the twentieth century, Communism and Nazism — both of which were hostile to the religions in their midst — runs to well over 100 million.

"For the historian of the year 3000, where will fanaticism lie? Where, the oppression of man by man? In the thirteenth century or the twentieth?" Regine Pernoud aptly wondered a quarter of a century ago.

Each religion is a separate story, admittedly, and the motives at play throughout the history of Islamic jihad have been notoriously difficult to disentangle. Yet even suicide terrorists, seemingly so foreign to the West, are not exactly unknown, even in the American heartland. Eric Harris and Dylan Klebold strode into Columbine High School knowing full well it was their final act, and neither cared a fig about religious faith.

This Is a Religious War
Andrew Sullivan, *New York Times Magazine*, October 7, 2001

Perhaps the most admirable part of the response to the conflict that began on September 11 has been a general reluctance to call it a religious war. Officials and commentators have rightly stressed that this is not a battle between the Muslim world and the West, that the murderers are not representative of Islam. President Bush went to the Islamic Center in Washington to reinforce the point. At prayer meetings across the United States and throughout the world, Muslim leaders have been included alongside Christians, Jews, and Buddhists.

The only problem with this otherwise laudable effort is that it doesn't hold up under inspection. The religious dimension of this conflict is central to its meaning. The words of Osama bin Laden are saturated with religious argument and theological language. Whatever else the Taliban regime is in Afghanistan, it is fanatically religious. Although some Muslim leaders have criticized the terrorists, and even Saudi Arabia's rulers have distanced themselves from the militants, other Muslims in the Middle East and elsewhere have not denounced these acts, have been conspicuously silent, or have indeed celebrated them. The terrorists' strain of Islam is clearly not shared by most Muslims and is deeply unrepresentative of Islam's glorious, civilized, and peaceful past. But it surely represents a part of Islam — a radical, fundamentalist part — that simply cannot be ignored or denied.

In that sense, this surely is a religious war — but not of Islam versus Christianity and Judaism. Rather, it is a war of fundamentalism against faiths of all kinds that are at peace with freedom and modernity. This war even has far gentler echoes in America's own religious conflicts — between newer, more virulent strands of Christian fundamentalism and mainstream Protestantism and Catholicism. These conflicts have ancient roots, but they seem to be gaining new force as modernity spreads and deepens. They are our new wars of religion — and their victims are in all likelihood going to mount with each passing year.

Osama bin Laden himself couldn't be clearer about the religious underpinnings of his campaign of terror.

In 1998, he told his followers, "The call to wage war against America was made because America has spear-headed the crusade against the Islamic nation, sending tens of thousands of its troops to the land of the two holy mosques over and above its meddling in its affairs and its politics and its support of the oppressive, corrupt and tyrannical regime that is in control." Notice the use of the word "crusade," an explicitly religious term, and one that simply ignores the fact that the last few major American interventions abroad — in Kuwait, Somalia, and the Balkans — were all conducted in defense of Muslims.

Notice also that as bin Laden understands it, the "crusade" America is alleged to be leading is not against Arabs but against the Islamic nation, which spans many ethnicities. This nation knows no nation-states as they actually exist in the region — which is why this form of Islamic fundamentalism is also so worrying to the rulers of many Middle Eastern states. Notice also that bin Laden's beef is with American troops defiling the land of Saudi Arabia — "the land of the two holy mosques," in Mecca and Medina. In 1998, he also told followers that his terrorism was "of the commendable kind, for it is directed at the tyrants and the aggressors and the enemies of Allah." He has a litany of grievances against Israel as well, but his concerns are not primarily territorial or procedural. "Our religion is under attack," he said baldly. The attackers are Christians and Jews. When asked to sum up his message to the people of the West, bin Laden couldn't have been clearer: "Our call is the call of Islam that was revealed to Muhammad. It is a call to all mankind. We have been entrusted with good cause to follow in the foot-

steps of the messenger and to communicate his message
to all nations."

This is a religious war against "unbelief and unbelievers," in bin Laden's words. Are these cynical words
designed merely to use Islam for nefarious ends? We cannot know the precise motives of bin Laden, but we can
know that he would not use these words if he did not
think they had salience among the people he wishes to
inspire and provoke. This form of Islam is not restricted
to bin Laden alone.

Its roots lie in an extreme and violent strain in Islam
that emerged in the eighteenth century in opposition to
what was seen by some Muslims as Ottoman decadence
but has gained greater strength in the twentieth. For the
past two decades, this form of Islamic fundamentalism
has racked the Middle East. It has targeted almost every
regime in the region and, as it failed to make progress,
has extended its hostility into the West. From the assassination of Anwar Sadat to the fatwa against Salman
Rushdie to the decade-long campaign of bin Laden to the
destruction of ancient Buddhist statues and the hideous
persecution of women and homosexuals by the Taliban
to the World Trade Center massacre, there is a single line.
That line is a fundamentalist, religious one. And it is an
Islamic one.

Most interpreters of the Koran find no arguments in
it for the murder of innocents. But it would be naive to
ignore in Islam a deep thread of intolerance toward unbelievers, especially if those unbelievers are believed to be
a threat to the Islamic world. There are many passages
in the Koran urging mercy toward others, tolerance, respect for life, and so on. But there are also passages as

violent as this: "And when the sacred months are passed, kill those who join other gods with God wherever ye shall find them; and seize them, besiege them, and lay wait for them with every kind of ambush." And this: "Believers! Wage war against such of the infidels as are your neighbors, and let them find you rigorous." Bernard Lewis, the great scholar of Islam, writes of the dissonance within Islam: "There is something in the religious culture of Islam which inspired, in even the humblest peasant or peddler, a dignity and a courtesy toward others never exceeded and rarely equaled in other civilizations. And yet, in moments of upheaval and disruption, when the deeper passions are stirred, this dignity and courtesy toward others can give way to an explosive mixture of rage and hatred which impels even the government of an ancient and civilized country — even the spokesman of a great spiritual and ethical religion — to espouse kidnapping and assassination, and try to find, in the life of their prophet, approval and indeed precedent for such actions." Since Muhammad was, unlike many other religious leaders, not simply a sage or a prophet but a ruler in his own right, this exploitation of his politics is not as great a stretch as some would argue.

This use of religion for extreme repression, and even terror, is not of course restricted to Islam. For most of its history, Christianity has had a worse record. From the Crusades to the Inquisition to the bloody religious wars of the sixteenth and seventeenth centuries, Europe saw far more blood spilled for religion's sake than the Muslim world did. And given how expressly nonviolent the teachings of the Gospels are, the perversion of Christianity in this respect was arguably greater than bin Laden's

selective use of Islam. But it is there nonetheless. It seems
almost as if there is something inherent in religious mono-
theism that lends itself to this kind of terrorist temptation.
And our bland attempts to ignore this — to speak of this
violence as if it did not have religious roots — is some
kind of denial. We don't want to denigrate religion as
such, and so we deny that religion is at the heart of this.
But we would understand this conflict better, perhaps, if
we first acknowledged that religion is responsible in some
way, and then figured out how and why.

The first mistake is surely to condescend to fundamentalism. We may disagree with it, but it has attracted
millions of adherents for centuries, and for a good reason.
It elevates and comforts. It provides a sense of meaning and direction to those lost in a disorienting world.
The blind recourse to texts embraced as literal truth, the
injunction to follow the commandments of God before
anything else, the subjugation of reason and judgment
and even conscience to the dictates of dogma: these can be
exhilarating and transformative. They have led human beings to perform extraordinary acts of both good and evil.
And they have an internal logic to them. If you believe that
there is an eternal afterlife and that endless indescribable
torture awaits those who disobey God's law, then it requires no huge stretch of imagination to make sure that
you not only conform to each diktat but that you also
encourage and, if necessary, coerce others to do the same.
The logic behind this is impeccable. Sin begets sin. The
sin of others can corrupt you as well. The only solution
is to construct a world in which such sin is outlawed and
punished and constantly purged — by force if necessary.
It is not crazy to act this way if you believe these things

strongly enough. In some ways, it's crazier to believe these things and not act this way.

In a world of absolute truth, in matters graver than life and death, there is no room for dissent and no room for theological doubt. Hence the reliance on literal interpretations of texts — because interpretation can lead to error, and error can lead to damnation. Hence also the ancient Catholic insistence on absolute church authority. Without infallibility, there can be no guarantee of truth. Without such a guarantee, confusion can lead to hell.

Dostoyevsky's Grand Inquisitor makes the case perhaps as well as anyone. In the story told by Ivan Karamazov in *The Brothers Karamazov,* Jesus returns to earth during the Spanish Inquisition. On a day when hundreds have been burned at the stake for heresy, Jesus performs miracles. Alarmed, the Inquisitor arrests Jesus and imprisons him with the intent of burning him at the stake as well. What follows is a conversation between the Inquisitor and Jesus. Except it isn't a conversation because Jesus says nothing. It is really a dialogue between two modes of religion, an exploration of the tension between the extraordinary, transcendent claims of religion and human beings' inability to live up to them, or even fully believe them.

According to the Inquisitor, Jesus' crime was revealing that salvation was possible but still allowing humans the freedom to refuse it. And this, to the Inquisitor, was a form of cruelty. When the truth involves the most important things imaginable — the meaning of life, the fate of one's eternal soul, the difference between good and evil — it is not enough to premise it on the capacity of human choice. That is too great a burden. Choice leads to unbe-

lief or distraction or negligence or despair. What human
beings really need is the certainty of truth, and they need
to see it reflected in everything around them — in the cultures in which they live, enveloping them in a seamless
fabric of faith that helps them resist the terror of choice
and the abyss of unbelief. This need is what the Inquisitor calls the "fundamental secret of human nature." He
explains: "These pitiful creatures are concerned not only
to find what one or the other can worship, but to find
something that all would believe in and worship; what
is essential is that all may be together in it. This crav-
ing for community of worship is the chief misery of every
man individually and of all humanity since the beginning
of time."

This is the voice of fundamentalism. Faith cannot exist
alone in a single person. Indeed, faith needs others for it
to survive — and the more complete the culture of faith,
the wider it is, and the more total its infiltration of the
world, the better. It is hard for us to wrap our minds
around this today, but it is quite clear from the accounts
of the Inquisition and, indeed, of the religious wars that
continued to rage in Europe for nearly three centuries,
that many of the fanatics who burned human beings at
the stake were acting out of what they genuinely thought
were the best interests of the victims. With the power of
the state, they used fire, as opposed to simple execution,
because it was thought to be spiritually cleansing. A few
minutes of hideous torture on earth were deemed a small
price to pay for helping such souls avoid eternal torture in
the afterlife. Moreover, the example of such government-
sponsored executions helped create a culture in which
certain truths were reinforced and in which it was eas-

ier for more weak people to find faith. The burden of this duty to uphold the faith lay on the men required to torture, persecute, and murder the unfaithful. And many of them believed, as no doubt some Islamic fundamentalists believe, that they were acting out of mercy and godliness.

This is the authentic voice of the Taliban. It also finds itself replicated in secular form. What, after all, were the totalitarian societies of Nazi Germany or Soviet Russia if not an exact replica of this kind of fusion of politics and ultimate meaning? Under Lenin's and Stalin's rules, the imminence of salvation through revolutionary consciousness was in perpetual danger of being undermined by those too weak to have faith — the bourgeois or the kulaks or the intellectuals. So they had to be liquidated or purged. Similarly, it is easy for us to dismiss the Nazis as evil, as they surely were. It is harder for us to understand that in some twisted fashion, they truly believed that they were creating a new dawn for humanity, a place where all the doubts that freedom brings could be dispelled in a rapture of racial purity and destiny. Hence the destruction of all dissidents and the Jews — carried out by fire as the Inquisitors had before, an act of purification different merely in its scale, efficiency, and Godlessness.

Perhaps the most important thing for us to realize today is that the defeat of each of these fundamentalisms required a long and arduous effort. The conflict with Islamic fundamentalism is likely to take as long. For unlike Europe's religious wars, which taught Christians the futility of fighting to the death over something beyond human understanding and so immune to any definitive resolution, there has been no such educative conflict in the Muslim world. Only Iran and Afghanistan have experienced the full horror of revolutionary fundamentalism, and only Iran has so far seen reason to moderate to some extent. From everything we see, the lessons Europe learned in its bloody history have yet to be absorbed within the Muslim world. There, as in sixteenth-century Europe, the promise of purity and salvation seems far more enticing than the mundane allure of mere peace. That means that we are not at the end of this conflict but in its very early stages.

America is not a neophyte in this struggle. The United States has seen several waves of religious fervor since its founding. But American evangelicalism has always kept its distance from governmental power. The Christian separation between what is God's and what is Caesar's — drawn from the Gospels — helped restrain the fundamentalist temptation. The last few decades have proved an exception, however. As modernity advanced, and the certitudes of fundamentalist faith seemed mocked by an increasingly liberal society, evangelicals mobilized and entered politics. Their faith sharpened, their zeal intensified, the temptation to fuse political and religious authority beckoned more insistently.

Mercifully, violence has not been a significant feature of this trend — but it has not been absent. The murders of abortion providers show what such zeal can lead to. And indeed, if people truly believe that abortion is the same as mass murder, then you can see the awful logic of the terrorism it has spawned. This is the same logic as bin Laden's. If faith is that strong, and it dictates a choice between action or eternal damnation, then violence can easily be justified. In retrospect, we should be amazed not that violence has occurred — but that it hasn't occurred more often.

The critical link between Western and Middle Eastern fundamentalism is surely the pace of social change. If you take your beliefs from books written more than a thousand years ago, and you believe in these texts literally, then the appearance of the modern world must truly terrify. If you believe that women should be consigned to polygamous, concealed servitude, then Manhattan must appear like Gomorrah. If you believe that homosexuality is a crime punishable by death, as both fundamentalist Islam and the Bible dictate, then a world of same-sex marriage is surely Sodom. It is not a big step to argue that such centers of evil should be destroyed or undermined, as bin Laden does, or to believe that their destruction is somehow a consequence of their sin, as Jerry Falwell argued. Look again at Falwell's now infamous words in the wake of September 11: "I really believe that the pagans, and the abortionists, and the feminists, and the gays and lesbians who are actively trying to make that an alternative lifestyle, the ACLU, People for the American Way — all of them who have tried to secularize America — I point the finger in their face and say, 'You helped this happen.' "

And why wouldn't he believe that? He has subsequently apologized for the insensitivity of the remark but not for its theological underpinning. He cannot repudiate the theology — because it is the essence of what he believes in and must believe in for his faith to remain alive.

The other critical aspect of this kind of faith is insecurity. American fundamentalists know they are losing the culture war. They are terrified of failure and of the Godless world they believe is about to engulf or crush them. They speak and think defensively. They talk about renewal, but in their private discourse they expect damnation for an America that has lost sight of the fundamentalist notion of God.

Similarly, Muslims know that the era of Islam's imperial triumph has long since gone. For many centuries, the civilization of Islam was the center of the world. It eclipsed Europe in the Dark Ages, fostered great learning, and expanded territorially well into Europe and Asia. But it has all been downhill from there. From the collapse of the Ottoman Empire onward, it has been on the losing side of history. The response to this has been an intermittent flirtation with Westernization but far more emphatically a reaffirmation of the most irredentist and extreme forms of the culture under threat. Hence the odd phenomenon of Islamic extremism beginning in earnest only in the last two hundred years.

With Islam, this has worse implications than for other cultures that have had rises and falls. For Islam's religious tolerance has always been premised on its own power. It was tolerant when it controlled the territory and called the shots. When it lost territory and saw itself eclipsed by the West in power and civilization, tolerance evaporated. To cite Lewis again on Islam: "What is truly evil and unacceptable is the domination of infidels over true believers. For true believers to rule misbelievers is proper and natural, since this provides for the maintenance of the holy law and gives the misbelievers both the opportunity and the incentive to embrace the true faith. But for misbelievers to rule over true believers is blasphemous and unnatural, since it leads to the corruption of religion and morality in society and to the flouting or even the abrogation of God's law."

Thus the horror at the establishment of the State of Israel, an infidel country in Muslim lands, a bitter reminder of the eclipse of Islam in the modern world. Thus also the revulsion at American bases in Saudi Arabia. While colonialism of different degrees is merely political oppression for some cultures, for Islam it was far worse. It was blasphemy that had to be avenged and countered.

I cannot help thinking of this defensiveness when I read stories of the suicide bombers sitting poolside in Florida or racking up a $48 vodka tab in an American restaurant. We tend to think that this assimilation into the West might bring Islamic fundamentalists around somewhat, temper their zeal. But in fact, the opposite is the case. The temptation of American and Western culture — indeed, the very allure of such culture — may well require a repression all the more brutal if it is to be overcome. The transmission of American culture into the heart of what bin Laden calls the Islamic nation requires only two responses — capitulation to unbelief or a radical strike against it. There is little room in the fundamentalist psyche for a moderate accommodation. The very psychological dynamics that lead repressed homosexuals to be viciously homophobic or that entice sexually tempted preachers to inveigh against immorality are the very dynamics that lead vodka-drinking fundamentalists to steer planes into buildings. It is not designed to achieve anything, construct anything, argue anything. It is a violent acting out of internal conflict.

And America is the perfect arena for such acting out. For the question of religious fundamentalism was not only familiar to the founding fathers. In many ways, it was the central question that led to America's existence.

The first American immigrants, after all, were refugees from the religious wars that engulfed England and that intensified under England's Taliban, Oliver Cromwell. One central influence on the founders' political thought was John Locke, the English liberal who wrote the now famous "Letter on Toleration." In it, Locke argued that true salvation could not be a result of coercion, that faith had to be freely chosen to be genuine. and that any other interpretation was counter to the Gospels. Following Locke, the founders established as a central element of the new American order a stark separation of church and state, ensuring that no single religion could use political means to enforce its own orthodoxies.

We cite this as a platitude today without absorbing or even realizing its radical nature in human history — and the deep human predicament it was designed to solve. It was an attempt to answer the eternal human question of how to pursue the goal of religious salvation for ourselves and others and yet also maintain civil peace. What the founders and Locke were saying was that the ultimate claims of religion should simply not be allowed to interfere with political and religious freedom. They did this to preserve peace above all — but also to preserve true religion itself.

The security against an American Taliban is therefore relatively simple: it's the Constitution. And the surprising consequence of this separation is not that it led to a collapse of religious faith in America — as weak human beings found themselves unable to believe without social and political reinforcement — but that it led to one of the most vibrantly religious civil societies on earth. No other country has achieved this. And it is this achievement that the Taliban and bin Laden have now decided to challenge. It is a living, tangible rebuke to everything they believe in.

That is why this coming conflict is indeed as momentous and as grave as the last major conflicts, against Nazism and Communism, and why it is not hyperbole to see it in these epic terms. What is at stake is yet another battle against a religion that is succumbing to the temptation Jesus refused in the desert — to rule by force. The difference is that this conflict is against a more formidable enemy than Nazism or Communism. The secular totalitarianisms of the twentieth century were, in President Bush's memorable words, "discarded lies." They were fundamentalisms built on the very weak intellectual conceits of a master race and a Communist revolution.

But Islamic fundamentalism is based on a glorious civilization and a great faith. It can harness and co-opt and corrupt true and good believers if it has a propitious and toxic enough environment. It has a more powerful logic than either Stalin's or Hitler's Godless ideology, and it can serve as a focal point for all the other societies in the world, whose resentment of Western success and civilization comes more easily than the arduous task of accommodation to modernity. We have to somehow defeat this without defeating or even opposing a great religion that is nonetheless extremely inexperienced in the toleration of other ascendant and more powerful faiths. It is hard to underestimate the extreme delicacy and difficulty of this task.

In this sense, the symbol of this conflict should not be Old Glory, however stirring it is. What is really at issue here is the simple but immensely difficult principle of the separation of politics and religion. We are fighting not for

our country as such or for our flag. We are fighting for the
universal principles of our Constitution — and the possibility of free religious faith it guarantees. We are fighting
for religion against one of the deepest strains in religion
there is. And not only our lives but our souls are at stake.

Strict Wahhabism:
A Split Branch or Islamic Diversity?
Larry Witham, *Washington Times*, October 11, 2001

An obscure sectarian divide in U.S. Islam is gaining more
attention as the nation tries to understand the world's
second-largest faith.

Wahhabism, a strict form of Muslim orthodoxy backed
by Saudi Arabia's wealth and its members' missionary
zeal, may have overshadowed alternative strands of Islam
here, its critics say.

Others say Wahhabism, which is more likely to claim
it is "true Islam" and expect other Muslims to conform,
is merely part of the faith's diversity.

"Wahhabism is identifiable only with American Muslims in Saudi religious organizations," said Sulayman
Nyang, a professor of Islam at Howard University. "But
it doesn't influence American Muslims linked to" other
branches of Islam.

Said to be the strictest of four legal schools of Islam, it
was revived by a religious leader named Muhammad Abd
al-Wahhab, who joined forces with the military founder
of the Saudi dynasty.

Mr. Nyang said it grew from a sect backed by the Saudi
royal family to a world movement, especially during the
Cold War. "The royals, in alliance with the United States,

used Wahhabism in the Middle East to drum up support against secular socialism," he said. "So there's unintended consequences."

Wahhabi Islam hopes to enforce a more literal interpretation of the Koran, Islam's holy book, in social custom and criminal law, said Khalid Duran, a Muslim scholar who is of the Sufi, or more mystical, persuasion.

"What we see today is some leaders demanding a rigidity that is really not Islamic," he said. "They want to show off as being more pious. They are all Wahhabis, though the term is a little bit loose."

He said they call themselves "Islamist."

He said Muslims abroad use the Wahhabi term negatively "to mean fundamentalist, fascist," and that in Western countries it can be divisive in its missionary zeal.

But Azizah al-Hibri, a law professor at the University of Richmond, said Wahhabism is merely part of religious diversity working itself out in America, not a major split among the faithful.

"The problem is that some ideas have more funding than others," she said, responding to the point about Saudi funding of Wahhabi schools, literature, and religious teachers.

But she said its influence in the United States, imported with immigration, has softened over the years.

"It has a strong presence, and that makes it an issue for people who are not Wahhabi. But it's not a split in Islam. It is part of the marketplace of ideas."

Wahhabism also has been characterized as an ardent political critic of Muslim regimes that secularize and of sects that are less legalistic, such as Sufism.

One Sufi leader, Sheik Hisham Kabbani, who founded

the Islamic Supreme Council of America as an alternative to Wahhabi influence, stirred an explosive debate on the issue in 1999.

In a State Department hearing, he said that 80 percent of the nation's mosques had been taken over by imams (Islamic clergy) with Wahhabi-like loyalties.

Estimates of the number of mosques, or prayer centers, in the United States range from twelve hundred to three thousand.

For his testimony, Mr. Kabbani was denounced by a coalition of established Muslim political groups here, and called a "hippie" or "guru" by orthodox Muslims who look askance at Sufism.

Mr. Nyang of Howard University said the sheik spread the Wahhabi label too liberally across U.S. Muslim leadership.

Mrs. al-Hibri rejected the sheik's charge that policy groups such as the American Muslim Council (AMC) harbor Wahhabism. "The AMC is not Wahhabi," she said.

3

Thy Will Be Done
on Earth As It Is in Heaven

The Providence of God:
How Could God Allow Such a Thing
to Happen?

Maybe That's Good Enough for Today

Libba Bray, writer, Brooklyn, New York, Reflections on a Week,
for the Presbyterian News Service, Presbyterian Church (U.S.A.),
September 2001

BROOKLYN, N.Y., September 18 — I cleaned soot off
my windowsills today.

I thought I'd gotten all of it yesterday and the day before, but somehow, splotches of black dust keep making
it through the windows of my Brooklyn apartment, re-
minders of a grief that also cannot be contained. This
week is being hailed by our mayor as "the worst week
in New York City's history." It is a week that has also
brought out the best in New York, a city of eight million strangers who came together as one family for many
horrible days and nights.

Here, then, is one account of the week that was.

Tuesday, September 11

The morning starts as most mornings do in my house, which is to say, in a chaotic fashion.

There is the mad scramble to get my son off to preschool complete with lunchbox, stuffed bunny, water cup. At 8:45 a.m., just about the time the first plane hits the North Tower of the World Trade Center, I hug my son goodbye and stroll out into a perfect, blue-skied day. It is 70 degrees and breezy. I'm anxious to get to my computer and begin work on a new book. First, I step into my local corner grocery store — bodegas, as we call them here in the melting pot. It's now 9:10. The radio is on. I put my milk on the counter as the DJ breaks in, sounding confused and breathless. There is a report about a second plane hitting the World Trade Center. The words "second" and "plane" barely register. My first thought is that a small Cessna with an inexperienced pilot has had some very unfortunate accident. Three more words try to make their way in: "deliberate terrorist attacks." The girl behind the counter stops, her hands dangling in the cash drawer. For a moment, we are frozen. And then she hands me my change, the store comes alive again, and I'm hurrying the two blocks to my apartment building.

A dark, angry plume of smoke streaks up into the blue sky. And now I am running up four flights of stairs and into my apartment where my husband has the TV on. We see the horrible footage of the towers on fire. It does not seem real. A neighbor rings my doorbell and asks if we have heard the news. Together, we go up one more flight to the roof of our building where we can see the two towers burning and smoking. Many of my neighbors are there. Someone passes around binoculars. I take a closer look. The fire is massive, engulfing a good twenty stories or so. It leaps out the broken windows. More unsettling are the millions of pieces of paper falling from office windows and blanketing the city like confetti. Someone gasps. A body has fallen from the windows. I can't look at this, and I pass the binoculars on.

Thirty minutes later, the unthinkable happens. There is a whooshing sound that becomes a roar as the South Tower, Tower 2, collapses in on itself. It's hard to tell exactly what's happening. Our minds won't accept what we see. The smoke rushes over lower Manhattan like an avalanche, enveloping the city. If I didn't know better, I'd think it was a special effect, a disaster film about a blinding snowstorm. But I do know better. The smoke pushes out into the Hudson River where the Statue of Liberty watches it all. It's fast, this cloud of dust and ash, and we run downstairs and into the safety of our living room where we huddle around the TV, blinking, unbelieving.

When Tower 1 falls, we are numb. Images of rubble, screaming people, and burned-out fire trucks assault us. My husband and I call our son's school. The children are all fine. They're napping, in fact. I resist the urge to run the seven blocks to the Methodist church that houses the school and scoop up my child. Where would we run?

The call goes out: blood donors are needed. My husband and I head to our local hospital, six blocks away. Out on the street, people are wandering, dazed. A businessman covered in gray ash stands on a corner talking to another man who keeps his hand on the guy's shoulder, as if anchoring him there. Our favorite coffee shop is closed. A hastily penned sign implores us to give blood. A neighbor is home safe from his office only two blocks from "Ground Zero" as it will come to be called. As Manhattan's assistant D.A., he has put drug dealers behind bars and been blasé about it. Today, he shakes when he tells me about seeing the building nearly come down on his head, turning and running hard and fast, all the way across the Manhattan Bridge. He was halfway through the streets of Brooklyn before he realized he could stop.

There is a two-hour wait at the hospital. People spill out onto the lawn. They ask us to come back later that night. By 1:00, the wind blows the smoke across the Hudson, directly into our neighborhood. The air is a solid, living thing with a distinctive, charred plastic odor. You can actually taste the air, and the sky has turned a jaundiced color. Breathing is difficult. Some people wear masks. Others breathe through T-shirts or sweaters.

We collect our son from preschool and try to act "normal," though we know there will have to be a new kind of normal for all of us. We're worried about the air, so we arrange a play date at the home of friends. They are waiting to hear from a sister who works blocks from the World Trade Center. The phone lines are all down, as is cellular and Internet service. She arrives, dusty and exhausted, an hour later, part of a mass exodus that made its way by foot across the closed Brooklyn Bridge. By 5:00, we know that we can't bear to leave the comfort of each other. We order pizza and stay till 7:30. My son is asleep by 8:00. My husband and I can't stop watching the news. The city that never sleeps has come to a dead stop. There are no subways, no ferries, no buses, no planes. Everything is closed. In just twelve hours, everything has changed.

Wednesday, September 12

Sleep proved impossible. I am used to the ceaseless noise of urban life. The comfort of planes, cars, chatter and yelling and music on the streets. There is something deeply disturbing about the silence. It is broken only by emergency sirens and the deafening rumble of low-flying fighter jets that shake my building when they pass overhead.

7:00 a.m. I turn on the *Today* show. My three-year-old son looks up from his train set to see the horrifying images of planes bursting into flames.

"Mommy, what happened?" he asks, clearly disturbed.

I take a deep breath and explain that there was an accident and a fire, but that the fire is out now. I hope this will suffice for a curious preschooler. It doesn't. "Mommy," he says, "that scares me."

"It scared us all, honey." It is the truest thing I will say all day. We turn off the TV.

Thursday, September 13

Schools are open. The hospitals can take no more blood. They're asking for supplies and clothes. We learn that our local firehouse, Squad 1, was one of the first rescue teams on the scene the day of the attacks. The entire company has been lost. The empty firehouse on Union Street has become a shrine filled with flowers and candles.

People look less numb, more determined. They fly into action. Outside the YMCA, they collect supplies for the rescue workers and offer housing to the displaced. It has become common to pass acquaintances on the streets with "Everyone on your end okay?"

In line at the grocery store, a man behind me tells of being "there." At 8:40, he stepped out of the World Trade Center to get coffee and a donut, narrowly escaping the plane that crashed into what had been his floor. He can't stop talking to me, and I listen, even though my frozen foods are completely inedible by the time I reach home.

Friday, September 14

Rain comes down hard and cold. It turns the rescue site into a slippery, dangerous mess.

My Southern Woman Defense System kicks in and I find myself in the kitchen, doubling the recipe for everything. Finally, in the middle of baking approximately ten dozen chocolate chip cookies, I break down. I grip the counter and sob, not caring how loud I am. It feels good to howl.

I take the cookies to the other firehouse in my neighborhood, but they've posted a sign imploring us to stop feeding them. I take the cookies to my son's school where the kids think Christmas has just come early.

For the first time in days, I'm smiling and laughing, taking in their chocolate-smeared faces and ingenious excuses for needing a second and third cookie.

Saturday, September 15

My husband is scheduled to work at the New York Public Library in Chinatown, adjacent to lower Manhattan. We don't know if he should report to work — we've had no word since the phone lines are still out. We decide to go in together as a family. There is a wonderful playground only blocks from the library.

The library is closed "due to emergency," the sign reads.

We walk under the huge shadow of the Manhattan Bridge, afraid to look up and see the blank spot where the Twin Towers used to be. Instead, I spot the same flyer stuck to every light pole: "Missing, Jennifer Y. Wong, age 22."

Jennifer Y. Wong is young, beautiful, shining. She could be running for office or selling us long-distance service. She is not. She never will.

But I will always remember her name.

Sunday, September 16

I take my son to church today. I don't want to go alone, and so attend a Catholic mass with my friends who also have young children. I have come seeking comfort, guidance, and answers, though I know there are none. But it is my son who has all the questions: "Who is God?" "What is pray?" "Why you pray?" Through that Tourette's stream of consciousness unique to three-year-olds, he has hit on the essential nature of faith. I can only offer three lame replies, "God is the Mommy and Daddy of us all," "Praying is talking to and listening to God," and "Because."

There is more black soot on my windowsills. I let it stand.

Monday, September 17

I have a meeting in the city. It's tempting to cancel, but I find my desire to be with other people outweighs my fear. Still, taking the F train through darkened subway tunnels by myself makes my heart beat hard against my chest. When the train rounds a piece of elevated track, I have a clear view of lower Manhattan. The smoke still rises through the remaining buildings. The skyline seems bare. The city is missing its gateposts. I could be looking at any city. For a few seconds, my brain doesn't register this new horizon. It isn't until I find the Empire State Building and follow the line down to the now unfamiliar view that I realize they are truly gone. And then we are moving, the F train dipping back down into blackness.

In the city, I see the flyers. Every flat surface has become a paper memorial. Handmade posters are taped to bus stops, kiosks, drugstores, apartment buildings, restaurants. Faces smile out at me. A young father holds his baby daughter. A businessman stands in a group of beaming employees. A laughing college grad loops an arm around her best friends. They are tan and happy. Facts stay with me. 5′11″. 180 lbs. Wears glasses. Gall bladder scar. Celtic tattoo on left shoulder. Might be wearing a silver ball on a chain. Blood type O+. Worked for Cantor-Fitzgerald, 104th floor. Windows on the World, 106th floor. 81st floor. 95th floor. 101st. 74th. Last seen . . . last seen . . . last seen . . .

I can't read anymore. I can't carry any more lives with me on this trip. At Sixth Avenue, the Avenue of the Americas, I cross against the light, a New Yorker's game of chicken. I try not to look at anything else, but something catches my eye. It's a small yellow sticker, smaller than a postcard, stuck to a rusted-out dumpster. It reads simply, I WILL NOT BE TERRORIZED.

People pass by, their voices and scents linger and trail off, but the yellow sticker remains, small, bold, undeniable.

For a minute, I forget to be afraid.

Tuesday, September 18

4:45 a.m. The digital clock confirms the ungodly hour. I am awake. At 5:30, I'm still awake and no longer delusional that I'm going to get any more sleep, so I make coffee. The coffee is strong and good. The rooftops of Brooklyn pinken and glisten in the early morning light. It's going to be another gorgeous day in New York, except for the persistent burning ash smell.

Today heralds the Jewish New Year, 5762. We are an interfaith family, a Jewish-Presbyterian-Russian-Irish-Texas-California-Kansas mix. We're much like the city itself, not so much one thing as a blend of flavors, colors, accents, creeds. Later, my husband will most likely attend services. He might take our son and take his turn answering the questions about God and prayer and what makes the water come up through the water fountain and why can't we eat M&Ms for breakfast.

I wish my husband luck.

In one week, I have had so many questions of my own. I have seen devastation and destruction and fear. And I have seen people race into burning buildings to save others. I have seen neighbors embrace each other at mailboxes and in the dry cleaners. I have seen strangers give everything of themselves, even blood.

I have seen that children will look to you for answers, that they will ask you why you pray and the answer, beyond all ideology, is this: We pray because we are human and we need each other. We pray because when something of such a magnitude happens, we must turn to something greater than ourselves and greater than tragedy to sustain us. We pray because life goes on, and we must always go toward the life-affirming, and, in fact, we have just proved that we do. We pray because we can't seem to stop ourselves. We pray because.

Children's questions, like soot, like grief, like catastrophe, cannot all be measured and contained. They cannot be answered to satisfaction. This is the best that I can do.

I'm still thinking that it is a new year, and maybe that thought is enough for today.

How Do We Keep Our Faith When God Seems to Be Silent?

Most Rev. Jose Gomez, auxiliary bishop of Denver, homily on National Day of Prayer and Remembrance for terrorism victims, September 14, 2001

On the day of the World Trade Center attack, a friend asked me, "How can a God of love allow this kind of evil and suffering?" I answered him that God made us free, and because we're free, we can freely choose to do terrible things. God can't interfere with our freedom without also taking away our dignity as His children. The struggle between good and evil isn't "outside" us in the big world somewhere. It runs right through the center of each human heart. What separates us from every other creature is our ability to know and do what is right. Our love means something because it's not just an instinct. It's a gift that we can freely choose to give or withhold.

Another friend asked me, "How can we keep our faith when a tragedy like this occurs, and God seems to be silent?" I answered him: What do we expect God to do — be available when we need Him, and then go away when we don't? Because that's the way many of us act. We ignore Him, or we pay Him lip service — and then we expect Him to show up like a paramedic when we dial 911. That's not "loving" God. That's just using Him. And if you and I don't like to be used, what makes us think that God does?

Of course, Scripture tells us that God's ways are not our ways. He loves us better than we love ourselves. And so He *does* answer us every time we call on Him. In fact, *God never leaves us.* He's never silent. He's never absent. But if we fill our lives with noise, we can't hear Him speak. If we crowd our hearts with confusion and distractions, we forget how to listen.

How do we keep our faith in the face of tragedy? I think that's the wrong question. Faith untested is faith that's not real. Tragedy and suffering are where we find our faith. Suffering is what God uses to wake us up to our purpose in the world.

The great Jewish Christian writer Leon Bloy once said that "man has places in his heart which do not yet exist — and into them enters suffering, in order that they may have existence." It's suffering, not comfort, that draws us into the heart of God. It's suffering, not comfort, that teaches us how to live as children of God. This is the lesson of all of Scripture. It's why Pope John Paul once described the Bible as God's "great book about suffering." From Genesis to Job to the Book of Revelation, the human heart only finds God when it's humble and broken.

We Americans like to think that this present moment in which we live is entirely new and different from anything in the past. This illusion is part of our vanity. We like to think that no one has ever had our power. No one has ever had our technology or wealth. But as I prayed over our First Reading from Numbers today, I realized how little has changed about the human condition in four thousand years.

Then and now, we're made from exactly the same clay. God delivers the Israelites from slavery, and they immediately begin forgetting and complaining. God gives Americans incredible opportunities and privilege, and so many of us repay Him by removing Him from our public life and our private behavior. The Scripture today says that God sent the serpents to punish the Israelites, but God never chastises us except to teach us where our real security lies. He sent the serpents, and He also sent a *deliverance* from the serpents, so that His people would turn their eyes to Him.

In our psalm this afternoon, God tells us, "Hearken my people to my teaching, incline your ears to words of my mouth." These aren't the words of an angry judge. They're the words of a Father who loves His children, but who knows that they have trouble listening. It was only when God pressed His people that "they sought Him and inquired after God again, remembering that God was their rock and the Most High God, their redeemer." So it is with us today.

What our readings remind us — what the pain of this entire week teaches us — is that only God is our security and strength. The tremendous suffering inflicted on so many innocent people Tuesday, the wound our whole country now bears, is a call to conversion. Today's Gospel says, "For God so loved the world that He gave His only son. . . . God did not send His Son into the world to condemn the world, but that the world might be saved through Him."

Yesterday a friend said that she hoped we could find a way to put Tuesday's attack behind us and get back to normalcy as soon as possible. I understand her feelings. All of us yearn, in a way, for the routine concerns we had on Monday. But if "normalcy" is the self-absorption, division, and discontent we've created for ourselves as a nation over the last decade, God grant that we never go back to it. We owe the victims, their survivors, and our own children, more than that.

In the midst of all the suffering of the past week, God is still with us. He still speaks to us. Today is one of the great feasts of the church year — the Feast of the Exaltation of the Cross. It's no accident that for two thousand years, an instrument of execution has been the greatest symbol of human hope. The cross is a hard gift, but a great gift. God created us to be His children, to be his cooperators in redeeming and sanctifying the world.

And so the real question facing us today isn't, "How can God allow the kind of evil that happened on Tuesday?"

The real question is: *What are we going to do about it?* In the days and weeks ahead, are we going to choose to hate as the murderers hated on Tuesday? Or will we try to live and love as Jesus did — no matter what the cost?

The Mystery of Goodness

Rev. Andrew C. Mead, rector, St. Thomas Church Fifth Avenue
in the City of New York, sermon preached on September 16, 2001

In the Name of God the Father, God the Son, and God the Holy Ghost. Amen.

The lessons from Holy Scripture, which were read this morning, are the ones appointed by the Church's Book of Common Prayer for this Sunday in September. They are all on the theme of God's mercy, culminating with Jesus' parables of the Lost Sheep and the Lost Coin. It is important to know and remember that God is, above all, loving and merciful. But this is a unique time with special demands. My other "text" is what has been happening since last Tuesday, September 11.

The question everyone is constantly asking is, Why, How, can God allow this to happen? I have struggled with this question in other grievous situations over the thirty years of my ministry in the Church. It is the same question posed by the Book of Job. Billy Graham posed it on Friday at the National Cathedral. The answer is, I don't know. It is a mystery. Evil is a deep mystery, going all the way back to the Devil and his own rebellion against the Creator. Jesus has taught us that God is both almighty and good; why God permits evil of this kind is a mystery. And as we know from the horrible scene a few miles downtown, evil can be destructive and malicious beyond our capacity to imagine.

On the other hand, no one asks, Why does good happen? Do you know, that is a deep mystery too? Goodness is a mystery. That is what I am going to speak about this morning: the mystery of goodness.

Jesus Christ taught us, among other things, that God is almighty and good, his almighty and good Father and ours as well, if we follow Jesus' lead. The very existence of the world is God's act of good will: "Let there be light." And the salvation of the world through Christ is God's act of love. Christ came that we might have eternal life.

All week our attention has been focused on death and dying. The victims at the World Trade Center, the Pentagon, and in the hijacked airplanes did not get up last Tuesday expecting to die. They all got up thinking they had time to work on or finish all sorts of plans, projects, and relationships. Don't we all!

God, who is indeed almighty and good, will take care of those victims. The ones who died are in the arms of his mercy. They are delivered from the burden of the flesh. Their souls are in the Lord's good hands.

And God will bless the injured, and the families and friends of the victims. If they are willing, if they ask him, they will discover God's grace and mercy even in their pain.

God also will bless our country, and the many good nations that will join us, to fight the great wickedness that has assaulted America and the rest of the free world, to defeat terrorism. We will have to be courageous and resolute in this war. And we must pray that our "quiet, unyielding anger" (to quote the President's speech) is purified and prevented from turning into the same kind of ungodly rage (at home and abroad) that has been visited upon us. That would be a great defeat, God forbid; it would be a victory for the Evil One himself.

But let's talk a little more about the dying and the mystery of goodness. First of all let's understand something. This morning, when you got up and looked in the mirror, you saw one of the dying. We all know this, but in order to function "normally," we push this thought out of our minds. Yet we all know, and should not try to deny or forget, that not one of us is going to get out of this world alive. Each of us has an appointment with death.

The victims at the World Trade Center, at the Pentagon, and in the hijacked airplanes had this appointment, which we all realize but do not often seriously entertain — they had this appointment thrust in their faces Tuesday morning. They knew they had only a very little time left, a few minutes. What some of those victims did with those minutes provides us with a priceless gift, a lesson from the dying on how to live, a lesson about the mystery of goodness.

There was the man on the plane that crashed in rural Pennsylvania instead of God knows where the hijackers intended. He called his family to say he and his fellow passengers knew they were doomed; they knew what the hijackers were up to; but they were *"going to do something about this."* It appears that they did, and may well have averted yet another catastrophe.

Then there were the people in the Twin Towers, the ones who knew they could not escape from the inferno caused by the exploding planes that hit the buildings. They called their families and loved ones to tell them they loved them. In the midst of all that hell, those magic, mysterious words were spoken: *"I love you."*

Then there are the firefighters and the police, so many of whom lost their lives, because, as the hymn "America the Beautiful" says, they "loved mercy more than life." They are joined by the living: their comrades and the soldiers and the rescue and medical workers, counselors, clergy of all sorts, volunteers of every kind. And behind them countless people who want to do something to help. This is an overwhelming multitude, a great body of compassion and love, a mighty army of good will and prayer.

On Friday, we were caught flat-footed at our noon Eucharist. We had expected perhaps a few hundred people at that Mass. After all, the President had asked us to pray. But instead of a few hundred, we had standing room only, probably two thousand. We were caught by surprise, but the Lord provided wonderfully. It was very moving. Similar scenes occurred in many places.

This great army of good will is not only in the city but also in the nation and around the world. Just here at Saint Thomas, we have been inundated by messages of love and offers to help, not just from New York or the United States; from North India to Uruguay, to England and Ireland, to Germany to Japan. This is the great mystery of goodness, and it connects us to the almighty and good God, the Father of our Lord Jesus Christ.

If you think your little acts of goodness do not count, you are mistaken. Think again. Think of those good, brave victims on the planes and in the buildings. Think of the police and firefighters. Think of the nurses and doctors. Think of the great multitude, that mighty army of good will, which they represent. You and I have been called to be soldiers in that army.

We have already said that God created the world out of good will and that he has saved his world by Christ out of love. There is one more thing. The mystery of goodness not only has the first word, it also has the last word. God will also *judge* the world, including us, by the standard of goodness. What did Jesus say? He said that the King will draw up all the nations before him at the End, to judge them for all eternity. And the difference between the sheep and the goats consists of the "little" acts of goodness. The Lord is very clear and precise — "I was hungry, thirsty, sick, in prison, naked, dying, suffering, and you ministered to me. And inasmuch as you did this to the least, you did it to me."

So, my brothers and sisters, let us remember to do goodness. Let us never forget just two sentences said by the people who knew they were dying, who had only a few more minutes to live. "*We're going to do something about this.*" "*I love you.*" This is the mystery of goodness. Time is short and precious; eternity is long. These things we do really matter. The great thing is, if we embrace goodness, if we, like the firefighters, "love mercy more than life," we will not die. *We will have life forever, life in the almighty, good God.*

In the Name of God the Father, God the Son, and God the Holy Ghost. Amen.

God's Care Is beyond Reason
Rev. Dr. John Clinton Evans, interim pastor, Madison Avenue Presbyterian Church, New York, September 16, 2001

Why? Why such hatred? Why such horrible death? Why such carnage? Why would God allow this to happen? Was this God's will? Why questions ask only for answers to why questions. What we have been faced with is a tragedy of unimagined horror and proportion. Thousands of precious lives have been senselessly snuffed out, people representing every racial, religious, ethnic, economic, professional, and caring part of this city and world. Mothers, fathers, sisters and brothers, sons and daughters, relatives and friends and coworkers. And there were the fire, police, and emergency care workers. What do we say?

We can say that September 11 was not God's will.

Never would God will such horror! God is such depth of love that God respects and values us enough to grant us free will. We can reflect that love or we can turn that love in upon ourselves, or outward as hatred toward others, and God suffers. Yes, "For God so loved the world that he gave his only Son, so that everyone who believes in him may not perish but may have eternal life," the ultimate example of God's care beyond reason! And we die, die in every imaginable way from natural causes, tragic diseases, to the unexplainable horror we watched on September 11. God does not will tragedy, death, and destruction. Love, forgiveness, and reconciliation are the fruits of God who created this world and called it good.

In light of this week, the lectionary passages of scripture needed to be studied afresh. Jeremiah was called to be a mouthpiece for God at a time when the Assyrian control had tired and the Covenant people of God were able to enjoy some of the freedom and material blessings of the good life. Jeremiah was aware of Egypt seeking to flex its strength at that time. Jeremiah also was mindful of the power of the Babylonians posturing for control on two flanks. It looked like God might use aggressors to humble God's people, bringing them to their knees and even taking them from their own country. We hear Jeremiah's anguish as he spills out the words, "Your ways and your doings have brought this upon you. This is your doom, and it is bitter; it has reached your very heart." And God is saying, "For my people are foolish, they do not know me; they are stupid children, they have no understanding. They are skilled in doing evil, but do not know how to do good." Though these are very strong words, God was in no way abandoning them. Their own ways had startled them, thinking that they had pulled God along with them to bless their ways. Their reasoning had everything in order.

Tragedies like September 11 remind us that all of our best efforts to build our society, its structures, safeguards, and values, are never quite enough. We reason that we have everything in order. So we will assess the situation and struggle to build better, safer systems that will serve us for a few more years. Twelve years ago San Francisco began rebuilding the city to withstand earthquakes of greater magnitude. All of this and what will be done to rebuild the trade and financial center will be better. What God was asking of the covenant community was to understand the gift of their lives and goodness of love that was given them to share. How much of Jeremiah's community lost the power of his prophesy through his poetry and missed God speaking through it to their own reasoned, other-directed lives.

The depth of the poetry was pointing beyond what often is seen as God's wrath, to the deeper love of God that is always forgiving and redeeming. Remember God's words to Jeremiah, "Before I formed you in the womb I knew you, and before you were born I consecrated you; ... " So too, with God's covenant children and with us, we hurt God and wander from God's presence. The power of God's love is there, even in our darkest days of our history. " ... the whole land shall be a desolation; yet I will not make a full end." Thank God, God's care is beyond reason.

T. S. Eliot wrote, "What we call the beginning is often the end and to make an end is to make a beginning. The end is where we start from." And you and I know that the trade and financial centers will rise again in NYC!

In the Gospel lectionary passage, Jesus was dealing with the ending of separation of the righteous and the outcasts. He was being criticized for turning his energy to publicans and sinners, so he told a parable to the holy and righteous ones who were the keepers of the faith and society. The parable reflected their situation seeing Jesus caring for those who were lost.

It is a parable for today. It brings back that Sunday School picture of a just-washed cute lamb resting on Jesus' shoulder. It is a valuable image for today, of being rescued. We like it also because we wander off following our lusts, greed, self-image, and finally we stumble over something, look around, and realize that we are lost, really lost. We need today, in spite of all others, to have one who cares, who respects us, who can comfort us, who can return us to the right direction for our lives. Rescue us Lord. PLEASE!

The image of God seeking the lost sheep is very much God seeking and finding each and every one of the thousands who died in the rubble and planes, along with those deep in shock and struggling with grief. That old Sunday School picture has new meaning, and we see those huge arms surrounding all of those children of God in that rubble. The understanding we have of the shepherd leaving the flock in order to search and find the lost sheep misses the depth of the parable. The parable is really about the owner of the flock. The owner is God. And it is God who never leaves each one within the flock while, at the same time, is there to rescue the lost one. There is only and always God's care and redeeming forgiving love. We speak of revenge, just response, and growing hatred. God's care is beyond reason. God's love is right here, when the days are beautiful, when the storms of life overtake us, when tragedies happen, yea, when death comes. God's love is our comfort, the way through the valley of the shadow of death, and our future direction.

May we reflect God's love more fully in these days ahead.

In the name of the Father, Son, and Holy Spirit. Amen.

God Almighty Is Lifting His Protection
Pat Robertson, president, Christian Broadcasting Network, press release, September 27, 2001

America has enjoyed unprecedented peace and prosperity throughout its history. Though we have been involved in wars on our own soil — the last was the Civil War — the United States of America has not experienced the anguish of invasion by a foreign power since the War of 1812.

We have imagined ourselves invulnerable and have been consumed by the pursuit of financial gain. The focus of many in America has been on the pursuit of health, wealth, material pleasures, and sexuality. Sadly, those in the churches have been as self-indulgent as those in the world.

We have allowed rampant pornography on the Internet, and rampant secularism and the occult, etc. to be broadcast on television. We have permitted somewhere in the neighborhood of 35–40 million unborn babies to be slaughtered by our society.

We have a court that has essentially stuck its finger in God's eye and said, "We are going to legislate You out of the schools and take Your commandments from the courthouses in various states. We are not going to let little children read the commandments of God. We are not going to allow the Bible or prayer in our schools."

We have insulted God at the highest level of our government. Then, we say, "Why does this happen?" It is happening because God Almighty is lifting His protection from us. Once that protection is gone, we are vulnerable because we are a free society.

We lie naked before these terrorists who have infiltrated our country. There are probably tens of thousands of them in America right now. They have been raising money and preaching their hate. Overseas, they have been spewing out venom against the United States for years.

All over the Arab world there is venom against America being poured into people's minds, and the only thing that is going to sustain us is the umbrella power of Almighty God. That is the only thing that we have going for us.

Yes, we can put up a nuclear shield, but they are not coming in with missiles. We can beef up marshals on airplanes, but then they will come in with car bombs. There is always some way they can get at us. The means of these rogue states are awesome.

Yes, we will mobilize now and our country is moving together. But I want to say as firmly as I can, the Scripture for this time is — "If My people who are called by My name will humble themselves, pray, seek My face and turn from their wicked ways, then I will hear from heaven, forgive their sin, and heal their land."

Now, I am filled with compassion. It just tears my heart when I think of the families of these suffering. But I want to say as surely as I am sitting here today, this is only a foretaste, a little warning, of what is going to happen.

We have not seen the massive destruction of life in our

urban centers that can take place with sarin gas and with the biological and chemical warfare that is available to these rogue people, not to mention suitcase nuclear bombs that they probably have available as well. We must come back to God as a people.

So what we say to you today is, if you are not right with God then get your life right with God. Think of the things in your life that are wrong. Think of the careless indifference. Think of the poor who you could have helped. Think of the Scripture you have ignored. Think of the time you should have been spending in prayer, when you were watching television or focusing on pornography or tuned into the Internet. Think of the things you have done in your own life and think of the indifference to the sin of this nation that you have just passed by and said, "Well, that is just the way it is. We have to have freedom." Think of it!

Don't ask why did it happen. It happened because people are evil. It also happened because God is lifting His protection from this nation and we must pray and ask Him for revival so that once again we will be His people, the planting of His righteousness, so that He will come to our defense and protect us as a nation. That is what I want to see and why we say we must have revival.

We must have a spiritual revival. The churches need to be full. We must pray for our pastors. We must pray for the churches. We must ask God to send a mighty, powerful revival in the midst of His people. That is what is needed for this land.

I want us to pray right now for America. I want us to pray for you and your families. I want us to pray particularly for those mothers, those fathers, those husbands and wives, those brothers and sisters who have lost loved ones. Their hearts are breaking right now. As they see this thing happen and they say "Why, Why?" And their hearts are broken.

We may find that as many as twenty thousand innocent civilians have been killed in this tragedy. We don't know what the full number is yet. It may not be that high, but that is one estimate.

Please join with me as we all pray right now.

Father, we come before You, and we share the pain and the grief of those who are suffering. We saw those people with their little posters held up before TV cameras with the pictures of their loved ones. Surely, you have seen this man. He is 5′10″ and he weighs so and so and he's got a cute smile. Oh, God in heaven, we pray that You would comfort them — that You will comfort those who suffer and grieve in this manner.

And Lord, we pray for our nation. We have sinned against Almighty God. At the highest level of government we have stuck our finger in Your eye. The Supreme Court has insulted You over and over again, Lord. They have taken Your Bible away from the schools. They have forbidden little children to pray. Organizations have gone to court to take the knowledge of God out of the public squares of America. Then people say, "Why isn't God looking after us?"

We have sinned against You, Lord. We ask that You might forgive us. And that You might bring us to the place where we are truly sorry for our sins, and as a Nation we repent before You. And Almighty God, we ask for a spiritual revival, a cleansing of our Nation, a cleansing of the hearts of Your people.

We pray for pastors, anoint them, Lord. We pray, oh God, for the churches. Give them the fire of God. And Lord, may millions come to the knowledge of Jesus Christ. Do a miracle in this land, we pray, that Your name might be honored. And Lord, we ask that You would bind up our wounds and heal our land. We receive this, Lord, in Jesus' name. Amen.

I Blame No One but the Hijackers

Jerry Falwell, senior pastor, Thomas Road Baptist Church,
Lynchburg, Virginia, statement of apology, September 17, 2001

Last Thursday during an appearance on the 700 Club, in the midst of the shock and mourning of a dark week for America, I made a statement that I should not have made and which I sincerely regret. [Falwell said that "the pagans, the abortionists, the feminists, the gays and lesbians..., the ACLU...helped this happen."] I apologize that, during a week when everyone appropriately dropped all labels and no one was seen as liberal or conservative, Democrat or Republican, religious or secular, I singled out for blame certain groups of Americans.

This was insensitive, uncalled for at the time, and unnecessary as part of the commentary on this destruction. The only label any of us needs in such a terrible time of crisis is that of "American."

I obviously did not state my theological convictions very well and I stated them at a bad time. During the difficult weeks ahead there will be much discussion about the judgment of God. It is a worthy discussion for all of us at a time when we are reminded of the fleeting nature of life itself, but it is a complicated discussion.

I do not know if the horrific events of September 11 are the judgment of God, but if they are, that judgment is on all of America — including me and all fellow sinners — and not on any particular group.

My statements were understandably called divisive by some, including those whom I mentioned by name in the interview. This grieves me, as I had no intention of being divisive.

In conclusion, I blame no one but the hijackers and terrorists for the barbaric happenings of September 11.

We know, as Abraham Lincoln anguished in his second inaugural address, that "The Almighty has his own purposes," but as he said, "The judgments of the Lord are true and righteous altogether."

Not without Criticism
**James Skillen, president, Center for Public Justice,
Annapolis, Maryland, September 17, 2001**

A multitude of concerns occupies America's leaders as a consequence of the September 11 terrorist attacks. One interpretation of those events that we must not allow to pass without criticism was offered by Jerry Falwell and Pat Robertson on CBN's 700 Club, September 13.

In conversation, the two agreed that the terrorist attacks should be understood theologically as God's judgment on America because of the secularization of our society caused by pagans, abortionists, feminists, gays, and lesbians. "I point the finger in their face and say, 'You helped this happen,'" Falwell said.

"And when we destroy 40 million little innocent babies, we make God mad," Falwell added. "When a nation deserts God and expels God from the culture . . . the result is not good."

From a biblical point of view these comments are deplorable on at least three counts. The first error is the pretension of the speakers to know the secret will of God. Falwell asserts that America's "secular and anti-Christian environment" left us open to God's judgment rather than protection. But why would Falwell adopt this rather than some other interpretation? Maybe God loves America so much that he thwarted other terrorist plans, allowing only three planes to reach their targets and saving thousands more people from destruction. How does Falwell know that God's judgment and not God's protection explains the events? False prophets have always abounded, claiming to know too much.

The second error is that the two television preachers confuse America with God's chosen people. When Falwell, with Robertson's agreement, criticizes all "who have tried to secularize America," his underlying assumption is that there once was a time when America was not secularized, when it met with God's approval as his chosen nation. Falwell speaks as a modern Jeremiah lamenting the sins of God's new Israel, America. The roots of this mind-set reach back to the Puritans who established a new covenant community in New England — a city set on a hill. But modern, new-Israelite nationalism has no biblical justification. On New Testament grounds, the chosen people of God are the faithful in Jesus Christ throughout the world, not the citizens of America or any other state. Moreover, even as a political entity, the American republic was, from the beginning, shot through with injustices deserving of God's judgment. The Falwell/

Robertson theology of church and state is fundamentally unbiblical.

Finally, Falwell and Robertson exhibit one of the sins most condemned by Jesus and his disciples, namely, self-righteousness. These pretentious priests of God's supposedly chosen nation point an authoritative finger to a circle of sinners that happens not to include them. If it weren't for the abortionists, gays, and lesbians, God would apparently have had no reason to judge America. If America was filled with the members of Falwell's church and the listeners/donors to the 700 Club, the attack would perhaps not have been necessary.

Did it ever cross the mind of either man that if God is judging America, it might be, in part, because of the self-righteous, ungodly practices of those who claim to be Christians and who are preaching and practicing a way of life that, on biblical grounds, is disobedient?

Christians should be spending their time ministering to the suffering and conveying the good news of God's forgiving love in Jesus Christ, who is fashioning a new people drawn from all nations on earth. And in their civic capacities, Christians should be helping to design and support just public policies to protect the innocent and to punish those who take vengeance into their own hands.

God at the Ritz

Lorenzo Albacete, professor at the Seminary of the Archdiocese of New York, from *God at the Ritz* (Crossroad, 2002)

As soon as we began to grasp what happened, it became clear that the ultimate nature of the attack against us was religious. By destroying the Twin Towers and part of the

Pentagon, the terrorists did not think they were going to mortally wound American power. The targets were chosen as symbols of power. This was a symbolic gesture, so to speak, the type of statement or affirmation typical of religious behavior. The people who crashed those planes into the World Trade Center and the Pentagon saw themselves as religious martyrs. We have unavoidable proof of that in the literature left behind by one of them in the car he took to the airport, literature urging him to think of the paradise that awaited him and not to be afraid of death. But rather than face it as such, all kinds of ways were found to avoid the issue. It was said that the terrorists were not authentically religious, that they were using religion to justify their hatred, or that they were just completely insane.

Religious people went out of the way to insist that this kind of behavior is absolutely incompatible with any authentic religion, even more so of Islam, which the terrorists saw themselves as following. But that is not the question. The question is not why any particular religion was being used to justify the hatred that inspired such acts; the question is the religious nature of the hatred itself. This is what many had trouble facing.

During that first week after the horror I heard two people trying to understand the religious nature of what had happened. One was David Letterman. His show may not be the best forum for religious discussion, but again and again Letterman said he wanted to understand how it was possible to claim a religious motivation for such violence against innocent people. For a week he brought into the show the usual parade of TV gurus of culture, and they could not answer — nor even really understand — the question. By the end of the week Letterman had given up and the deepest level reached was, as usual, the psychological, or maybe even the "philosophical," in particular, a conflict between views about freedom and human rights.

The other person who publicly recognized the ultimately religious nature of the conflict was Jerry Falwell, before he was led to claim that he had not expressed himself properly. The statement attributed to him was wrong, but at least he recognized that there is a relation between what happened and our own religious behavior. It is important to try to rescue this insight.

In order to do this, we must absolutely reject all suggestions of moral equivalence, as if were a matter of numbers or interchangeable evil acts. There is absolutely nothing that anyone did at any time that justifies the death of a single innocent person, not to mention over six thousand. Such a suggestion is obscene. I believe we must also reject the view that God allowed what happened on September 11 to awaken us to our culture's offenses against life and human nature. I don't know how we can say things like that and not see ourselves in the company of those theologians and religious friends of Job who tried to explain to him the reason for his sufferings. God, remember, rejected their arguments and offered Job no explanation for what had happened. Instead, he asked him questions that led Job to recognize that God would always be a Mystery beyond human comprehension. What mattered was to know that this Mystery was not his enemy.

Andrew Sullivan also recognized the religious nature of what is happening in an article in the *New York Times Magazine* [reprinted in this volume, p. 83]....

I do not know how truly religious are the personal motivations of the leaders who planned this attack. But even if they are motivated purely by a desire for power, their success is due to their appeal to the religious sense of their followers. It is true that the targeting of the United States is due to the realities of American political, military, and economic involvement in "their" world, but it is to a religious interpretation of the ultimate meaning of this involvement that they appeal to justify their war as a "holy" war.

Some argue that this is about a "conflict between civilizations." I think we have to be very careful when we say this. There is indeed a conflict between civilizations in the world today — actually, many such conflicts. The breakdown in national frontiers characteristic of the so-called "global village" and the spread of American-style culture everywhere is certainly being perceived as a threat by people who have not been exposed to the changes of modernity. (It is interesting to note also that within the present dominant global culture there are people afraid of the growing presence in our midst of people from the very cultures threatened by our influence and power.) This situation is the background for the present crisis, but it is just that, a background for the manifestation of another conflict, one that has been present from the beginning of human history. The conflict with the terrorists feeds from this other conflict characteristic of the present time, but it is an ancient conflict.

This deeper conflict is not between one civilization and another; this conflict is between all civilizations and an anti-civilization. Civilization is a triumph against the forces of indiscriminate violence, intolerance, and pursuit of power that can be embodied in terrorism, and terrorism has existed within all civilizations, threatening their best achievement.

To repeat again, at the deepest level this is a religious conflict. It is amazing that the first global war of the twenty-first century, the beginning of the new millennium, is a war of religion. It shows that the twentieth century was not that secular after all; what was often held to be secularism was really another form of religion; it was religion without real transcendence.

This is not a conflict between one religion, Islam, and Western secularism. This is a conflict within the religious world itself in which secularism is often a religious position. It is a conflict between different forms of our relation to transcendence and Mystery. This conflict exists within Western civilization itself, as it exists within Islamic civilization. It exists within all human civilizations. It is a conflict within the very structure of humankind.

The human being is characterized by the religious sense, that is, the search for the meaning of life, for what makes life valuable. If not thrown off course by something external to this human impulse, the religious sense will bring men and women to the recognition that this source of meaning, value, and purpose is located, so to speak, in a Mystery beyond anything that can be grasped or imagined by our understanding, but with which we need to be connected in order to live according to all the possibilities, all the desires in the human heart. However, because of the frustration in not being able to reach this Mystery, as well as a mysterious wound — a malfunctioning — within the religious sense itself, this quest for the Mystery is cut short, and human beings equate the ultimate source of meaning with a reality that is not the Mystery.

This reality can be within or beyond this world. The religious conflict is the conflict between religion open to the Infinite Mystery and a religion that has created idols, substitutes for the Mystery, for which sacrifices are willingly made.

The idol to which the terrorists appeal is an abstract ideology constructed by a distorted religious sense. They may equate it with "Islamic civilization," but civilization is precisely the triumph over their way of thinking. The terrorists represent a conflict within the Islamic world, just as other terrorists have represented conflicts within the Jewish and Christian worlds. The very foundations of all civilization are being attacked, not by the Islamic faith, but by an idol created by presumed adherents to Islamic faith. Islamic civilization is also under attack. We should not fall into the error of constructing our own idol and call it "Western Civilization." Instead, as a civilization, ours is one that has originated exactly where Islam did, namely, within a religious experience of Mystery associated with a historical event called "the election of Abraham." A true dialogue between the West and the Islamic world should be based on this common origin and its implications. Western civilization must itself try to rediscover what its own origin in Abraham's call means in terms of its view of the religious sense.

Therefore, beyond the need (and the moral obligation), which cannot be denied, to protect our freedom and the achievements of our civilization by a defensive military campaign, the most important thing to do is purify our own civilization from the idols that have been created in it. That is, we must seek to retrieve again the fundamental insights and convictions that gave rise to our civilizing efforts, to the ideals, values, and convictions to which we appeal in order to formulate the rules for living and working together.

The fundamental value is the dignity of the human person. Everything else depends on this. Respect for the dignity of the human person is the ethical norm that should guide our behavior and our view of progress. But this dignity comes from the human person's link with transcendence, indeed with the human person's vocation to transcendence, the vocation to establish a relation with an infinite Mystery that defines the range of human possibilities for the fulfillment of our desire for happiness. This vocation is the only secure basis for what we experience when we speak of freedom.

The link between so-called Western civilization and the Mystery has been the religious experience preserved in Judaism and inherited by the Christian faith. We must retrieve this original insight in order to be faithful to our authentic culture-building, civilizing tradition. This requires that we refuse to identify this Mystery with anything that originates in human efforts to avoid falling into an idolatry or ideology that seeks to force human life to conform to its restricted view of the Mystery. The affirmation of a true transcendence is the basis that will preserve and defend our cultural achievements, especially our understanding of freedom. From this too comes an authentic respect for tolerance, diversity, and human rights. This is also the best defense from being manipulated by Power, including the power of the State, or the Power of those who control the resources needed for human growth and development. Finally, this conviction is also the basis for our view of the primacy of freely chosen interpersonal relations over all social arrangements proposed or even imposed on us by the power of majorities.

The ideals that animate our civilizations reflect the human heart's cry for justice and peace in the pursuit of happiness. The problem is when these ideals are "wrapped in theory," to use the words of the American novelist Flannery O'Connor. When ideals are wrapped in theory they can actually become dangerous and deadly, used to justify all kinds of acts that are really motivated by anger and the desire for revenge. But how can the religious sense be protected from degenerating into a "theory" that gives rise to destruction and violence?

The twentieth century could not resolve the dilemma about the need and the danger of religion. This will be the great question of our new century. But in order to answer it, I believe we must look beyond religion to the experience that has been called "grace."

A World Out of Touch with Itself

Rabbi Michael Lerner, editor, *Tikkun* magazine, September 17, 2001 (www.tikkunmagazine.org)

There is never any justification for acts of terror against innocent civilians — it is the quintessential act of dehumanization and not recognizing the sanctity of others, and a visible symbol of a world increasingly irrational and out of control.

It's understandable why many of us, after grieving and consoling the mourners, will feel anger — and while some demagogues in Congress have already sought to manipulate that feeling into a growing militarism (more spies, legalize assassinations of foreign leaders, increase the defense budget at the expense of domestic programs), the more "responsible" leaders are seeking to narrow America's response to targeted attacks on countries that allegedly harbor the terrorists.

The perpetrators deserve to be punished, and I personally would be happy if all the people involved in this act were to be imprisoned for the rest of their lives. Let's not be naive: these are evil people who planned this and perpetrated it, just as are many who are engaged in acts of terror against Israel. They should not be excused or forgiven for their acts.

Yet in some ways this narrow focus allows us to avoid dealing with the underlying issues. When violence becomes so prevalent throughout the planet, it's too easy to simply talk of "deranged minds." We need to ask ourselves, "What is it in the way that we are living, organizing our societies, and treating each other that makes violence seem plausible to so many people?"

We in the spiritual world will see this as a growing global incapacity to recognize the spirit of God in each other — what we call the sanctity of each human being.

But even if you reject religious language, you can see that the willingness of people to hurt each other to advance their own interests has become a global problem, and it's only the dramatic level of this particular attack which distinguishes it from the violence and insensitivity to each other that is part of our daily lives.

We may tell ourselves that the current violence has "nothing to do" with the way that we've learned to close our ears when told that one out of every three people on this planet does not have enough food, and that one billion are literally starving.

We may reassure ourselves that the hoarding of the world's resources by the richest society in world history, and our frantic attempts to accelerate globalization with its attendant inequalities of wealth, has nothing to do with the resentment that others feel toward us.

We may tell ourselves that the suffering of refugees and the oppressed have nothing to do with us — that that's a different story that is going on somewhere else.

But we live in one world, increasingly interconnected with everyone, and the forces that lead people to feel outrage, anger, and desperation eventually impact on our own daily lives.

The same inability to feel the pain of others is the pathology that shapes the minds of these terrorists. Raise children in circumstances where no one is there to take care of them, or where they must live by begging or selling their bodies in prostitution, put them in refugee camps and tell them that they have "no right of return" to their homes, treat them as though they are less valuable and deserving of respect because they are part of some despised national or ethnic group, surround them with a media that extols the rich and makes everyone who is not economically successful and physically trim and conventionally "beautiful" feel bad about themselves, offer them jobs whose sole goal is to enrich the "bottom line" of someone else, and teach them that "looking out for number one" is the only thing anyone "really" cares about and that any who believe in love and social justice are merely naive idealists who are destined to always remain powerless, and you will produce a worldwide population of people feeling depressed, angry, unable to care about others, and in various ways dysfunctional.

I see this in Israel, where Israelis have taken to dismissing the entire Palestinian people as "terrorists" but never ask themselves: "What have we done to make this seem to Palestinians to be a reasonable path of action today?" Of course there were always some hateful people and some religious fundamentalists who want to act in hurtful ways against Israel, no matter what the circumstances.

Yet, in the situation of 1993–96 when Israel under Yitzhak Rabin was pursuing a path of negotiations and peace, the fundamentalists had little following and there were few acts of violence. On the other hand, when Israel failed to withdraw from the West Bank, and instead expanded the number of its settlers, the fundamentalists and haters had a far easier time convincing many decent Palestinians that there might be no other alternative.

Similarly, if the U.S. turns its back on global agreements to preserve the environment, unilaterally cancels its treaties to not build a missile defense, accelerates the processes by which a global economy has made some people in the third world richer but many poorer, shows that it cares nothing for the fate of refugees who have been homeless for decades, and otherwise turns its back on ethical norms, it becomes far easier for the haters and the fundamentalists to recruit people who are willing to kill themselves in strikes against what they perceive to be an evil American empire represented by the Pentagon and the World Trade Center.

Most Americans will feel puzzled by any reference to this "larger picture." It seems baffling to imagine that somehow we are part of a world system which is slowly destroying the life support system of the planet, and quickly transferring the wealth of the world into our own pockets.

We don't feel personally responsible when an American corporation runs a sweat shop in the Philippines or crushes efforts of workers to organize in Singapore. We don't see ourselves implicated when the U.S. refuses to consider the plight of Palestinian refugees or uses the excuse of fighting drugs to support repression in Colombia or other parts of Central America. We don't even see the symbolism when terrorists attack America's military center and our trade center — we talk of them as buildings, though others see them as centers of the forces that are causing the world so much pain.

We have narrowed our own attention to "getting through" or "doing well" in our own personal lives, and who has time to focus on all the rest of this? Most of us are leading perfectly reasonable lives within the options that we have available to us — so why should others be angry at us, much less strike out against us?

And the truth is, our anger is also understandable: the striking out by others in acts of terror against us is just as irrational as the world-system that it seeks to confront. Yet our acts of counterterror will also be counterproductive. We should have learned from the current phase of the Israel-Palestinian struggle — responding to terror with more violence rather than asking ourselves what we could do to change the conditions that generated it in the first place — will only ensure more violence against us in the future.

Luckily, most people don't act out in violent ways — they tend to act out more against themselves, drowning themselves in alcohol or drugs or personal despair. Others turn toward fundamentalist religions or ultra-nationalist extremism. Still others find themselves acting out against people that they love, acting angry or hurtful toward children or relationship partners.

This is a world out of touch with itself, filled with people who have forgotten how to recognize and respond to the sacred in each other because we are so used to looking at others from the standpoint of what they can do for us, how we can use them toward our own ends. The alternatives are stark: either start caring about the fate of everyone on this planet or be prepared for a slippery slope toward violence that will eventually dominate our daily lives.

Let's not be naive about the perpetrators of this terror. Many are evil people, as are some of the fundamentalists and ultra-nationalists who demean and are willing to destroy others. But these evil people are often marginalized when societal dynamics are moving toward peace and hope (e.g., in Israel while Yitzhak Rabin was prime minister) and they become much more influential and able to recruit people to give their lives to their cause when ordinary and otherwise decent people despair of peace and justice, as when Israel from 1996 to 2000 dramatically increased the number of settlers.

So here is what would marginalize those who hate the United States. Imagine if the bin Ladens of the world had to recruit people against America at a time when:

- America was using its economic resources to end world hunger and redistribute the wealth of the planet so that everyone had enough.

- America was the leading voice championing an ethos of generosity and caring for others — and it required that as the standard for its own corporations.

- America was restructuring its own internal life so
  that all social practices and institutions were being judged "productive or efficient or rational"
  not only because they maximized profit, but also
  to the extent that they maximized love and caring, ethical/spiritual/ecological sensitivity, and an
  approach to the universe based on awe and wonder
  at the grandeur of creation.

Think it's naive and impossible to move America in
that direction? Well, here are two reasons why, even if it's
a long shot, it's an approach that deserves your support:

- It's even more naive to imagine that military assaults,
  more spies, or repression can stop someone willing to
  lose his life while hijacking an airplane, letting loose
  a biochemical assault, or using new technologies to
  wreak havoc.

- The response of people to the World Trade Center attack was an outpouring of loving energy and
  generosity which shows the degree to which people
  really do care about each other. If we could legitimate Americans allowing that part of themselves to
  come out without having to wait for a disaster, we
  would not be "socially engineering" a "new kind of
  humanity" but rather empowering a part of every
  human being which our social order marginalizes.
  There's lots of goodness in Americans.

We should pray for the victims and the families of those
who have been hurt or murdered in these crazy acts. We
should also pray that America does not return to "business as usual," but rather turns to a period of reflection,

coming back into touch with our common humanity, asking ourselves how our institutions can best embody our highest values.

We may need a global day of atonement and repentance dedicated to finding a way to turn the direction of our society at every level, a return to the notion that every human life is sacred, that "the bottom line" should be the creation of a world of love and caring, and that the best way to prevent these kinds of acts is not to turn ourselves into a police state, but turn ourselves into a society in which social justice, love, and compassion are so prevalent that violence becomes only a distant memory.

Where was God on September 11?

Rabbi Daniel F. Polish, director of the Commission
on Social Action of Reform Judaism, October 12, 2001

On the days immediately after September 11, I found my thoughts returning to the opening words of the Book of Lamentations:

> How does the city sit deserted,
> She who was
> Once great with people,
> Is become like a widow.
> The princess among states
> Has become like one in thrall.
>
> Bitterly she weeps in the night.
> Her cheeks wet with tears . . .
>
> Her enemies are now her masters.
> Her foes are at ease.

I know that in the wake of these profoundly tragic events many people asked the question, "Where was God?" But as a Jew born in the twentieth century, that was not a question that came to my mind on September 11. I had had to grapple with it already — indeed all of my life. For no Jew with any sense of historical consciousness has not already asked, Where was God on November 9, 1938, Kristallnacht. Where was God when the gas chambers and crematoria were being conceived, and built — and used? And the answers with which I had already furnished my intellectual and spiritual inner chamber were the same answers I would have offered anyone who asked me as I made my way through the streets of Manhattan on September 11.

Not insignificantly, the High Holy Day period of the most profound introspection and theological attentiveness came quickly on the heels of these horrendous events. And it is from the raw material of the liturgy, lectionary, and ideology of these days that I have constructed the answers to the question of where is God that have sustained me through my own times of asking it.

We Jews are not taught that the world is the arena of dueling powers and principalities. We do not see human events as driven by the battle of two competing forces. Rather, we believe in the one God who can say:

> I form light and create darkness,
> I make peace and create evil.
> I the Lord do all these things.
>
> (Isa. 45:7)

This is a stunning, perhaps troubling, way to articulate the oneness of God, so stark and disturbing that when we include it in our liturgy, we take recourse to the euphemistic reformulation that says more gently that God "makes peace and creates everything." Still, it recognizes the workings of God behind all we experience. The same idea is put even more pointedly in the Book of Deuteronomy:

> See, then, that I, I am He;
> There is no god beside Me.
> I deal death and give life;
> I wound and I heal...
> (Deut. 32:39)

So why this horror, why the unbearably overwhelming tragedy of the Shoah? It is not our theology that must challenge us here, but our anthropology. For God has, for God's own reasons, chosen to contract and constrict enough to leave room for human beings to act as they see fit. "Everything is in the hands of heaven," our Rabbis teach us, "except obedience to heaven." On Yom Kippur, the Torah portion we read reminds us:

> See, I set before you today, life and good, death and evil....I call heaven and earth to witness against you this day. I put before you life and death, the blessing and the curse. Choose life that you may live, you and your children after you. (Deut. 30:15, 19)

The words of Torah are clear enough which way people should behave, and yet we are given the power to choose. We are not created all good; nor, in the eyes of Jewish tradition, with any kind of inherent wickedness. We were created with inclinations pulling us in any number of directions. We can do acts of great goodness, even emulating

God in righteousness. Or we can respond to our impulse to destructiveness and wickedness. The choice, Jewish religious tradition reminds us, is in our hands: "I place before you today . . . " Even with the injunction "choose life," we have the freedom of will to choose for the curse and evil and death.

Throughout history there have been those who have chosen for the wrong. We hear them described in the Book of Psalms:

> Why boastest thou thyself of evil, O mighty man?
> Thy tongue deviseth destruction
> Like a sharp razor. (Ps. 52:3–4)

> My soul is among lions, I do lie down among them
>   that are aflame;
> Even the sons of men whose teeth are spears and
>   arrows
> And their tongues like a sharp sword. (Ps. 57:5)

> He is like a lion that is eager to tear to pieces,
> Like a young lion lurking in secret places.
>   (Ps. 17:12)

We human beings were not created to be that way. Those individuals were not born like that. They made choices. And what they chose, they became.

The question is not, Where was God? It never has been. It is, Where were we human beings? How could flesh and blood have made the decision to turn other flesh and blood to smoke and ash? It is almost too easy to blame God; harder, much harder, to blame those who were, at least in origin — and in potential — like ourselves.

Where was God? Some saw God in the people who made other choices, who risked their lives to save others, who rushed to help, who performed acts of kindness small and great, to console and comfort and make gentle the lives of people they did not even know to whom great wrong had been done.

Where was God? A lovely rabbinic commentary to Psalm 137 is based on an apparently extraneous word on the first verse. Literally translated, the text reads, "by the rivers of Babylon, there we sat down, also we wept when we remembered Zion." The Rabbis ask why the verse includes the word *gam* (also). And they teach that it connotes that the weeping of the people at the cataclysm of the destruction of their Temple and at their exile was so intense that it caused God to weep *gam* — also, alongside them. Where was God? Grieving beside the people in the time of its most profound sorrow. So I did not find myself asking that question, Where was God? Instead, I found myself asking the harder question: Humanity, where were you?

And yet we know that, in the end, the ultimate control of the course of human history is with God. As Joseph instructs his brothers when he finally reveals his identity to them:

> I am your brother Joseph whom you sold into Egypt. Now do not be discomforted or reproach yourselves because you sold me here. For it was to save life that God sent me ahead of you. . . . So it was not you who sent me here, but God. (Gen. 45:4, 8)

Beyond the self-willed deeds of human beings is the overarching design of God. Even in the face of our individual actions, God creates the great pattern of history. We know that sorrow can be overtaken by gladness: "Weeping may tarry for the night, but joy comes in the morning" (Ps. 30:5). The exile that is lamented in Psalm 137 did come to an end, and the people ultimately were restored to their homeland.

> When the Lord brought back those that returned to
>   Zion,
> We were like those that dream
>
> Then was our mouth filled with laughter,
> And our tongue with singing.... (Ps. 126:1–2)

We have even seen that out of terrible evil can come great good. But when we are in it, we cannot imagine how. From the vantage of this moment in history, the exodus from Egypt was more than an important event in biblical history. It was an occasion of rebirth and renewal. To the people who lived through those forty years in the wilderness, it was nothing but sand, heat, thirst, and terrible suffering. Only from the perspective of after the experience can later generations look back and see the good in it.

Now is our time of suffering. We cannot imagine a good that can come from this — as none of the generation of the wilderness could imagine the good that would emerge from their ordeal. But faith instructs us that such good may come, even if it is too far beyond our horizon to perceive. Where is God? Directing even these events toward that, for us unknown and unknowable, good.

May that be God's will. May it come speedily... and in our day.

The God Who Forsakes Us

Dietrich Bonhoeffer, German Lutheran pastor and theologian
who resisted the Nazis and was imprisoned and executed
in Germany in 1945 near the end of World War II

The Absence of God

The God who is with us is the God who forsakes us (Mark
15:34). The God who lets us live in the world without
the working hypothesis of God is the God before whom
we stand continually. Before God and with God we live
without God. God lets himself be pushed out of the world
on to the cross. He is weak and powerless in the world,
and that is precisely the way...in which he is with us
and helps us. (*Letters and Papers from Prison,* edited by
Eberhard Bethge [Macmillan, 1953, repr. 1971], 360)

The world that has come of age is more godless, and perhaps for that very reason, nearer to God than the world
before its coming of age. (Ibid., 362)

The one who has found Jesus Christ on the cross knows
how wondrously God hides in this world and how he is
just there, closest, where we believe him to be farthest.

The crucifixion of Jesus Christ is the necessary proof
that God's love is equally near and equally far at all
times. (*The Mystery of Easter,* edited by Manfred Weber
[Crossroad, 1997], 34)

God's Presence

I am God's claim on you; you are God's claim on me —
God himself — and with this recognition our vision
breaks through to the fullness of divine life in this world.

Now life within the human community receives divine meaning. The community is itself a form of God's revelation. God is with us, as long as there is community. This is the deepest meaning of our being bound to social life, that through it we are bound all the closer to God. See, I will be with you always until the end of time. Again, the last things are spoken about. "I am the first and the last," "Jesus Christ yesterday, today, and tomorrow." Jesus is the Lord of times, he is with his people always, even when it is hard, and he will stay with us, this is our consolation. Should affliction and fear overcome us, Jesus is with us and guides us into God's eternal kingdom. Jesus Christ is the expanse of our life. Jesus Christ is the center of our community. Jesus Christ is with us until the end of the world. (Ibid., 35)

Blessed Be the Lord for His Miracles

Elie Wiesel, *The Trial of God* (Schocken Books, 1995), 146–47

MENDEL: Sabbath morning. A crowded synagogue — more crowded than usual. I stood on the bimah before the open scrolls and read. That Shabbat we read the commandment to celebrate our holidays in joy. I had hardly finished the sentence when the doors were pushed open. The mob took over. The killers were laughing. I remember their laughter as I remember their shiny swords. Minutes later, it was all over. Not one Jew cried out; we didn't have the time. As I heard the echo of my own words: "And you shall celebrate your holidays in joy" — I found myself without a community. I was still standing; I stood throughout the slaughter. Standing before the open parchments. Why was I spared? Is is possible that they failed to see me because I was standing? I saw blood, only blood. I felt swept by madness. I whispered over and over again: "And you shall celebrate your holidays in joy, in joy, in joy." And I backed out and left.

SAM: Blessed be the Lord for His miracles.

MENDEL: A whole community was massacred, and you talk of miracles?

SAM: A Jew survived, and you ignore them?

4

Give Us This Day
Our Daily Bread

How Should We Respond?
Justice and Peace

The Case for Rage
Lance Morrow, *Time*, October 22, 2001

For once, let's have no "grief counselors" standing by with banal consolations, as if the purpose, in the midst of all this, were merely to make everyone feel better as quickly as possible. We shouldn't feel better.

For once, let's have no fatuous rhetoric about "healing." Healing is inappropriate now, and dangerous. There will be time later for the tears of sorrow.

A day cannot live in infamy without the nourishment of rage. Let's have rage.

What's needed is a unified, unifying, Pearl Harbor sort of purple American fury — a ruthless indignation that doesn't leak away in a week or two, wandering off into Prozac-induced forgetfulness or into the next media sensation . . . or into a corruptly thoughtful relativism. . . .

Let America explore the rich reciprocal possibilities of the *fatwa*. A policy of focused brutality does not

come easily to a self-conscious, self-indulgent, contradictory, diverse, humane nation with a short attention
span. America needs to relearn a lost discipline, self-
confident relentlessness — and to relearn why human
nature has equipped us all with a weapon (abhorred in
decent peacetime societies) called hatred.

As the bodies are counted, into the thousands and thousands, hatred will not, I think, be a difficult emotion
to summon. Is the medicine too strong? Call it, rather,
a wholesome and intelligent enmity — the sort that impels even such a prosperous, messily tolerant organism as
America to act. Anyone who does not loathe the people
who did these things, and the people who cheer them on,
is too philosophical for decent company.

It's a practical matter, anyway. In war, enemies are enemies. You find them and put them out of business, on
the sound principle that that's what they are trying to
do to you. If what happened on Tuesday does not give
Americans the political will needed to exterminate men
like Osama bin Laden and those who conspire with them
in evil mischief, then nothing ever will and we are in for
a procession of black Tuesdays.

This was terrorism brought to near perfection as a
dramatic form. Never has the evil business had such
production values. Normally, the audience sees only the
smoking aftermath — the blown-up embassy, the ruined
barracks, the ship with a blackened hole at the waterline.
This time the first plane striking the first tower acted as a
shill. It alerted the media, brought cameras to the scene so
that they might be set up to record the vivid surreal bloom
of the second strike ("Am I seeing this?") and then —
could they be such engineering geniuses, so deft at de-

molition? — the catastrophic collapse of the two towers, one after the other, and a sequence of panic in the streets that might have been shot for a remake of *The War of the Worlds* or for *Independence Day*. Evil possesses an instinct for theater, which is why, in an era of gaudy and gifted media, evil may vastly magnify its damage by the power of horrific images.

It is important not to be transfixed. The police screamed to the people running from the towers, "Don't look back!" — a biblical warning against the power of the image. Terrorism is sometimes described (in frustrated, oh-the-burdens-of-great-power tone of voice) as "asymmetrical warfare." So what? Most of history is a pageant of asymmetries. It is mostly the asymmetries that cause history to happened — an obscure Schickelgruber nearly destroys Europe; a mere atom, artfully diddled, incinerates a city. Elegant perplexity puts too much emphasis on the "asymmetrical" side of the phrase and not enough on the fact that it is indeed real warfare. Asymmetry is a concept. War is, as we see, blood and death.

It is not a bad idea to repeat a line from the nineteenth-century French anarchist thinker Pierre-Joseph Proudhon: "The fecundity of the unexpected far exceeds the prudence of statesmen." America, in the spasms of a few hours, became a changed country. It turned the corner at last, out of the 1990s. The menu of American priorities was rearranged. The presidency of George W. Bush begins now. What seemed important a few days ago (in the media at least) became instantly trivial. If Gary Condit is mentioned once in the next six months on cable television, I will be astonished.

During World War II, John Kennedy wrote home to

his parents from the Pacific. He remarked that Americans are at their best during very good times or very bad times; the in-between periods, he thought, cause them trouble. I'm not sure that is true. Good times sometimes have a tendency to make Americans squalid. The worst times, as we see, separate the civilized of the world from the uncivilized. This is the moment of clarity. Let the civilized toughen up, and let the uncivilized take their chances in the game they started.

The Return of History

Saul Singer, *Jerusalem Post*, September 23, 2001

It is beginning to sink in that what happened on September 11 was not a single terrorist attack on a single country, but the Pearl Harbor of Islamism in its war against the West. In 1941, Americans were surprised by the Japanese attack, but at least knew what and where Japan was.

In retrospect, the great defeated "isms" of the last century, Nazism and Communism, are well understood. Now we are groping for an understanding of the new "ism" that has declared war on us.

The first shocker, of course, is that someone is out to get the West in the first place. For the past decade, the West has been operating under a paradigm characterized by the title of Francis Fukuyama's celebrated article, "The End of History?" (*National Interest*, 1989). As Fukuyama put it then, "we are witnessing not just the end of the Cold War, or a passing of a particular period of history, but the end of history as such: that is the end point of mankind's ideological evolution and the universalization of Western liberal democracy as the final form of human government."

Just as this new paradigm was settling in, Harvard professor Samuel Huntington wrote a blazingly contrarian article that now looks prescient. In "The Clash of Civilizations?" (*Foreign Affairs*, 1993), Huntington suggested the conflicts that had dominated the twentieth century were essentially "Western civil wars," while this century would be dominated by conflicts between the West and other civilizations, primarily the Islamic world.

"The West's next confrontation," according to M. J. Akbar, an Indian Muslim author quoted by Huntington, "is definitely going to come from the Muslim world. It is in the sweep of the Islamic nations from the Maghreb to Pakistan that the struggle for a new world order will begin."

Huntington predicted that the thirteen-hundred-year-old conflict between Islam and the West, far from declining, "could become more virulent."

The full-blown revival of this conflict is Osama bin Laden's dream. It is no coincidence that he describes his enemy as "Judeo-Crusaders," accurately lumping together two former foes, while recalling the ancient Christian wars against Islam.

Does this mean the West is now at war with Islam? Not yet, not exactly. In some ways, Islamists such as bin Laden understand the situation much better than we do. They realize the struggle is whether Islamism — a militant, politicized form of Islam — or Western liberal democracy will define the political structure of the Islamic world.

In this struggle, the West has an enormous head start. Islamists provide no cultural competition within the West, but the West is a profound source of attraction and influence within the Islamic world. All the Islamists have to offer is war, oppression, and stagnation, while the West represents the opposite.

Judaism and Christianity both went through militant phases, but outgrew them many centuries ago. The "end of history" paradigm pretended that Islam's militant phase was similarly buried, but that was a tad optimistic. Now the question is whether or not the Islamic world can, as Judaism and Christianity did, reinvent itself in a manner consistent with modernity.

It is not enough for the Muslim political and religious leaders to condemn terrorism; they must provide positive competition to militant Islamism. The founder of modern Turkey, Kamal Ataturk, provided such a positive vision, melding Islam and democracy. But such voices are few and far between in the Arab world and other places infected with Islamism.

In a column calling on the Arab world to extradite all terrorists, Lebanese writer Hazem Saghiyeh listed all the ways that the September 11 attack "eliminated, one by one, the political elements of the Arab strategy." Saghiyeh blasted bin Laden's "madness" for causing "injury to millions of Muslims in the West: to their lives, their bodies, their freedom; ... [and] insult to the Arab and Muslim role in world civilization...."

The most important way for the West to help those brave enough to stand up for an alternative, modern, peaceful vision of Islam is to defeat radical anti-Western regimes such as Iran and Iraq. The last century pitted the God of the democracies against the pagan, anti-religious ideologies of Nazism and Communism. In the Bible, ancient peoples would fight each other to prove whose god was stronger.

Our weapons now include cruise missiles and radio broadcasts, but not that much has changed. Now we are back to the basic struggle over visions of God, a struggle in which the fate of both Islam and the West hang in the balance.

"Relentlessly and Thoroughly": The Only Way to Respond

Paul Johnson, historian and journalist, from the October 15, 2001, issue of the *National Review*

Old and uncompromising words were spoken by American (and British) leaders in the immediate response to the Manhattan Massacre. But they may be succeeded by creeping appeasement unless public opinion insists that these leaders stick to their initial resolve to destroy international terrorism completely. One central reason why appeasement is so tempting to Western governments is that attacking terrorism at its roots necessarily involves conflict with the second-largest religious community in the world.

It is widely said that Islamic terrorists are wholly unorthodox in their belief that their religion sanctions what they do, and promises the immediate reward of heaven to what we call "suicide bombers" but they insist are martyrs to the faith. This line is bolstered by the assertion that Islam is essentially a religion of peace and that the very word "Islam" means "peace." Alas, not so. Islam means "submission," a very different matter, and one of the functions of Islam, in its more militant aspect, is to obtain that submission from all, if necessary by force.

Islam is an imperialist religion, more so than Christianity has ever been, and in contrast to Judaism. The Koran, Sura 5, verse 85, describes the inevitable enmity between Moslems and non-Moslems: "Strongest among men in enmity to the Believers wilt thou find the Jews and Pagans." Sura 9, verse 5, adds: "Then fight and slay the pagans wherever you find them. And seize them, beleaguer them and lie in wait for them, in every stratagem [of war]." Then nations, however mighty, the Koran insists, must be fought "until they embrace Islam."

These canonical commands cannot be explained away or softened by modern theological exegesis, because there is no such science in Islam. Unlike Christianity, which, since the Reformation and Counter Reformation, has continually updated itself and adapted to changed conditions, and unlike Judaism, which has experienced what is called the eighteenth-century Jewish enlightenment, Islam remains a religion of the Dark Ages. The seventh-century Koran is still taught as the immutable word of God, any teaching of which is literally true. In other words, mainstream Islam is essentially akin to the most extreme form of biblical fundamentalism. It is true it contains many sects and tendencies, quite apart from the broad division between Sunni Moslems, the majority, who are comparatively moderate and include most of the ruling families of the Gulf, and Shia Moslems, far more extreme, who dominate Iran. But virtually all these tendencies are more militant and uncompromising than the orthodox, which is moderate only by comparison, and by our own standards is extreme. It believes, for instance, in a theocratic state, ruled by religious law, inflicting (as in Saudi Arabia) grotesquely cruel punishments, which were becoming obsolete in Western Europe in the early Middle Ages.

Moreover, Koranic teaching that the faith or "submission" can be, and in suitable circumstances must be, imposed by force, has never been ignored. On the contrary, the history of Islam has essentially been a history of conquest and reconquest. The seventh-century "breakout" of Islam from Arabia was followed by the rapid conquest of North Africa, the invasion and virtual conquest of Spain, and a thrust into France that carried the crescent to the gates of Paris. It took half a millennium of reconquest to expel the Moslems from Western Europe. The Crusades, far from being an outrageous prototype of Western imperialism, as is taught in most of our schools, were a mere episode in a struggle that has lasted fourteen hundred years, and were one of the few occasions when Christians took the offensive to regain the "occupied territories" of the Holy Land.

The Crusades, as it happened, fatally weakened the Greek Orthodox Byzantine Empire, the main barrier to the spread of Islam into southeast and central Europe. As a result of the fall of Constantinople to the ultramilitant Ottoman Sultans, Islam took over the entire Balkans, and was threatening to capture Vienna and move into the heart of Europe as recently as the 1680s.

This millennial struggle continues in a variety of ways. The recent conflicts in Bosnia and Kosovo were a savage reaction by the Orthodox Christians of Serbia to the spread of Islam in their historic heartlands, chiefly by virtue of a higher birthrate. Indeed, in the West, the battle is largely demographic, though it is likely to take a more militant turn at any moment. Moslems from the Balkans and North Africa are surging over established frontiers on a huge scale, rather as the pressure of the eastern tribes brought about the collapse of the Roman Empire of the West in the fourth and fifth centuries A.D. The number of Moslems penetrating and settling in Europe is now beyond computation because most of them are illegals. They are getting into Spain and Italy in such numbers that, should present trends continue, both these traditionally Catholic countries will become majority Moslem during the twenty-first century.

The West is not alone in being under threat from Islamic expansion. While the Ottomans moved into southeast Europe, the Moghul invasion of India destroyed much of Hindu and Buddhist civilization there. The recent destruction by Moslems in Afghanistan of colossal Buddhist statues is a reminder of what happened to temples and shrines, on an enormous scale, when Islam took over. The writer V. S. Naipaul has recently pointed out that the destructiveness of the Moslem Conquest is at the root of India's appalling poverty today. Indeed, looked at historically, the record shows that Moslem rule has tended both to promote and to perpetuate poverty. Meanwhile, the religion of "submission" continues to advance, as a rule by force, in Africa in part of Nigeria and Sudan, and in Asia, notably in Indonesia, where non-Moslems are given the choice of conversion or death. And in all countries where Islamic law is applied, converts, whether compulsory or not, who revert to their earlier faith, are punished by death.

The survival and expansion of militant Islam in the twentieth century came as a surprise. After the First World

War, many believed that Turkey, where the Kemal Ataturk regime imposed secularization by force, would set the pattern for the future, and that Islam would at last be reformed and modernized. Though secularism has — so far — survived in Turkey, in the rest of Islam fundamentalism, or orthodoxy, as it is more properly called, has increased its grip on both the rulers and the masses. There are at present eighteen predominantly Islamic states, some of them under Koranic law and all ruled by groups that have good reason to fear extremists.

Hence American policymakers, in planning to uproot Islamic terrorism once and for all, have to steer a narrow path. They have the military power to do what they want, but they need a broad-based global coalition to back their action, preferably with military contributions as well as words, and ideally including such states as Pakistan, Jordan, Saudi Arabia, and Egypt. To get this kind of support is not easy, for moderate Moslem rulers are far more frightened of the terrorists than of Americans, and fear for their lives and families. The danger is that they will insist on qualification of American action that will amount, in effect, to appeasement, and that this in turn will divide and weaken both the administration and U.S. public opinion.

It is vitally important that America stick to the essentials of its military response and carry it through relentlessly and thoroughly. Although only Britain can be guaranteed to back the White House in every contingency, it is better in the long run for America to act without many allies, or even alone, than to engage in a messy compromise dictated by nervousness and cowardice. That would be the worst of all solutions and would be certain to lead to more terrorism, in more places, and on an ever-increasing scale. Now is the ideal moment for the United States to use all its physical capacity to eliminate large-scale international terrorism. The cause is overwhelmingly just, the nation is united, the hopes of decent, law-abiding men and women everywhere go with American arms. Such a moment may never recur.

The great William Gladstone, in resisting terrorism, once used the phrase, "The resources of civilisation are not yet exhausted." That is true today. Those resources are largely in American hands, and the nation — "the last, best hope of mankind" — has an overwhelming duty to use them with purposeful justification and to the full, in the defense of the lives, property, and freedom of all of us. This is the central point to keep in mind when the weasel words of cowardice and surrender are pronounced.

The Relevance of Niebuhrian Irony

Martin E. Marty, Fairfax M. Cone Distinguished Service Professor Emeritus, University of Chicago Divinity School, October 8, 2001, in *Sightings*, a publication of the Martin Marty Center, University of Chicago Divinity School

As I read those columns and responses, and so many more opinions on what we ought to do in the wake of September 11, I am thrown back to my favorite, often-used, treatment of this kind of subject. Reinhold Niebuhr wrote *The Irony of American History*, exactly fifty years ago as we were realizing involvement in the Cold War. It was immediately relevant. I made much use of it during the Vietnam War. And now it speaks to the present moment, as we mobilize against terrorists at home and abroad.

Niebuhr also wrote amidst often-heavy cross-fire. He was a theological cold warrior, attacking the Soviet Union, and was applauded by all except the pacifists, and the few on the religious far left. But after providing a stinging critique of the Soviet Union, he did what theologians and prophets should: he asked whether America was perfect, or whether it too stood distant from the will of God, equally under divine judgment. His text for that was Psalm 2:4, in which God is pictured as the one who sits in the heavens and laughs, and holds human pretensions ("the princes") in derision.

Let me paraphrase: Niebuhr said that the "good" side — that is, our side, once again — also has to be aware that there is enough guilt tucked into our innocence, enough vice in inner war with our virtue, enough insecurity undercutting our security, enough ignorance to go with our knowledge, that when we undertake action, "ironically," some of it will go wrong. And we will have been, as we always are, partial agents of the going wrong. Always.

Niebuhr did not leave things there. Awareness of our own guilt, vice, insecurity, and ignorance, in the eyes of a laughing God, and in the eyes of beholders who use ironic perspective, is not to be an excuse for apathy, cynicism, or scrupulosity in self-judgment to the point that we turn paralyzed. Indeed not. The same God who wants us to keep ourselves and our causes in perspective also holds us responsible for wise action. Niebuhr always said that the God who laughs at human pretension does not disdain legitimate human aspiration.

I picture Reinhold Niebuhr urging us on in pursuit of the terrorists, and encouraging us to keep our cause, our side, our flag, our nation, our ways of life "under exam-ination," so we give each other freedom and space and leeway to criticize — and to affirm.

How Should Christians Respond?
Ron Sider, president, Evangelicals for Social Action,
reprinted from the ESA bi-weekly *E-Pistle*, www.esa-online.org,
September 2001

The most important — and perhaps the hardest — task is to be Christians first before we are Americans or Europeans or Palestinians. History shows that especially in times of national crisis and heightened patriotism, Christians often equate God and country; often quickly identify perceived national self-interest with the will of God; often inappropriately apply biblical texts about the people of God to their nation.

Especially at this moment, it is enormously important that the church in the United States refuse to blur the distinction between the body of Christ and America. The first responsibility of the church — whether one stands within the just war or the pacifist tradition — is to be the church.

God has not suspended the biblical commands to "do good to all" (Gal. 6:10) and "love your enemies" (Matt. 5:44). They still apply after September 11. Let's ask God to show us how Christians everywhere and especially in America could take some dramatic steps to demonstrate our love for Middle Eastern Muslims, even — or perhaps especially — the people of Afghanistan.

It is also crucial that the church offers a biblical answer to the question on so many minds: Why did this happen?

Jerry Falwell and Pat Robertson disgraced all Christians, especially evangelicals, with their terrible comments on September 13 saying that "the pagans and the abortionists and the feminists and the gays and the lesbians [and] the ACLU" all "helped this happen."

Our all-wise, all-powerful God chose to create free human beings capable of rejecting God's will and harming their neighbors. Since we are communal beings, our sinful acts regularly create terrible consequences for our neighbors. God could always prevent evil people from harming their neighbors, but that would destroy both our freedom and our very existence as communal beings. So God allows terrorist attacks and holocausts, not because God wants that, but because God desires free persons.

God's goodness to us, however, does not stop with the gift of freedom. The cross tells us that God cares so much about the way that we abuse our freedom to defy God and devastate our neighbors that the Creator of the universe actually dies for our sins. God stands weeping, with open arms, pleading with us to repent, accept his astonishing forgiveness, and turn from hurting our neighbors. Today, perhaps, we have a special opportunity to share this wonderful gospel with gentle love and confidence. But we also need to remember that as long as history lasts, God will continue to grant persons freedom, even when they choose to do terrible things. That's why the dastardly evil of September 11 happened.

Another part of what the Bible tells us is also important, albeit easily distorted. The Creator who gave us freedom also embedded a moral order in the very structure of the universe. Whether or not we acknowledge it, some things are right and others are wrong. As Romans 1 says, violating that moral order has consequences, not just eternally, but within history. Sin — whether sexual misconduct or economic injustice, disrespect for human life or racial prejudice — has consequences that work their way through our homes and nations. Societies that defy the moral order God placed in the universe will suffer consequences.

But that does not mean that we should connect specific tragedies with specific sins. People in Jesus' day thought specific illnesses resulted from specific sins. Jesus clearly rejected that view (John 9:1–3). On occasion, God directly revealed to the prophets of the Old Testament that specific tragedies resulted from specific disobedience in Israel and Judah. But no Christian today dare claim that kind of special revelation. Never, therefore, should Christians today connect an evil like the terrorist attack with specific sinful acts.

To be sure, there is a truth here that is crucial. This nation like all others is a tragic mix of good and evil — which is *not* to say that all societies are equally good and bad; the relative difference between relatively free, relatively just America and the Taliban's unjust, repressive Afghanistan is a good to be treasured. Our nation, however, has done evil things in the world which help explain why significant numbers of people hate us. Christians in America need to be humble enough to face that honestly (but I will have to postpone further comment on that topic for a longer discussion of what American Christians should do *as citizens*).

But to engage in honest self-evaluation and also to be able to condemn the attack on September 11 as evil (rather than merely personally distasteful) we need precisely the universal moral norm given by the Creator. American intellectuals who have embraced postmodernism's radical relativism cannot condemn the attacks on September 11 as wrong and immoral; they can only say some groups feel good about the attacks and others do not. It is surely illuminating that on September 22, the *New York Times* ran a long Op-Ed pointing out that the "attacks on the U.S. challenge the perspective of postmodern true believers." The author clearly rejected postmodernism as "ethically perverse."

Gently and prayerfully, Christians today should use this teachable moment to answer the question "Why?" To explain the moral order of the universe. To invite everyone to trust in the God who loves his free, disobedient creatures so much that God dies to overcome evil. To love even those who despitefully use us and thereby demonstrate that our highest loyalty is not to our nation, but to the Middle-Eastern carpenter who is Lord and Savior of the world.

Violence Will Only Increase the Cycle of Violence
The Dalai Lama's letter to the president of the United States of America, September 12, 2001

Your Excellency,

I am deeply shocked by the terrorist attacks that took place involving four apparently hijacked aircraft and the immense devastation these caused. It is a terrible tragedy that so many innocent lives have been lost, and it seems unbelievable that anyone would choose to target the World Trade Center in New York City and the Pentagon in Washington, D.C. We are deeply saddened. On behalf of the Tibetan people I would like to convey our deepest condolence and solidarity with the American people during this painful time. Our prayers go out to the many who have lost their lives, those who have been injured and the many more who have been traumatized by this senseless act of violence. I am attending a special prayer for the United States and its people at our main temple today.

I am confident that the United States as a great and powerful nation will be able to overcome this present tragedy. The American people have shown their resilience, courage, and determination when faced with such difficult and sad situations.

It may seem presumptuous on my part, but I personally believe we need to think seriously whether a violent action is the right thing to do and in the greater interest of the nation and people in the long run. I believe violence will only increase the cycle of violence. But how do we deal with hatred and anger, which are often the root causes of such senseless violence? This is a very difficult question, especially when it concerns a nation and we have certain fixed conceptions of how to deal with such attacks. I am sure that you will make the right decision.

With my prayers and good wishes

The Dalai Lama
Dharamsala, India

Not by a Blind Desire for Vengeance
Daniel Nagashima, general director, USA Buddhist Association,
September 14, 2001

We share with our fellow Americans the sense of shock and horror that goes beyond words in response to the explosions Tuesday morning at the World Trade Center and the Pentagon. While we do not yet know the full extent of loss, we know it is great, and our hearts and prayers go out to the families and loved ones of those who have been lost in this tragedy....

The cycle of hatred, violence, and retribution that lies at the root of this horror must end. I fully understand the desire for justice that arises when a tragedy like this occurs. It is my deepest hope, however, that our nation's response will not be driven by a blind desire for vengeance, but rather a renewed determination to work for a peaceful and just world. The single great evil that must be opposed is not one group or people or another, but rather the hatred that continues to find root in human hearts.

Let us now put our energies toward comforting those who are suffering. Then let us work to rise from the ashes of hatred with a sense of hope and resolve.

Be Living Letters of Compassion

Rev. Dr. Ronald Raiser, general secretary,
World Council of Churches, September 20, 2001

Dear Sisters and Brothers in Christ,

Grace and peace to you in our One Lord and Saviour, Jesus Christ.

In the brief message I sent you on behalf of the Executive Committee of the World Council of Churches on that tragic morning of September 11, I assured you of the prayers of your sister churches around the world. That was an affirmation of faith. Now you have had the evidence of those prayers in an almost unprecedented flood of messages of compassion, love, and solidarity from churches in East, West, North, and South.

This expression of unity in such a time of trial gives flesh to the words Paul wrote to the Church in Corinth: "Blessed be the God and Father of our Lord Jesus Christ, the Father of mercies and God of all comfort, who comforts us in all our affliction, so that we may be able to comfort those who are in any affliction, with the comfort with which we ourselves are comforted by God. For as we share abundantly in Christ's sufferings, so through Christ we share abundantly in comfort too.... Our hope for you is unshaken, for we know that as you share in our sufferings, you will also share in our comfort" (2 Cor. 1:3–7)....

In these days, you have sought to respond in faith to many contradictory voices. Some plead for a form of justice that would name the evil and identify those responsible and bring them to trial in appropriate courts of law. Others, however, want decisive military action to show the will of the nation to avenge its losses and deny victory to its enemies. Very many share the deep apprehension you have heard from churches abroad about the prospect of the United States striking out again with its uncontested military might. They fear that this would result in an ever-rising spiral of retributive violence and the loss of ever more lives.

Words of condemnation and the language of "war" come so quickly to the fore. Blame is easily assigned to "the enemy." These are reinforced by the images and messages streaming across all our television screens, wherever we live. It is far more difficult to regard ourselves in the mirror of such hatred, and to have the courage to recognize how deeply violence is rooted within ourselves, our communities, and even our churches. These are lessons we are all trying to learn in the Decade to Overcome Violence.

Among those who have contributed to the remarkable outpouring of sympathy with the U.S.A. have been other communities of faith. They share both your sufferings and your fears. Partly in response to this, but also out of your own sense of justice, you have reached out to those communities in your own nation and with them have spoken out clearly against threats or open acts of violence against Muslims and Arab Americans. This powerful witness must be heard both at home and abroad. No one should be allowed to forget that in the places often mentioned as primary targets of military retaliation, Muslims, Christians, and people of other faiths live side by side. Minority Christian communities and those majority communities with whom their lives are shared stand to suffer severely at the hands of religious extremists if the "Christian" West strikes out yet again.

People in your country and around the world have gathered together during this past week in sanctuaries of the churches for silent reflection, and to invoke the presence of the Holy Spirit, who stands beside us in our time of need and journeys with us through the valley of the shadow of death. In these safe spaces, Christians and others have sought to discern the deeper meaning of such thoughtless acts and the suffering they have inflicted. This is indeed a time for quiet discernment of the "signs of the times," for courage and wisdom, and to pray for God's guidance. As the prophet Isaiah says: "In quietness and trust shall be your strength" (Isa. 30:15).

The message to the church in Ephesus goes on, however: "But I have this against you, that you have abandoned the love you had at first. Remember then from what you have fallen, repent and do the works you did at first." The United States was one of the early architects of the United Nations and was once among the strongest advocates for the international rule of law. In recent times, however, it has repeatedly ignored its international obligations and declared its intention to ignore the rest of the world in pursuit of its own perceived self-interests. This it does to its own and the world's peril. The events of September 11 have again reminded all nations that all are vulnerable and that the only true security is common security. The United States, so often accused, has now been the beneficiary of the sympathy and solidarity of the whole world. It could respond in kind and with humility by reversing its course now and rejoining the global community in a common pursuit of justice for all. It could set aside its reliance on military might at whatever cost and invest in efforts to find non-violent solutions to conflicts generated by poverty, mistrust, greed, and intolerance.

As the writer of the Book of Revelation says, "He who has an ear, let him hear what the Spirit says to the churches."

It is one of the chief marks of the ecumenical movement that the churches understand Jesus' prayer that they all might be one, as he is one with the Father. They are being called to practice mutual love and to extend this love even to the enemy, to become, as our familiar hymn puts it, "one great fellowship of love in all the whole wide earth." No one can live alone, separated from the wider fellowship, for we share one humanity. When one hurts, all suffer together.

As an expression of that fellowship, the WCC Executive Committee has expressed its desire to send to you a delegation of church leaders from around the world as "living letters" of compassion, and to engage with you in a common reflection about how we can shape a shared witness to the world in a time of such great need. I hope that you will welcome and open your hearts to them as they will to you....

Yours in Christ, the Prince of Peace.

Our Responsibility to History Is Already Clear

President George W. Bush, remarks at National Day of Prayer and Remembrance Service, National Cathedral, Washington, D.C., September 14, 2001

We are here in the middle hour of our grief. So many have suffered so great a loss, and today we express our nation's sorrow. We come before God to pray for the missing and the dead, and for those who love them.

On Tuesday, our country was attacked with deliberate and massive cruelty. We have seen the images of fire and ashes, and bent steel.

Now come the names, the list of casualties we are only beginning to read. They are the names of men and women who began their day at a desk or in an airport, busy with life. They are the names of people who faced death, and in their last moments called home to say, be brave, and I love you.

They are the names of passengers who defied their murderers, and prevented the murder of others on the ground. They are the names of men and women who wore the uniform of the United States, and died at their posts.

They are the names of rescuers, the ones whom death found running up the stairs and into the fires to help others. We will read all these names. We will linger over them, and learn their stories, and many Americans will weep.

To the children and parents and spouses and families and friends of the lost, we offer the deepest sympathy of the nation. And I assure you, you are not alone.

Just three days removed from these events, Americans do not yet have the distance of history. But our responsibility to history is already clear: to answer these attacks and rid the world of evil.

War has been waged against us by stealth and deceit and murder. This nation is peaceful, but fierce when stirred to anger. This conflict was begun on the timing and terms of others. It will end in a way, and at an hour, of our choosing.

Our purpose as a nation is firm. Yet our wounds as a people are recent and unhealed, and lead us to pray. In many of our prayers this week, there is a searching, and an honesty. At St. Patrick's Cathedral in New York on Tuesday, a woman said, "I prayed to God to give us a sign that He is still here." Others have prayed for the same, searching hospital to hospital, carrying pictures of those still missing.

God's signs are not always the ones we look for. We learn in tragedy that his purposes are not always our own. Yet the prayers of private suffering, whether in our homes or in this great cathedral, are known and heard, and understood.

There are prayers that help us last through the day, or endure the night. There are prayers of friends and strangers, that give us strength for the journey. And there are prayers that yield our will to a will greater than our own.

This world He created is of moral design. Grief and tragedy and hatred are only for a time. Goodness, remembrance, and love have no end. And the Lord of life holds all who die, and all who mourn.

It is said that adversity introduces us to ourselves. This is true of a nation as well. In this trial, we have been reminded, and the world has seen, that our fellow Americans are generous and kind, resourceful and brave. We see our national character in rescuers working past exhaustion; in long lines of blood donors; in thousands of citizens who have asked to work and serve in any way possible.

And we have seen our national character in eloquent acts of sacrifice. Inside the World Trade Center, one man who could have saved himself stayed until the end at the side of his quadriplegic friend. A beloved priest died giving the last rites to a firefighter. Two office workers, finding a disabled stranger, carried her down sixty-eight floors to safety. A group of men drove through the night from Dallas to Washington to bring skin grafts for burn victims.

In these acts, and in many others, Americans showed a deep commitment to one another, and an abiding love for our country. Today, we feel what Franklin Roosevelt called the warm courage of national unity. This is a unity of every faith, and every background.

It has joined together political parties in both houses of Congress. It is evident in services of prayer and candlelight vigils, and American flags, which are displayed in pride, and wave in defiance.

Our unity is a kinship of grief, and a steadfast resolve to prevail against our enemies. And this unity against terror is now extending across the world.

America is a nation full of good fortune, with so much to be grateful for. But we are not spared from suffering. In every generation, the world has produced enemies of human freedom. They have attacked America, because we are freedom's home and defender. And the commitment of our fathers is now the calling of our time.

On this national day of prayer and remembrance, we ask almighty God to watch over our nation, and grant us patience and resolve in all that is to come. We pray that He will comfort and console those who now walk in sorrow. We thank Him for each life we now must mourn, and the promise of a life to come.

As we have been assured, neither death nor life, nor angels nor principalities nor powers, nor things present nor things to come, nor height nor depth, can separate us from God's love. May He bless the souls of the departed. May He comfort our own. And may He always guide our country.

God bless America.

Gratitude to President Bush

American Muslim Council statement, September 21, 2001

The American Muslim Council (AMC) commends President George W. Bush for showing great leadership as reflected in his speech to the American nation last night. AMC applauds President Bush's effort to join nations worldwide in the challenge against world terrorism.

AMC extends its gratitude to President Bush for reiterating his support for the American Muslim community and cautioning people to avoid making racial or religious slurs. AMC believes that any type of bigotry against American Muslims or Arab-Americans during this serious time of global crisis may lead to greater danger for the human rights of Americans.

AMC supports President Bush's struggle to bring the perpetrators of the attacks to justice. AMC also thanks the Senate Majority Leader Tom Daschle for restating his condemnation against harassment of American Muslims and Arab Americans.

The American Muslim community agrees with President Bush and Attorney General John Ashcroft on their encouragement to initiate a climate of tolerance in order to protect the civil and human rights of all Americans.

Khomeini's Curse

S. Rob Sobhani, adjunct professor, Georgetown University, and president, Caspian Energy Consulting, October 16, 2001

"Let the American president know that he is the most repulsive member of the human race today, because of the injustice he has imposed on the Muslim nation. Today the Koran has become his enemy." These are not the words of Osama bin Laden, but those of the late Ayatollah Khomeini, arguably the godfather of hate toward America. Indeed, the phenomenon called Osama bin Laden did not happen in a vacuum. The roots of Islamic terrorism against America were nurtured by the founding father of the Islamic Republic of Iran. Since his arrival on the international scene in 1979, the Ayatollah Khomeini was at the vanguard of hate-filled anti-American statements. And at every Friday prayer sermon since then for the last twenty-two years, the Islamic Republic of Iran has perpetuated the atmosphere of violence against the United States in the Middle East by chanting the refrain: "Death to America."

His hatred of America was not based on any religious precepts, but was purely a political power play. The man whom he replaced, the Shah of Iran, was modernizing his country with American assistance. The only way to do so was to limit the power of the members of the clergy who were rigidly opposed to modernization. Any move forward was viewed as an assault on the traditional power base of the clergy in Iran. Therefore, secular education, full participation of women in nation-building, and family planning were viewed as a direct threat.

The first victims of Khomeini's "Death to America" campaign were the American diplomats held hostage for 444 days. But it was not just Americans whom he held hostage. The Ayatollah Khomeini hijacked Islam in the process and held Islam hostage until his death in 1989. His successor, the Ayatollah Khamenei, continues to follow in the footsteps of his mentor. In the name of Islam, the government of Iran has waged a non-stop "jihad" against America, and its ally, Israel.

The word "Hezbollah" was never part of the Middle East lexicon until 1982. That year, Ali Akbar Mohtashemi-Pur, who currently serves as a member of parliament and a foreign policy adviser to the "moderate" President Khatami, founded this terrorist group while he was Iran's ambassador to Syria. He was instrumental in the 1983 suicide bombing in Beirut that resulted in 241 dead Marines.

Last June, the United States indicted Iranian officials and Iran-backed Saudi Hezbollah for their involvement in the 1996 attack against U.S. Air Force housing in Saudi Arabia that killed nineteen American servicemen. All of this murder and hate took place under the banner: "Party of God." But in fact, the name "Hezbollah, Party of God," is blasphemous, because in Islam there is only one God and he cannot have a party.

Herein lies the fundamental problem facing America and its war against terrorism: Muslims have allowed their beautiful religion to be hijacked and held hostage by fanatics intent on advancing their personal agendas. Not surprisingly, the handwritten words left behind by Mohamed Atta, one of the terrorists who carried out the September 11 attacks, resemble instructions Khomeini imparted in 1984 to the thousands of children who were given the "keys to paradise" before blowing themselves up on land mines during the Iran-Iraq war. Osama bin Laden is merely a continuation in the timeline of hatred toward America begun by Ayatollah Khomeini in 1979.

Muslims living in America must speak out loudly and with one voice: "Osama, stop manipulating our religion to feed your own megalomania." The leadership of the Muslim community in America must embark on a tour called "Free Islam." Fifty clerics representing the fifty states of the union must immediately begin this tour, starting in Egypt, which is home to a majority of the terrorists who attacked the World Trade Center and the Pentagon. They should say unequivocally: Those Egyptians who carried out this act are not going to end up in heaven as suggested by Osama bin Laden. They were criminals, not good Muslims. From Egypt, they should go to Lebanon, home to Hezbollah. They should condemn the members of Hezbollah for the blasphemous use of God's name. God, they should remind their fellow Muslims, is above politics and not a tool of the politicians.

The tour should then travel to Qatar, home of the Al-Jazeera television network, which is a major voice in the Arab world. Through Al-Jazeera, these American Muslims must denounce — in the strongest terms — attacks against America and demand that their fellow religious leaders in the region join them in this condemnation. The tour should end in Pakistan, home to 147 million Muslims, who have become increasingly politicized by Osama bin Laden. In Pakistan, they should directly accuse Osama bin Laden of murder and sacrilege and condemn all of his followers.

U.S. Special Forces are now in Afghanistan, on the front line of our war against terrorism. This is a war to safeguard the freedoms that we Americans — including American Muslims — enjoy. Therefore, it is the moral obligation and patriotic duty of the Muslim leadership of this country to start the campaign of wresting back control of Islam from the violent extremists.

The tragedy of September 11 was the result of a vitriolic anti-American hatred started by one fanatic, Ayatollah Khomeini, and put into action by Osama bin Laden. The onus now rests on the Muslims in America to begin the campaign of reversing this atmosphere of hate by actively joining in the war against terrorism with all the means at their disposal. In the process, they will have freed millions of peace-loving Muslims around the world who are enslaved by the perversion of their religion.

The UN Must Draw a Line

New York Mayor Rudolph W. Giuliani, opening remarks to the
United Nations General Assembly Special Session on Terrorism,
October 1, 2001

Thank you, President of the General Assembly Dr. Han
Seung-Soo. Thank you, Secretary General Kofi Annan. . . .

On September 11, 2001, New York City — the most
diverse city in the world — was viciously attacked in an
unprovoked act of war. More than five thousand innocent
men, women, and children of every race, religion, and
ethnicity are lost. Among these were people from eighty
different nations. To their representatives here today, I
offer my condolences to you as well on behalf of all New
Yorkers who share this loss with you. This was the dead-
liest terrorist attack in history. It claimed more lives than
Pearl Harbor or D-Day.

This was not just an attack on the City of New York
or on the United States of America. It was an attack on
the very idea of a free, inclusive, and civil society.

It was a direct assault on the founding principles of the
United Nations itself. The Preamble to the U.N. Charter
states that this organization exists "to reaffirm faith in
fundamental human rights, in the dignity and worth of the
human person . . . to practice tolerance and live together in
peace as good neighbors . . . [and] to unite our strength to
maintain international peace and security."

Indeed, this vicious attack places in jeopardy the whole
purpose of the United Nations.

Terrorism is based on the persistent and deliberate violation of fundamental human rights. With bullets and
bombs — and now with hijacked airplanes — terrorists

deny the dignity of human life. Terrorism preys particularly on cultures and communities that practice openness and tolerance. Their targeting of innocent civilians mocks the efforts of those who seek to live together in peace as neighbors. It defies the very notion of being a neighbor.

This massive attack was intended to break our spirit. It has not done that. It has made us stronger, more determined, and more resolved.

The bravery of our firefighters, our police officers, our emergency workers, and civilians we may never learn of, in saving over twenty-five thousand lives that day — carrying out the most effective rescue operation in our history — inspires all of us. I am very honored to have with me, as their representative, the Fire Commissioner of New York City, Tom Von Essen, and the Police Commissioner of New York City, Bernard Kerik.

The determination, resolve, and leadership of President George W. Bush has unified America and all decent men and women around the world.

The response of many of your nations — your leaders and people — spontaneously demonstrating in the days after the attack your support for New York and America, and your understanding of what needs to be done to remove the threat of terrorism, gives us great, great hope that we will prevail.

The strength of America's response, please understand, flows from the principles upon which we stand.

Americans are not a single ethnic group.

Americans are not of one race or one religion.

Americans emerge from all your nations.

We are defined as Americans by our beliefs — not by our ethnic origins, our race, or our religion. Our beliefs in

religious freedom, political freedom, and economic freedom — that's what makes an American. Our belief in
democracy, the rule of law, and respect for human life —
that's how you become an American. It is these very principles — and the opportunities these principles give to so
many to create a better life for themselves and their families — that make America, and New York, a "shining city
on a hill."

There is no nation, and no city, in the history of the
world that has seen more immigrants, in less time, than
America. People continue to come here in large numbers
to seek freedom, opportunity, decency, and civility.

Each of your nations — I am certain — has contributed
citizens to the United States and to New York. I believe I
can take every one of you someplace in New York City,
where you can find someone from your country, someone from your village or town, that speaks your language
and practices your religion. In each of your lands there
are many who are Americans in spirit, by virtue of their
commitment to our shared principles.

It is tragic and perverse that it is because of these very
principles — particularly our religious, political, and economic freedoms — that we find ourselves under attack by
terrorists.

Our freedom threatens them, because they know that if
our ideas of freedom gain a foothold among their people
it will destroy their power. So they strike out against us
to keep those ideas from reaching their people.

The best long-term deterrent to terrorism — obviously — is the spread of our principles of freedom,
democracy, the rule of law, and respect for human life.
The more that spreads around the globe, the safer we will

all be. These are very powerful ideas, and once they gain a foothold, they cannot be stopped.

In fact, the rise that we have seen in terrorism and terrorist groups, I believe, is in no small measure a response to the spread of these ideas of freedom and democracy to many nations, particularly over the past fifteen years.

The terrorists have no ideas or ideals with which to combat freedom and democracy. So their only defense is to strike out against innocent civilians, destroying human life in massive numbers and hoping to deter all of us from our pursuit and expansion of freedom.

But the long-term deterrent of spreading our ideals throughout the world is just not enough, and may never be realized, if we do not act — and act together — to remove the clear and present danger posed by terrorism and terrorists.

The United Nations must hold accountable any country that supports or condones terrorism, otherwise you will fail in your primary mission as peacekeeper.

It must ostracize any nation that supports terrorism.

It must isolate any nation that remains neutral in the fight against terrorism.

Now is the time, in the words of the UN Charter, "to unite our strength to maintain international peace and security." This is not a time for further study or vague directives. The evidence of terrorism's brutality and inhumanity — of its contempt for life and the concept of peace — is lying beneath the rubble of the World Trade Center less than two miles from where we meet today.

Look at that destruction, that massive, senseless, cruel loss of human life... and then I ask you to look in your hearts and recognize that there is no room for neutrality on the issue of terrorism. You're either with civilization or with terrorists.

On one side is democracy, the rule of law, and respect for human life; on the other is tyranny, arbitrary executions, and mass murder.

We're right and they're wrong. It's as simple as that.

And by that I mean that America and its allies are right about democracy, about religious, political, and economic freedom.

The terrorists are wrong, and in fact evil, in their mass destruction of human life in the name of addressing alleged injustices.

Let those who say that we must understand the reasons for terrorism come with me to the thousands of funerals we are having in New York City and explain those insane, maniacal reasons to the children who will grow up without fathers and mothers, to the parents who have had their children ripped from them for no reason at all.

Instead, I ask each of you to allow me to say at those funerals that your nation stands with America in making a solemn promise and pledge that we will achieve unconditional victory over terrorism and terrorists.

There is no excuse for mass murder, just as there is no excuse for genocide. Those who practice terrorism — murdering or victimizing innocent civilians — lose any right to have their cause understood by decent people and lawful nations.

On this issue — terrorism — the United Nations must draw a line. The era of moral relativism between those who practice or condone terrorism, and those nations who stand up against it, must end. Moral relativism does not have a place in this discussion and debate.

There is no moral way to sympathize with grossly immoral actions. And by trying to do that, unfortunately, a fertile field has been created in which terrorism has grown.

A Just War?

Thomas Reese, S.J., editor, *America* magazine, in *America* magazine, October 8, 2001

The United States is going to wage a war against terrorists, says President George W. Bush. Is this a just war according to the principles of the Catholic just war theory? For this issue of *America* we asked experts in the just war theory to examine this question and present their views.

Before looking at the U.S. response, it is important to make clear that the terrorists' attacks violated almost every principle of the just war theory. First, wars can be waged only by legitimate authorities of a state. They cannot be declared by anyone who feels he has a just cause. The terrorists are not government officials. Second, the attack on the World Trade Center was directed at civilians who, according the principle of civilian immunity, should not be targeted. And even if the Pentagon could be considered a military target, using a plane loaded with innocent civilians as a bomb is unacceptable.

By their actions, the terrorists have declared war on the United States, and we certainly have the right under the just war theory to defend ourselves with military force. But before we go too far down this path, we should ask if the use of the word "war" is apt. The use of the word by the president is rhetorically satisfying. It makes clear that this is an effort that is serious and will take great effort and sacrifice. But calling our response "war" gives the terrorists a stature that they do not deserve. It treats them like a government when in fact they are more like organized criminals — mass murderers, not soldiers. Treating terrorists as criminals does not mean that the use of deadly force is ruled out. Police have the right to use deadly force to protect themselves and others from harm.

The rhetoric of war also makes it easier for the president to argue that we will treat nations that support terrorism in the same way that we deal with terrorists. This is easy to say, but difficult to carry out. If we discover that a foreign intelligence service gave money, arms, or forged documents to Osama bin Laden, do we bomb the country? Do we bomb the offices of the intelligence service? What if the government did not know the resources were going to be used in the attack on the United States? Since the U.S. government has stated that a number of countries support terrorist groups, we could quickly be at war on many fronts.

But granting that the rhetoric of war has captured the day, it is appropriate to use the just war theory to guide us in our response. The fact that the terrorists acted immorally, against every standard of military conduct, does not mean that we have the right to do the same in response. We must not become what we hate. The just war theory emphasizes that waging war is a last resort, not a first option. Diplomatic efforts are to be preferred, not only because they are less violent but also because, in the long run, only with the cooperation of other nations will we make the world safe from terrorism. Killing those responsible for these crimes will no more stop terrorism than killing some drug lords will stop drugs from flooding into our country.

The just war theory examines the legitimacy of the reasons for going to war (*ad bellum*) and the means that are used in war (*in bello*). The use of military forces by a country to defend itself and others from terrorist attack is legitimate if all else fails. But these forces must be directed against those responsible, not against civilian populations and civilian infrastructures (like power plants and water supplies).

During the Persian Gulf War, the U.S. military attempted to keep civilian casualties low, but the destruction of civilian infrastructures, along with economic sanctions, resulted in the deaths of thousands of Iraqi civilians. Killing thousands of Afghan civilians would be a sacrilegious memorial to those killed in the United States. After decades of war and bad government, Afghanistan is already a basket case with millions of refugees. To "bomb it back into the stone age," as some suggest, would simply increase the suffering of a people who have little if any power over their rulers.

The terrorists should be brought to justice because of their crimes and because of the danger they pose to life in this country and elsewhere. If this cannot be done peacefully, then they are legitimate targets of military action. But in the use of military force we should not lose sight of our ultimate goal of rallying the world community — including the Islamic world — in a concerted effort to root out terrorism.

The importance of Islamic public opinion must not be underestimated if we are to achieve our long-term objective of eliminating terrorism. The president's unfortunate use of the term "crusade," for which he apologized, shows how ignorant Washington still can be when dealing with

Muslim nations. Washington should instead be studying and using Islamic just war theory to isolate bin Laden and present a rationale for U.S. action. The United States has won worldwide sympathy as a result of these attacks. We must not dissipate that good will through intemperate action.

Getting "Just-War" Straight

George Weigel, senior fellow of the Ethics and Public Policy Center, Washington, D.C., October 8, 2001

Catholic commentary on the grave moral issues involved in responding to the attack on the United States on September 11, 2001, and in taking effective measures to rid the world of terrorism and its capacity for mass violence, has been burdened by a disturbing shift in just-war thinking. The shift began decades ago, but its full import is only now coming into clear focus.

It's important, at the outset, to understand what the just-war tradition is, and isn't. The just-war tradition is not an algebra that provides custom-made, clear-cut answers under all circumstances. Rather, it is a kind of ethical calculus, in which moral reasoning and rigorous empirical analysis are meant to work together, in order to provide guidance to public authorities on whom the responsibilities of decision-making fall.

From its beginnings in St. Augustine, just-war thinking has been based on the presumption — better, the classic moral judgment — that rightly constituted public authorities have the moral duty to pursue justice — even at risk to themselves and those for whom they are responsible. That is why, for example, St. Thomas Aquinas discussed just war under the broader subject of the meaning of "charity," and why the eminent Protestant theologian Paul Ramsey argued that the just-war tradition is an attempt to think through the public meaning of the commandment of love-of-neighbor. In today's international context, "justice" includes the defense of freedom (especially religious freedom), and the defense of a minimum of order in international affairs. For these are the crucial components of the peace that is possible in a fallen world.

This presumption — that the pursuit of justice is a moral obligation of statecraft — shapes the first set of moral criteria in the just-war tradition, which scholars call the "ius ad bellum" or "war-decision law": Is the cause a just one? Will the war be conducted by a responsible public authority? Is there a "right intention" (which, among other things, precludes acts of vengeance or reprisal)? Is the contemplated action "proportionate": is it appropriate to the goal (or just cause); is the good to be accomplished likely to be greater than the evil that would be suffered if nothing were done, or if the use of armed force were avoided for the sake of other types of measures? Have other remedies been tried and found wanting or are other remedies prima facie unlikely to be effective? Is there a reasonable chance of success?

It is only when these prior moral questions have been answered that the second set of just-war criteria — what scholars call the "ius in bello" or "war-conduct law" — come into play, logically. The positive answers to the first set of questions, the "war-decision" questions, create the moral framework for addressing the two great "war-conduct" issues: "proportionality," which requires the use of no more force than necessary to vindicate the just cause; and "discrimination," or what we today call "non-combatant immunity."

Under the moral pressures created by the threat of nuclear war, Catholic attention focused almost exclusively on "war-conduct" questions in the decades after World War II. This, in turn, led to what can only be described as an inversion of the just-war tradition: the claim, frequently encountered in both official and scholarly Catholic commentary today, that the just-war tradition "begins with a presumption against violence."

It does not. It did not begin with such a presumption historically, and it cannot begin with such a presumption theologically. For as one of America's most distinguished just-war theorists, James Turner Johnson, has put it, to do this — to effectively reduce the tradition to "war-conduct" questions — is to put virtually the entire weight of the tradition on what are inevitably contingent judgments. This error, in turn, distorts our moral and political vision, as it did when it led many Catholic thinkers to conclude, in the 1980s, that nuclear weapons, not communist regimes, were the primary threat to peace — a conclusion falsified by history in 1989.

That just-war fighting must observe the moral principle of non-combatant immunity goes without saying. That this is the place to begin the moral analysis is theologically muddled and unlikely to lead to wise statecraft. If "war-conduct" judgments drive the analysis, the moral foundations are knocked out from under the entire edifice.

The just-war tradition should also help us see more clearly the empirical reality of a situation and to draw the appropriate moral conclusions. What would the tradition teach us about what happened on September 11, 2001? It would teach us that these were acts of war, not simply "crimes" writ large. It would teach us that those who committed these acts, planned them, and supported them are combatants. It would teach us that our response to these attacks must be framed in terms of the appropriate just cause — which in this case is the punishment of evil and the defense of an essential minimum of order in world politics.

It would teach us that a "Yes, but . . . " response to September 11 — "Yes, we deplore what was done, but we have problems with U.S. policy in the Middle East"; "Yes, what happened on September 11 was terrible, but American economic imperialism is really at fault"; etc., etc. — is morally unacceptable. The mass murder of innocents for political ends is to be condemned unequivocally. No "buts" are acceptable among morally serious people.

Finally, the tradition would teach us that the peace that is possible in this world is the peace of public order, an order informed by justice and freedom. It is not the peace of personal right-standing before God, and it is not the peace of a world without conflict. The world cannot give those kinds of peace. What the world can strive toward is a peace that provides for the resolution of conflict by negotiation, agreement, and law, not by indiscriminate mass violence. Terrorism is a threat to peace, not only because it is violent, but because it attempts to destroy the minimum of order that has been achieved in world politics. That is why it must be resisted, through the only mechanism, unfortunately, to which terrorists respond. A just war against terrorism is a war ordered to the pursuit of the kind of peace possible in this world.

Five Major Changes
Rev. Richard John Neuhaus, publisher, *First Things Magazine,*
November 2001

For years to come, I expect, we will speak of "before" and
"after" September 11. I was on my way to say the nine
o'clock Mass at Immaculate Conception, on 14th Street
and First Avenue, when the hijacked airline hit the first
tower. There was a small crowd at the corner of 14th,
and I remarked that there seemed to be a fire at the
World Trade Center and we should pray for the people
there. But I could not stay or I would be late for Mass.
Only after Mass did I discover what had happened. How
strange beyond understanding, I thought, that as we were
at the altar offering up, as Catholics believe, the sacrifice
of Christ on the cross, only a little to the south of us was
rising, in flames and mountains of smoke, a holocaust
of suffering and death. That, too, was subsumed and offered on Calvary. It occurred to me that Friday, only three
days away, is the feast called The Triumph of the Cross.
Exactly.

The first commentary I heard was from a woman
coming out of the church: "That's what we get for un-
conditionally supporting Israel." I wondered how many
others would draw that lesson. Watching television during the day, the question was several times asked, "Why
do they hate us so much?" And the answer given in one
word was "Israel." The further question implied was, Is
our support for Israel worth this? What justice requires
us to do in order to punish the perpetrators and ward
off even greater evil is done for Israel, of course, but it
is done, much more comprehensively, for the civilization

that Christians, Jews, and everyone else will now come to see more clearly as it is seen by others: the Christian West.

My part of Manhattan is a long string of hospitals, and I went to be of whatever help I could. After a couple of hours it became obvious that very few of the injured were coming into the hospitals. The doleful conclusion is that, except for the many who were able to get out and away, the people at ground zero are dead. Many thousands they are saying today; no doubt we will find out how many in the days ahead. It will be a city of funerals for weeks to come, as bodies and pieces of bodies are identified. The church, the residence, and our offices are all north of 14th Street. At the house and office, everyone is safe. I am sure the same is not true of all our parishioners. It is weird. We can look down the avenues and see the still billowing smoke, as though watching a foreign country under attack, but of course it is our city, and our country.

Before and after September 11, what difference will it make? That's the subject of endless chatter and nobody knows. For what it's worth, I anticipate five major changes. It will inaugurate a time of national unity and sobriety in a society that has been obsessed by fake pluralisms while on a long and hedonistic holiday from history.

Second, there will be an understandable passion for retaliation and revenge that could easily veer into reckless bellicosity. That is a danger. The other danger is that fear of that danger will compromise the imperative to protect and punish.

Third, a legitimate concern for increased security will spark a legitimate concern for personal freedoms. Many will warn that freedom cannot be protected by denying freedom, and such warnings should not be lightly dismissed, even as we know that the liberty we cherish is not unbridled license but ordered liberty. Without order there can be no liberty; it is for liberty that we surrender license. I expect that many Americans who never understood that will now be having long second thoughts.

Fourth, after some initial sortings out, America will identify itself even more closely with Israel. Disagreements over the justice of how Israel was founded and how it has maintained itself in existence will not disappear. But the diabolical face of the evil that threatens Israel, and us, is now unveiled. Among Americans and all who are part of our civilization, it will be understood that we must never surrender, or appear to be surrendering, to that evil.

Finally, the question of "the West and the rest" will be powerfully sharpened, including a greatly heightened awareness of the global threats posed by militant Islam. Innocent Muslims in this country and Europe are undoubtedly in for some nastiness, and we must do our best to communicate the distinction between Islam and Islamism, knowing that the latter is the monistic fanaticism embraced by only a minority of Muslims. But almost inevitably, given the passions aroused and the difficulties of enforcing the law among people who are largely alien in their ways, such distinctions will sometimes get lost. We can only try to do our best by those Muslims who have truly chosen our side in "the clash of civilizations." It seems likely also that, after September 11, discussion about immigration policy will become more intense, and more candid.

That's a mixed bag of possible consequences, and, of

course, I may be wrong about any or all of them. These are but first thoughts one day after. Only a little south of here thousands are buried under the rubble. So it is now to the tasks at hand. It will be the work of weeks, perhaps months, to give them a proper burial. The consolation of the living is a work without end.

5

Forgive Us Our Trespasses
As We Forgive Those
Who Trespass Against Us

Forgiveness and Understanding

Forgiveness: A Hard Saying

Austin Ruse, president, Catholic Family and Human Rights
Institute, New York, October 8, 2001

I must forgive them. I have no choice. God tells me
to. God calls me to a radical forgiveness that is practically incomprehensible. But there it is. It is why he came
here. Asked twice, twice he answered, "I came to teach
forgiveness."

A survivor of the Shoah said so deep was his hatred, if
anyone licked his heart, they would surely die of poison.
But our Church teaches that love, like the Body of Christ,
is indivisible. Hatred in one's heart blocks the entrance
that God uses, just as surely as the stairwell was blocked
on the 104th floor. They died there, and so shall I die if
hatred blocks my heart.

But this just doesn't make sense. I stood on First Avenue
just before 9 a.m. and saw the rude gash of black smoke,
like torn skin, violating the purest sky of the year. I

watched on TV as they jumped from the upper floors. I ventured near the site and smelled the smoke and wet ashes permeating everything north to Canal Street. I stood before the ruins of tall buildings and knew instantly that no one could have survived riding this vulgar mess down from the sky.

A woman, trapped with others in an elevator, called 911 and asked for someone to get them out. She called again, more frantic, and said smoke was coming into the elevator. She called again and said everyone was dying. Then the building collapsed. She is called to forgive. So are we all.

Forgive us our trespasses as we forgive those who trespass against us.

This is a hard saying.

An Anguished Cry from America's Heartland for Forgiveness

Rev. Catherine M. Waynick, bishop of the Diocese
of Indianapolis, letter from New York to her diocese,
September 12, 2001

Dear Friends:

First, and foremost, I want the first words you read from me to be these — I love you and am very proud of you. I know from conversations with Bob Giannini and others that you have all risen to provide comfort and pastoral care to our members and to the communities served by our parishes. I only wish I could have been among you during these past few days.

When I arrived in NYC on Monday evening I expected to be attending a meeting of the Committee on Abundance for the Church Pension Fund and to return home on Wednesday afternoon.

Staying with friends at 80th and Lexington, I was about five miles from the Trade Center when the attacks took place. My friends left early Tuesday morning to attend a taping at Trinity on Wall Street with Archbishop Rowen Williams of Wales. They arrived just as the first plane hit. I watched the breaking news reports not knowing whether they were safe — thanks be to God they are, along with all who were in the church that morning.

The devastation here is something I cannot adequately describe to you — and I am fully aware that I have not even come close to really allowing my feelings free reign. I have not yet been able to cry ... but that will come.

What I feel certain about is what I have said to you over and over — our life of prayer shapes our ministry; and this is a time which calls for prayer. Prayer for those who have died, for those who are mourning their beloved family and friends, for those who may yet be alive and awaiting rescue, for those who are working tirelessly to find them and to begin the heartbreaking work or clearing away the rubble of "the wrecks of time," ... but also for those whose hatred led them to these acts.

It may not be honest yet to pray for forgiveness — the truest forgiveness comes after we have become fully aware of the extent of our hurt and pain. But we must pray for discernment. God's heart is aching for us to know the most faithful response to this tragedy and we cannot jump to conclusions or assume we know what God's will for us is in this. We must "wait on the Lord," and open our hearts to listen. When we do, one of the things we risk hearing is that we have brothers and sisters all over the world whose lives are wracked with this kind of pain and fear day in and out. For us to lay claim to entitlement about security and safety — and the illusion of control of our lives — may be the height of arrogance.... Our hearts have been given what Rowan Williams has called "a bitter gift": the ability we have never had before to enter into the sufferings of others and to take Christ with us. This is the gift God gave us in the Incarnation — the gift of entering into the fullness of human life, with all the worst we can do to each other, and then transforming it. When we become able to acknowledge our terror, our grief, and our rage and hold alongside it empathy for all those who suffer in these ways and the holy hope of God's transforming grace and love, we have begun to "Grow into the full stature of Christ."

I am not saying that we deserved what we got; the point is that no one deserves this kind of thing, not even those we tend to think of as "other" or even enemy. If we consider basic safeties and freedoms necessities for ourselves, we must surely claim them as necessities for all others. I take this to be the meaning of the Great Commandment to love others as we love ourselves — and as Christ loves ... and so we must pray for wisdom and discernment and urge those around us to do the same. We simply cannot claim to immediately know the full heart and mind of God about this.

What we do know is this: nothing is stronger than love. Nothing can make us stop loving; and God's love is far stronger than our own. This is the message we can give to our frightened young children. We can't promise them that bad and scary things will not happen again — even to them. What we can promise them is that we will always love them — no matter what — and that God loves them even better than we.

I have said this to you over and over — our love is not tested and tried when all is well and things are going smoothly. It is proven when we are angry and hurt and refuse to walk away and abandon the relationship.

I think it will be the greatest of shames if we, as a Church, do not choose to learn from these devastating events that our dispute with each other cannot be resolved by schism. More on those sorts of thoughts later.

Let me finish for now by saying that I became aware late last night that one of the things I want most is to see you all....

Please greet one another with the kiss of peace — and pray for me as I long to come home to you.

The Heart of God

Miriam Pollard, O.C.S.O., Trappistine nun of Santa Rita Abbey, Sonoita, Arizona, September 17, 2001

For two nights we had rain. Imagine. You could hear it on the roof. Today's light is mellow, as if God were running a gentle finger along the jagged edges of our grief — a many-colored grief, holding the lost lives and the hearts left behind shattered and shocked. But also grief for what seems an impenetrable murk of little understanding, conflicting values, and the promise of more violence. The human condition has not improved very much over the centuries, has it? And here we are being wrung again between its tortured palms.

One of our sisters said she could not be angry. She was terribly sad, but sad as much for the men who chose to find such value in destruction, as for those whose mortal lives and economic security have been destroyed.... We are in a place of terrible pain, but that place is the heart of God, a quiet beyond answers, a scream beyond echo, where anger dies if we let it go and want something better, where darkness is the greatest light. There is a world beyond human depravity — our own and others'. There is kinship beyond hate and even heroism. There is a deep home in which we have to be willing to wait, because waiting is the best of what we are. Conflict is not the meaning of existence. Under the wreckage of today and yesterday and probably tomorrow lies a fallen God who measures the human condition in the beating of his own heart, someone who knows that we are greater than our degradation and inadequacy, that Resurrection is not a word but a reality and a future.

Can we never know peace on earth? Perhaps not, but in our own hearts at least, at least there. At least there, love and an effort toward understanding. Our brothers of Tiberhine in Algeria were killed by extremists, fundamentalists. They were loved by the local people, Muslims to a man. Their superior, Dom Christian, studied Islam and spoke Arabic fluently. He loved the people of the Prophet, and gave his life to them. He called his future murderer his friend — "my unknown friend who believes that in killing me he does service to Islam" — a friend whom he would embrace someday beyond the blood and blindness of this earthly life.

Well, yes there it is. Beyond this earthly life. We can more easily craft here a life of maturity and understanding out of the conviction that the darkly warped human condition is but a womb in which another life is being formed.

Somehow, it becomes easier to compromise, to let go of what might seem too dear were this the only life we have.

And when we get to the doorsill of eternity, what will we be able to justify in our reaction to this recent experience of the mystery of evil — our own and "theirs"? Yes, a hunting out and putting beyond the possibility of more destructive activity those individuals and groups which threaten ourselves and our brothers and sisters. But attacking nations whose innocent, oppressed, and hungry people have suffered more than enough already? A reprisal of immense magnitude is now an option too easily available to small numbers of people. It could come our way, wreckage on wreckage on wreckage, and what innocence would we have to defend against it, if we have covered the earth with bombs? Can't we be creative in our containment of harm, deliberate and thoughtful?

We can listen to the questions, or not, as we choose. The earth will be better if we find constructive answers, if we wrestle ourselves out of the spider web, if we act according to the measure of our own dignity.

We seem to have a new family [of deer] down the hill. . . . The other sisters have seen them too. One day they grazed right beside the sorting room of the Altar Bread building.

Develop the Spiritual Bonds That Unite Us
Statements on Islam by the Vatican Council and Pope John Paul II

Second Vatican Council, Nostra Aetate, *no. 3,* October 28, 1965

The Church has also a high regard for the Muslims. They worship God, who is one, living and subsistent, merciful and almighty, the Creator of heaven and earth [Cf. St. Gregory VII, Letter III, 21 to Anazir (Al-Nasir), King of Mauretania PL, 148. 451A.], who has spoken to men. They strive to submit themselves without reserve to the hidden decrees of God, just as Abraham submitted himself to God's plan, to whose faith Muslims eagerly link their own. Although not acknowledging him as God, they venerate Jesus as a prophet, his Virgin Mother they also honor, and even at times devoutly invoke. Further, they await the day of judgment and the reward of God following the resurrection of the dead. For this reason they highly esteem an upright life and worship God, especially by way of prayer, alms-deeds, and fasting.

Over the centuries many quarrels and dissensions have arisen between Christians and Muslims. The sacred Council now pleads with all to forget the past, and urges that a sincere effort be made to achieve mutual understanding; for the benefit of all men, let them together preserve and promote peace, social justice, and moral values.

John Paul II to the Catholic Community of Ankara (Turkey), November 29, 1979

My brothers, when I think of this spiritual heritage [Islam] and the value it has for man and for society, its capacity of offering, particularly in the young, guidance for life, filling the gap left by materialism, and giving a reliable foundation to social and juridical organization, I wonder if it is not urgent, precisely today when Christians and Muslims have entered a new period of history, to recognize and develop the spiritual bonds that unite us, in order to preserve and promote together for the benefit of all men "peace, liberty, social justice, and moral values," as the Council calls upon us to do (*Nostra Aetate*, no. 3).

John Paul II to the Young Muslims of Morocco, August 19, 1985

Christians and Muslims have many things in common, as believers and as human beings. We live in the same world, marked by many signs of hope, but also by multiple signs of anguish. For us, Abraham is a model of faith in God, of submission to his will, and of confidence in his goodness. We believe in the same God, the one God, the living God, the God who created the world and brings his creatures to their perfection.

John Paul II on His Arrival in Syria, May 5, 2001

Today, in a world that is increasingly complex and inter-dependent, there is a need for a new spirit of dialogue and cooperation between Christians and Muslims. Together we acknowledge the one indivisible God, the Creator of all that exists. Together we must proclaim to the world that the name of the one God is "a name of peace and a summons to peace" (*Novo Millennio Ineunte*, 55)!

John Paul II, Address at the Palace of Congresses in Astana, Kazakhstan, September 24, 2001

Again let us listen to the great teacher Abai Kunanbai [Kazak philosopher and sage]: "All people, whatever their religion, attribute to God love and justice. Love and justice are the origin of humanity. Those in whom sentiments of love and justice prevail are the truly wise" (*Sayings of Abai*, chap. 45).

In this context, and precisely here in this land of encounter and dialogue, and before this distinguished audience, I wish to reaffirm the Catholic Church's respect for Islam, for authentic Islam: the Islam that prays, that is concerned for those in need. Recalling the errors of the past, all believers ought to unite their efforts to ensure that God is never made the hostage of human ambitions. Hatred, fanaticism, and terrorism profane the name of God and disfigure the true image of man.

The One God Calls Us to Be Peoples of Peace
U.S. Catholic Bishops and Muslim Leaders joint statement, September 14, 2001

Catholics and Muslims meet regularly as friends and religious partners in dialogue and engage together in many community projects. We are fully committed to one another as friends, believers, and citizens of this great land. We abhor all terrorist acts and hate crimes and implore all American citizens to refrain from sinking to the mentality and immorality of the perpetrators of Tuesday's (September 11, 2001) crimes.

The U.S. Conference of Catholic Bishops and American Muslim Council, Islamic Circle of North America, Islamic Society of North America, Muslim American Society, and numerous Islamic centers and councils have co-sponsored dialogues on religious themes, and we commit ourselves to the many noble goals of interreligious cooperation. We believe that the one God calls us to be peoples of peace. Nothing in our Holy Scriptures, nothing in our understanding of God's revelation, nothing that is Christian or

Islamic justifies terrorist acts and disruption of millions of lives which we have witnessed this week. Together we condemn those actions as evil and diametrically opposed to true religion.

We urge all American citizens to unify during this national tragedy and encourage cooperation among all ethnic, cultural, racial, and religious groups constituting the mosaic of our society. We appeal to American citizens to come to the assistance of the countless victims of Tuesday's crimes and the victims of any crimes of hate in the aftermath of those awful events. We join in supporting our Government in the pursuit of those who were responsible for Tuesday's terrorist acts, always mindful of the moral imperative to act with restraint and respect for civilian lives. We appeal to law enforcement agencies and the general public to assist those who may be targets of hate crimes. We entreat Catholics and Muslims to join together and with all people of good will in services of prayer and community programs promoting peace.

Most Rev. Tod D. Brown
Bishop of Orange,
Chairman, Bishops' Committee
for Ecumenical and Interreligious
Affairs, U.S. Conference of
Catholic Bishops

Dr. Muzammil H. Siddiqi
Director
Islamic Society of Orange County,
Islamic Society of North America

Aly R. Abuzaakouk
Executive Director
American Muslim Council

Dr. Sayyid M. Syeed
Secretary General
Islamic Society of North America

Naeem Baig
Secretary General
Islamic Circle of North America

Imam W. D. Mohammed
Muslim American Society

Cover the Sins of Their Fellows
Charles le Gai Eaton, "Man," in *Islamic Spirituality I*,
edited by Syyed Hossein Nasr (Crossroad, 1991), 374

Beauty and goodness relate to God, Who is the supreme
Reality, and have their source in Him; ugliness and evil
relate to nothingness and have the insubstantiality of
shadows. Positive qualities are, in the proper sense of the
term, more real than negative ones. The pious Muslim,
therefore, averts his eyes with decent courtesy (which is
also a kind of courtesy toward the Divine Image) from the
sores on an otherwise healthy body and from the flaws
which may spoil but cannot annihilate the potential no-
bility of those around him, or he will do so as long as the
person concerned desires to be better than he is. It is the
direction that a man or woman tries to follow rather than
the stumbling on the way that is significant.

Muhammad promised his people that those who
"cover" the sins of their fellows in this world will have
their own sins "covered" by God when they come to
judgment, and he warned that those who go out of their
way to expose the sins of their fellows in this world
will have their own sins mercilessly exposed on Judgment Day. He told them also that one sin in the sight
of men may be worse than a hundred in the sight of
God. Social stability and the maintenance of "ties of relationship" are among the highest priorities in the Islamic
scale of values, and, while a private sin may be read-
ily forgiven, the setting of a bad example is an offense
against the sacred community, which is the vehicle of the
Faith. The Quran itself rigorously condemns all malicious
gossip and backbiting, and it compares the seeking out

of a man's past sins to "eating the dead flesh of your brother."

There is, moreover, in all gossip and in every effort to draw attention to the weakness of our fellows an unspoken assumption that we know all about them. In the Islamic view God alone knows all about anyone. He knows every thought and hears the secret whisperings of which the soul itself may be less than fully aware, for He is the sole Owner of our souls, our minds, and our senses. Above all, He knows the *sirr,* the secret or innermost nucleus of each being, and no man can know another's secret. In its deepest sense, therefore, respect for others derives from the hiddenness of each being's true identity; and since this identity is intimately linked to its Source, its Creator and Owner, we dare not presume that it is worthless.

Despair, Hope, and Forgiveness
John N. Jones, New York, selections from the Gansevoort Manifesto, September 19, 2001

Two stacks of newspapers and magazines sit by my desk, each one telling stories of human misery and physical suffering. The first stack contains articles written on or after September 11, 2001. In these articles, almost all examples of suffering and violence refer to the World Trade Center bombing. In the second stack are articles from the months preceding the attack. Both in number of people affected and depth of suffering, the tales of misery in these pages are no less grim than the WTC stories. Some stories are of accidents and "acts of God." In other stories, Central Africa continues to be ravaged by AIDS, and people die from hunger in every inhabited corner of the globe. And as for examples of overt human aggression, one need look no further than stories with bylines from Sri Lanka or Palestine.

The Earth is a violent planet. Humans protect themselves as best they can from hunger, cold, and physical attack. But few if any places are safe, and when one human decides to hurt another, he often succeeds, as the WTC and Pentagon bombings remind us.

Yet for a number of people, the recent bombings come not as a reminder but as a revelation of something new. "Everything has changed!" they cry, speaking not about the specific tactics of the violent, but the prevalence of violence. Their world is darker.

But have things changed? Is the world darker? These cries are not much different from those of World Wars I and II. So much hand-wringing and disbelief can be seen in the writings of the intellectuals of that day and thereafter. . . . The post–World War II writer Jürgen Moltmann, for instance, wrote of the theology of the cross — at the foot of the cross, all worldly hopes and ideologies die. To think in a christocentric way is, in part, to know despair. The despair that resonates from the pages of such writers — their plea for Christians not to put their hopes in false idols — still rings true. But the basis for their despair does not. Despair is not the privilege of the Christian confronting Golgotha or the Jew confronting millennia of anti-Jewish persecution. Anyone with eyes to see and ears to hear can despair, whatever her religion and at any time. Globally, nothing has changed; the change is merely local. Many intellectuals of World War I and World War II were living in bubbles of their own making. Reports of violence from South Africa and Russia did not lead them to despair — violence at home did. Today, too, people who think of Rwanda and Ireland as faraway places have suddenly seen violence break into their own bubble.

The essence of violence did not change in September 2001, only the location where it happened to land. When one learns despair, one learns not to pretend that the world is any better than it actually is.

At a meditation gathering held one week after the bombing, one participant observed how, for the Harlem students he tutors every day, the bombing had not changed much. Before the bombing, they had been poor and hungry, with inadequate medical care, surrounded by violence, and with little investment in mainstream society, and so they remained after the bombing. Goaded by the man's comments, I solicited reactions from others. A friend who is psychotic/schizophrenic — the doctors disagree in their assessment, and so have difficulty treating him effectively — remains so. His heart aches for the dead and their kin, but it is, he notes, an old and familiar ache, the same one he continues to feel, decades after the fact, for friends killed or wounded in the Vietnam War.

Another friend feels apprehension and uncertainty, but not to a noticeably greater degree than usual, as he prepares, year after year, for gender reassignment surgery and becomes ever more convinced that God either does not exist or does not love him enough to deliver him from a life of depression. One man on death row feels, if he feels anything at all, a sense of vindication, since for years he has been telling anyone who will listen his beliefs about the vulnerability of U.S. borders and the inevitability of a terrorist attack. A prostitute working Gansevoort and

Washington in the West Village knows only that drive-up traffic from out-of-state customers has plummeted since the bombing, and she wonders when it will pick up again, since even in ordinary times, she barely clears enough money to pay for her drug habit, food, and rent, and the taxi ride back to Queens every morning. . . .

The WTC was bombed on a Tuesday morning. Making deliveries in New York City that day, I was able to see and hear very different reactions evoked by the single event. Many people were simply numb in disbelief. Some people had radios glued to their ears, establishing themselves as conduits of information for others. Some enjoyed the excitement. Like the house servant in Agatha Christie's *Pocket Full of Rye*, they would never have actively caused violence themselves, but they welcomed the drama and intrigue introduced by someone else's act of violence. Two people openly expressed approval of the bombing, because for them the WTC buildings were symbols of an oppressive and evil economic system.

Hatred and anger were not much in evidence at first, and this is not surprising. Most people need time to register the reality of an action before they can feel anything, including hatred against its perpetrators. Soon enough, of course, the reality settled in, hatred formed, and the official line was set: "Find the bastards who organized the attack and kill them, preferably after torturing them." Some dissenting voices advised patience and even non-violence. But outright forgiveness was largely absent from the discussion.

In matters such as bombings and war, forgiveness is often seen as soft, flaccid, and unmasculine. It comes, it is said, from putting on blinders and ignoring "reality."

There is some truth in this claim. The person who ignores every unpleasant aspect of life may find it quite easy to forgive, because for him, there is nothing much to forgive. But alongside the person blind to these new acts of violence stands the person blind to the pervasiveness of violence in many times and places. This person is blinded by optimism — if only we deal with this example of violence, things will be better.

President George W. Bush participated in this blindness when he spoke of "eradicating evil" from the face of the earth. Which evil? Not the evil of tribal warfare or of gang violence in Los Angeles, but Evil, which for Bush was synonymous with Osama bin Laden. Some have criticized Bush for misspeaking but, despite his reputation for mangling the English language, here he spoke with perfect accuracy. The face of Bush's Earth, his bubble, is ordinarily devoid of obvious evil. He can hope to eradicate from his world everyone who performs grand acts of violence, because his is, after all, a small world, where things largely make sense and proceed without interruption. Bush has not known despair.

As a result, Bush's hope, and the hopes of all those who have not (to use Moltmann's words) been to the foot of the cross, must always remain ephemeral. It is a hope based on the fragile boundaries between the world as a whole and the extremely narrow piece of land one has erected as one's reality. The hopes of such a world are brittle, and the moment anyone lobs a stone, a bomb, a hijacked plane from outside, hopes are dashed, or people reassure themselves that the problem is merely isolated and can be gotten rid of, once one forgets again about the world "out there."

It is not possible to acknowledge all the suffering of humans everywhere in the world, all the time. But by acknowledging the pervasiveness of violence, we can stop acting surprised whenever it takes place. Constant surprise is the privilege of the ignorant. But what happens in despair, in the decision not to pretend the world is any better than it is? From this despair, and only from this despair, can come genuine hope. Despair does not mean depression, sadness, or abandonment. It simply means a refusal to hope for outcomes we know to be patently false and illusory. That most people in the world are secure and comfortable today — this is false. But that people may be less miserable tomorrow; that I may take some steps to alleviate misery tomorrow: this is genuine hope. It may well fail to come to pass — I may falter in my resolve, or the world may become even more full of misery — but these pitfalls are part of the nature of hope. Hope is always oriented toward that of which we have no worldly guarantee. The practice of despair frees us from having to deceive ourselves about the way things are, but it does not stunt our capacity to hope for other things. Despair is a way of training our hope.

Despair arises from honesty. Hope arises from despair, but it takes on different forms for different people. For Christians who take the scriptures seriously, hope must give rise to forgiveness. Jesus demands that his followers forgive without limit. This is a hard demand, and as a few theologians have confided to me since the bombing, there are times when one wishes one were not a Christian, so crushing is the requirement to forgive. In the Lord's Prayer, Jesus instructs his followers to pray "forgive us our trespasses, as we forgive those who trespass against us." The Father is our Father, and we forgive trespasses against us. The prayer presupposes that all who turn to the Father will be mindful of sins against any part of the whole. A Christian knows the pervasiveness of violence and misery — a Christian knows despair, and yet must find a way to forgive.

It is easier to forgive once we recognize that nothing "out there" has changed.... The world is no better than it is. But neither is it any worse, and instead of constructing a carefree but fragile world, we can find whatever beauty, joy, and hope for the future among the violence, not in denial of it. "Forgive us our trespasses." Despair is not the gnostic's distaste for a world out there, into which I, untainted and pure, have been born. I share in the world's trespasses. Do I hope for forgiveness? From self-interest, I hope for it; according to Jesus' command, I expect it. But in that same moment, I know that others can expect it as well.

Despair, hope, and forgiveness also come together at the crucifixion. What Christian can consider the fate of Jesus of Nazareth without concluding that this world can be a horrifyingly violent one? And who, Christian or not, could say that our world since that time has stopped being violent? We begin with despair. Yet Jesus adds: "Father, forgive them, for they know not what they do." ... What did Jesus feel at the moment he forgave? Was it a true sense of reconciliation, or did he make the declaration even in the midst of anger? We don't know. We do know that moments later, according to Luke, Jesus spoke to another of the men being crucified there: "Truly I say to you, today you will be with me in paradise."

This gesture of unmerited grace is the test case for a

Christian's ability to forgive. I as a Christian must forgive. A Christian society must forgive. In this world, this forgiveness may take many forms. Can it coexist alongside a military response or capital punishment for the agents of violence? Perhaps. Regarding the next world, however, the lines are drawn more clearly. To forgive as a Christian means that I recognize my own fallibility before the Father the moment I think of someone else's fallibility. Just as the Father sees the murderer's heart, he sees the murderous thoughts in my own heart.

As I anticipate paradise, I see other people hanging alongside Jesus. If I forgive — if my forgiveness is genuine, even in the midst of my anger — I must be willing to extend my hope for paradise to the other persons. Can I bear to see Jesus opening the gates of heaven to those guilty of heinous actions? If I cannot tolerate the possibility — indeed, if I cannot fervently hope for it — then my forgiveness, whatever else it may be, is simply not Christian. A Christian who hopes for heaven must hope, in the here and now, to hear Jesus say, "Truly, I say to you, bin Laden, today you will be with me in paradise."

Dialogue As Challenge
Hermann Herder, from *Ramon Lull: Book of the Gentile and the Three Wisemen* (Herder Publishers, Freiburg, Germany, 1986)

I have always been impressed by the story of this Catalan knight and troubadour who is said to have entered the cathedral of Palma de Mallorca high atop a horse. Ramon Lull (born in 1232 near Barcelona, Spain) — friend of kings, educator of princes, philosopher, missionary, holy man, and fool (as he called himself). He was a mystic and

a poet who contributed to the flourishing of the Catalan language and is therefore considered its founder. I am
convinced that in spite of all the differences in the historic situation Ramon Lull has something to say to us
today that no one else has expressed quite like him: the
grand vision of the unity of the world and of the loving
community of religions.

This unity of the world, facilitated by science and the
progress of technology, is about to become reality before
our eyes. This occurs at a significant cost, as we become
more and more aware of this process. And yet there is
no doubt: the world's peoples are en route to becoming
a single human family. What is needed then? The ability to communicate with one another. The "grand world
conversation" of which the German poet Hölderlin wrote
(in his most important work *Friedensfeier* [Celebration of
Peace] written between 1801 and 1803):

> We have experienced much;
> And found many names for the divine
> Since we have become one conversation,
> And hear one from the other.

For those who work in the service of such conversation
one book of Ramon Lull is especially meaningful: *The
Book of the Gentile and the Three Wisemen* (*Libre del
gentil e dels tres savis*). Few literary texts have reached
such depth of the encounter of others. And few historic
times have seen as many encounters between people of
different faiths as the later years of the crusades when Lull
lived. Most of those encounters lacked understanding of
the other and only fueled the bloody confrontations of
that era.

And yet there were also encounters of light. The genial work of Ramon Lull was assumedly based on a religious dialogue that took place in Barcelona in the year 1263. We don't know to what extent this was a dialogue by modern definition. Ramon Lull's autobiography clearly shows his missionary zeal. Indeed, the tension between dialogue and mission continues to be a challenge today. The command "to go and bring the good news to all people" has not been repealed for Christians. Yet we need to define it anew.

In 1299 Ramon Lull asked his king for special permission to preach "on Sabbaths and Sundays to the Jews in the synagogues, and on Fridays and Sundays to the Saracens in the Mosques." His hearers were invited, but not required, to respond to his preaching. The intention of the arrangement was to avoid superiority on the one side and inferiority on the side of the other.

Lull raises an issue that is crucial in religious dialogue. No translation can adequately convey the meaning of the original language. With much passion the Catalan saint pursued the study of Arabic, Syrian, and Latin, even founding Franciscan monasteries where the languages were taught. He advocated that the Roman Curia establish schools for the study of language across the world.

In the eighty-fifth year of his life Ramon Lull began the last of many travels that led him across the Mediterranean, to France, Sicily, North Africa, Cyprus, and even to distant Armenia. The last we know is that in Tunis he "disputed with the Saracens"; then no more messages were recorded. Yet after his death an unusually wide distribution of his writings occurred. Lull wrote more than three hundred works of philosophical, mystical, theological, and poetic content.

However one interprets Lull's work, his intentions, writings, and actions reflect a great vision. From a remarkably early point in history, he pointed to a direction that today is so crucial for our future. We live at the beginning of the third millennium, which will be shaped by a new global consciousness. On this path all believers are called, and each one of us has to seek our very own vocation.

6

Lead Us Not into Temptation but Deliver Us from Evil

Temptation and the Power of Evil

What the Face of Sheer Evil Looks Like

Rabbi Daniel Lapin, president, Toward Tradition, Seattle,
Washington, statement issued September 13, 2001

President Bush is currently formulating an American response to Tuesday's attacks. As an Orthodox rabbi I turn for guidance to the pages of that very Book from which our nation's seventeenth- and eighteenth-century founders were most comfortable seeking wisdom and solace. In the book of Exodus we find an apt biblical model for the situation at hand.

I refer to the Amalekite attack on the ancient Israelites shortly after their hurried departure from Egypt. For this, God commanded the Jews to make unceasing war on the Amalekites — but not only that. Jewish tradition points out that the stated location of the attack, Rephidim, is to be read not as the geographical name of any place but instead as a Hebrew word, a plural noun, alluding to the moral turpitude of the Children of Israel at the time

221

shortly prior to the attack. God suggested that Amalek's attack was to be analyzed as a call to self-examination.

From the Amalek story we may extract two lessons. First of all is the obligation to root out evil of the kind that sends airliners smashing into the World Trade Center. Second, not every victim is perfectly virtuous. I realize this may sound outrageously insensitive, for many Americans are committed to the view that being a victim, as America was victimized this week, should immediately grant you immunity from all criticism. Thus the equation of victimhood with virtue has led some observers of turmoil in the Middle East to blame Israel for the fact that more than twice as many Palestinians have died in the present conflict as have Israelis. The conclusion for the morally untutored is simple: because Palestinians are dying in greater numbers, they must be the morally justified party in the conflict. But it is simply wrong to grant moral prestige on the basis of suffering. It is a core Jewish value, when confronted with catastrophe, to probe broadly and arrive at a detailed moral balance sheet.

I advise that we Americans do the same thing. I can't speak to the strategic question of how best to identify and destroy our nation's enemies. But we have been guilty of three dreadful mistakes during the past few decades, and they need to be addressed as surely as our assailants need to be punished.

The first mistake we made was to forget, amid peace and prosperity, what the face of sheer evil looks like. This forgetting has been easy for us. We are taught it in the schools, where children are instructed that there is no such thing as evil, only differences in point of view.

You see, to admit the existence of evil means we would have to define evil according to someone's morality, and we all know that in a multicultural society this would be wrong.

Knowing that there is evil carries with it many practical advantages. For instance, captains of commercial airplanes used to carry side arms, but politicians who didn't believe in evil long ago disarmed them. Armed pilots could have made quite a difference for the good on Tuesday.

A second mistake was to emasculate the CIA. In recent years, international sanctimoniousness about human rights trumped considerations of American security. The entire CIA structure was methodically undermined and demoralized by penalizing all operatives who might have violated the human rights of their targets.

Third, we Americans have ignored the real-life lessons that many of us learned in our fourth-grade schoolyard. The class bully was always encouraged by passivity. Sooner or later, you realized, you would have to bloody his nose. The longer you took to do the inevitable, the more demoralized you became.

Or, do you remember the unpleasant rich kid? He used to try to buy friendship with money. Did he ever win a most-popular-kid-in-the-class award? Of course not. He won only contempt and resentment. That, I'm afraid, is what America gets for its foreign aid. We should tell Mr. Arafat, your people laughing and celebrating in the street at our agony has just ended your stipend.

When confronted with tragedy, the Jewish way is, then, to assess one's own moral condition. But — and here is the tricky part — while the victim gauges his faults he is also commanded to strike back in devastating force. In short the strategy is counterattack accompanied by an equally remorseless attempt to identify the flaws that made the attack possible in the first place. Let us pray that something positive may come out of our suffering. If we Americans contemplate the lessons of Amalek, I believe it will.

Apocalypse

From Gil Bailie, president and founder, Florilegia Institute, in *Violence Unveiled: Humanity at the Crossroads* (Crossroad, 1999), 14–15

"Man creates what he calls history as a screen to conceal the workings of the apocalypse from himself," wrote the literary critic Northrop Frye. This is a stunning insight. It cries out to be paired with the observation that the Nazi experience tests the limits of what "history" can explain. It implies that "history" pays a price in return for its explanatory power. It suggests that "history" conceals something in order to illuminate everything else. It implies what Cesareo Bandera made explicit when he called attention to "what literal historical reality itself hides or disguises in order to constitute itself as such, as meaningful historical reality." In other words, what makes "meaningful historical reality" meaningful is the concealing of something that might rob it of its meaning were it not concealed. If "the Nazi experience tests the limits of what history can explain," it is because the explanatory power of "history" begins and ends with its ability to explain away the victims and the violence vented against them.

Equally remarkable in Frye's lapidary statement is its implication that the end of "history" was inextricably bound up with the Bible, and that the biblical texts could not be fully comprehended if their apocalyptic features were neglected. Frye even went so far as to suggest that the "vision of the apocalypse is the vision of the total meaning of the Scriptures," though he erred when he took the next step, asserting that apocalyptic destruction "is what the Scripture is intended to achieve." On the contrary, what Scripture is intended to achieve is a conversion of the human heart that will allow humanity to dispense with organized violence without sliding into the abyss of uncontrollable violence, and the apocalyptic abyss.

The word "apocalypse" means "unveiling." What, then, is veiled, the unveiling of which can have apocalyptic consequences? The answer is: violence. Veiled violence is violence whose religious or historical justifications still provide it with an aura of respectability and give it a moral and religious monopoly over any "unofficial" violence whose claim to "official" status it preempts. Unveiled violence is apocalyptic violence precisely because, once shorn of its religious and historical justifications, it cannot sufficiently distinguish itself from the counterviolence it opposes. Without benefit of religious and cultural privilege, violence simply does what unveiled violence always does: it incites more violence. In such situations, the scope of violence grows while the ability of its perpetrators to reclaim that religious and moral privilege diminishes. The reciprocities of violence and counterviolence threaten to spin completely out of control.

A Hijackers' Prayer

Selections from document found in hijacker Nawaf al-Hazmi's car at Dulles Airport, September 11, 2001.

The Last Night

1. Pledge of allegiance for death and renewal of intent.

2. To be perfect plan very well all its aspects and expect reaction or resistance from the enemy.

3. Reading and understanding well the chapters Al-Anfaal and At-Tawba [or chapters 8 and 9 of the Holy Koran] and understanding their meanings very well and what Allah has prepared for the believers or the permanent bliss for the martyrs.

4. Reminding one's self of listening well and obeying that night for you are going to face critical situations, which require strict abiding and obeying (100 percent). So you should tame yourself and make it apprehend and convince it and incite it for that.

   The Most High says, "Obey Allah and His messenger and dispute not amongst yourselves, and be not divided amongst yourselves; otherwise you will fail and your power will vanish, and be patient for Allah is with those who are patient.

5. Pray in the middle of the night and ask Allah many times for victory....

6. Mention God many many times and be learned that the best of mentioning God is reciting or reading the Holy Koran....

7. Clean your heart and purify it from mishaps and forget completely a thing which is called worldly-

life for the time. For playing has passed and the true promise has come, how much did we waste from our years? Shouldn't we utilize these hours to offer obedience and closeness?

8. Check your weapons before departure, and before you leave and "Let every one of you sharpen his knife and kill his animal and bring about comfort and relief of his slaughter" before the journey....

13. And also do not let perplexity and confusion and nervous tension appear upon you. Be cheerful, happy, serene, and comforted because you are doing a job which God loves and accepts. Hence it will be a day that with God's permission you will spend with the most beautiful women in paradise.

Smile in the face of death, oh young man! For you are on your way to the everlasting paradise!

Notes from the Underground
Fyodor Dostoyevsky, *Notes from the Underground,* 1864

Oh, tell me, who was it first announced, who was it first proclaimed, that man only does evil things because he doesn't know his own interests; and that if he were enlightened, if his eyes were opened to his real normal interests, man would at once cease to do evil things? ... And what if it so happens that a man's advantage, sometimes, not only may, but even must, consist in his desiring in certain cases what is harmful to himself and not advantageous.... One's own free unfettered choice, one's own caprice — however wild it may be, one's own fancy worked up at times to frenzy — is that very most advantageous advantage which we have overlooked, which comes under no classification and against which all systems and theories are continually being shattered to atoms.... What man wants is simply independent choice, whatever that independence may cost and wherever it may lead.

War without Boundaries

Stratford Caldecott, co-director of the Centre for Faith & Culture, Oxford, England, co-editor of the Centre's journal *Second Spring*, October 21, 2001

Many parts of Europe have lived with the threat and the reality of terrorism for a long time. In recent years the United States has experienced sporadic outbursts of violence in the form of serial killings, the suicidal last stands of lunatic sectarians, and high school massacres — all evidence that the Devil is out there, on Main Street USA, seeking for a way into the hearts and minds of ordinary citizens. What was it, then, about the destruction of the Twin Towers on September 11 that so traumatized America?

The scale of the tragedy is not enough by itself to explain the full effect, though it is more than enough to justify the flood of grief. Something else was at work. This had been an act of symbolic terrorism. Someone had struck at the very nerve center of American identity. The World Trade Center and the Pentagon were not simply large buildings previously deemed safe from attack; they were the preeminent symbols of Western capitalism and military might. At a subliminal level, the symbolic power of these buildings was somehow magnified by their geometry, reminiscent of the Platonic solids. These buildings were the shadows or projections of archetypal objects: the terrorists had succeeded in attacking America and Western civilization not on the surface but at a deeper, much more primal level.

As a result of those events, many feel that a new era began for us all in 2001, in the first year of the new millennium. Often these are the very people who poured scorn on the historical significance of the "year of three zeroes." Thanks to the pervasive power of modern technology and the ease with which it can be turned to evil ends, the human race is now off the map and into unknown territory. The result of our first truly postmodern war, the "War against Terrorism," is likely not to be world peace but a world police state, a New World Order maintained by force and surveillance, and inherently unstable. It is indeed a "new kind of war," because it is not fought against nations or armies, but against networks and ideologies which disregard all those boundaries which used to be defensible: those of the old nation states and power blocs.

The enemy is getting closer. He is no longer on the other side of some national frontier, but in our airplanes, and in our streets. What we fear now is that he is coming even closer, into our very bodies. We fear the invasion that crosses the frontiers of our skin and implants germs within our blood.

The war without boundaries, which threatens to rage through every neighborhood and turn even our own bodies against us, is something new. But it is also very old. It is the image of an interior war that has raged since the beginning of time. As we approach the end of a major historical cycle, with the disconcerting sense that time is running faster and perhaps even running out, the veils over that spiritual war are being stripped away. In a way, this is a consoling thought. There is a map, after all. And on that map, all roads lead through a Cross, to an empty tomb.

Take Nothing Good for Granted

John K. Roth, Russell K. Pitzer Professor of Philosophy, Claremont McKenna College, Claremont, California, October 13, 2001

On September 10, 2001, I addressed the first-year class at Claremont McKenna College. This essay's title was my theme that night. Accenting points I wanted those young men and women to feel, I quoted Lawrence Ferlinghetti, whose *Pictures of the Gone World* contains a poem that begins by saying, "The world is a beautiful place / to be born into / if you don't mind happiness / not always being / so very much fun / if you don't mind a touch of hell / now and then / just when everything is fine."

I scarcely could have imagined what would happen twelve hours after my remarks concluded, but events have certainly driven home that taking nothing good for granted is much more than the cliché it seems to be. Writing in the *New York Times* on Saturday, September 15, columnist Frank Rich was only one of many to observe that "we live in a different America today than we did only the day before Tuesday." Symbolically and literally, by targeting the World Trade Center and the Pentagon, if not the White House, terrorists alerted us to our vulnerability. After September 11, Americans are not as likely to take national security and personal safety, indeed our entire American way of life, for granted in the ways we did before. Nevertheless, three examples suggest that it remains worthwhile to ask whether Americans are still taking too much for granted.

First, on Friday, September 14, President George W. Bush spoke at a service of remembrance and mourning at the Washington National Cathedral. He said that America's "responsibility to history" is nothing less than "to answer these attacks and rid the world of evil." What shall be made of rhetoric like that? To what extent do we Americans assume that we can rid the world of evil, even if we must and do answer the attacks? Americans are prone to embrace the view that we are an exceptional nation, different and better than others. As one who teaches about and believes in the American Dream, I know that view is not entirely wrong. If, on the other hand, we Americans uncritically assume that view to be simply true, then we very likely do so not only at the peril of others but at our own as well.

Second, Americans are hearing and saying, again and again, that we are at war. Thomas Friedman, another *New York Times* opinion writer, wonders if the United States understands that it is World War III that has begun. We will find out if he is right, although at the time of this mid-October writing, we are doing so in circumstances where the enemy remains ambiguous and difficult to discern. Nevertheless, if war is what we are in, and I think we are, then what do we assume about its nature and length? A war against terrorism cannot be simply about capturing the likes of Osama bin Laden or even, if we could do it, "obliterating" terrorists, as Richard Grasso, chairman of the New York Stock Exchange, put it when the National

Anthem accompanied the NYSE's post-attack reopening bell during the most patriotic start to Wall Street trading in recent memory. Neither capture nor obliteration can create the social and economic changes necessary to defuse the conditions that ignite terrorism. If we are really serious about bringing terrorism to an end, that struggle is likely to be much longer and deeper than we suppose. A just war against terrorism is a battle for hearts and minds. Therefore, it is likely to be unending.

Third, in the autumn weeks after September 11, news reports indicated that huge numbers of Americans attended religious observances. Invoking God became a national pastime as "God Bless America" replaced the traditional "Take Me Out to the Ball Game" during the run up to major league baseball's 2001 World Series. American religious rhetoric generally assumes, in one way or another, that God must be a kind of tribal deity who is on our side. To the extent that we Americans make an assumption like that, on what is it based?

The petitions of the Lord's Prayer include "lead us not into temptation, but deliver us from evil." Surely it may be too easily assumed that American policies and God's will are identical, which can lead to religious legitimation for all kinds of grief that we may inflict as well as experience ourselves. Taking nothing good for granted means not taking God for granted either.

Ferlinghetti got it right: In spite of the folly and corruption that "our fool flesh is heir to," the world remains a beautiful place. Taking nothing good for granted will be essential to keep it that way.

Fighting the Forces of Evil

Syed Ali Ashraf, "The Inner Meaning of the Islamic Rites: Prayer, Pilgrimage, Fasting, Jihad," in *Islamic Spirituality: Foundations,* edited by Syyed Hossein Nasr (Crossroad, 1999), 125–26

The primary meaning of jihad is exertion or use of effort, of which only a particular kind is identified with fighting. Even in this sense of the word, jihad means fighting in the Way of God against the forces of evil with life and wealth in order to make God's Way prevail on the earth and not fighting for any worldly cause. Sincerity and purity of motive and the condition of society must justify such an action. If anyone wants personal fame and glory, he is not a *mujahid,* a fighter in the Way of God. Someone asked the Prophet, "One man fights for booty, one for the reputation of fighting, and one for his quality of bravery to be witnessed: which of them is in God's Way?" The Prophet replied, "The one who fights that God's Word may have preeminence is following God's Way." The sincerity of the motive must also involve the degree of the fighter's love for God and the Prophet. A *mujahid* must love God, His Messenger, and striving in His Way more than his wealth, relations, and his own life. God says in the Quran, "O Prophet, tell them plainly, If your fathers and your sons and your brothers and your wives, and your near and dear ones and the wealth you have acquired and the trade you hold dear may decline and the homes which delight you — if all these things are dearer to you than God and His Messenger and striving in His Way, then wait until God passes judgment on you for God does not guide the wicked." All Muslims must be *mujahids* because they must resist evil individually and collectively. When the condition of society is such that there is danger of elimination of the faithful, then the faithful must try to resist the spread of evil through fighting with their works or their pen. If that is also not possible, then internally they should resist the evil and not allow it to conquer their hearts. The last alternative is to leave the land of corruption and go to some place where fighting in the Way of God may be carried.

Jihad, therefore, is a compulsory function of a Muslin for both internal and external fighting, and conquering the forces of evil. The test of this jihad lies in the sincerity with which the individual undertakes this task.

How Great Is My Inner Struggle

Abraham Isaac Kook (1865–1935), chief rabbi of Palestine, from *Abraham Isaac Kook*, edited by Ben Zion Bokser (Paulist Press, 1978), 377

How great is my inner struggle,
My heart is filled with an upward longing,
I crave that the divine delight
Spread through my being,
Not because I seek its delights,
But because this should be,
Because this is the true state of existence,
Because this is the true content of life,
And I am continually astir,
I cry in my inwardness with a loud voice,
Give me the light of God,
The delight of the living God,
The grandeur of visiting
The palace of the eternal King,
The God of my fathers,

To whose love I am committed
With my whole being,
By whose awe I am uplifted.
And my soul continues to soar,
To rise above lowliness, smallness, above boundaries
With which nature, the body, the environment,
    conformity
Surround it, confine it in bonds.

Evil and Necessity
David Birnbaum, *God and Evil* (KTAV, 1989), 94–96

With the creation of potential for good, which is required
for man to be able to reach his spiritual potential, potential for evil indirectly, but nevertheless, inexorably, came
into existence as a consequence.

> He [God] creates evil only insofar as he produces
> the corporeal element [good and existence] such as
> it actually is; it is always connected with negatives,
> and is on that account the source of all destruction
> and all evil. (Maimonides)

> I form the light, and create darkness; I make peace,
> and create evil; I am the Lord, Who has made all
> things. (Isaiah 45:7)

> There is no possible source of evil except good.
> (Aquinas)

> Evil has its source in the good. (Augustine)

> Without evil goodness would not be possible either.
> (Berkovits)

Man cannot quest for spiritual heights unless there is intense good to use as a "spiritual ladder." The creation of good, however, mandates the existence of its polarity, evil.

Good and evil form a duality. Creating potential for good, by definition, creates the inverse potential for evil along with it. Good only exists with its duality, evil. In order to create potential for good, potential for evil was, by definition, created. God's omnipotence or non-omnipotence is not the issue. It is rather a question of definition. By definition, good comes packaged with concomitant evil. . . .

Evil exists not (à la the Irenaean and Augustinian theodicies) because God necessarily had a productive need for evil to exist. Rather, it was in the Divine/cosmic interest for good to exist, and evil is the inevitable duality of good. Evil exists because dualities are inherent in the universe. In a world of active Divine intervention, gross evil is held at bay by the omnipotent intervening Divinity. In a world of lesser intervention, as in a world where the Divine is in a state of greater contraction of here-and-now omniscience, evil gains power.

In a world where mortals lower their "moral guard," evil has a chance to achieve "critical mass" and emerge with increased destructiveness.

Can Good Be the Cause of Evil?
St. Thomas Aquinas (1226–1274), *Summa Theologica,*
Part 1, Question 49, translated from the Latin by John Farina

We next inquire into the cause of evil. Concerning this there are three points of inquiry: (1) Whether good can be the cause of evil. (2) Whether the supreme good, God, is the cause of evil. (3) Whether there be any supreme evil, which is the first cause of all evils.

We Proceed Thus to the First Article:

Objection 1. It would seem that good cannot be the cause of evil. For it is said (Matt. 7:18), "A good tree cannot bring forth evil fruit."

Objection 2. Further, one contrary cannot be the cause of another. But evil is the contrary to good. Therefore good cannot be the cause of evil.

Objection 3. Further, a deficient effect can proceed only from a deficient cause. But evil is a deficient effect. Therefore its cause, if it has one, is deficient. But everything deficient is an evil. Therefore the cause of evil can only be evil.

Objection 4. Further, Dionysius says (*Divine Names,* chap. 4) that evil has no cause. Therefore good is not the cause of evil.

On the contrary, Augustine says: "There is no possible source of evil except good."

I answer that it must be said that every evil in some way has a cause. For evil is the absence of the good, which is natural and due to a thing. But that anything fail from its natural and due disposition, can come only from some cause drawing it out of its proper disposition. For a heavy thing is not moved upwards except by some impelling force; nor does an agent fail in its action except from some impediment. But only good can be a cause except inasmuch as it is a being, and every being, as such, is good.

And if we consider the special kinds of causes, we see that the agent, the form, and the end, import some kind of perfection which belongs to the notion of good. Even matter, as a potentiality to good, has the nature of good. Now that good is the cause of evil by way of the material cause was shown above. . . . For it was shown that good is the subject of evil. But evil has no formal cause, rather it is a privation of form; likewise, neither has it a final cause, but rather is it a privation of order to the proper end, since not only the end has the nature of good, but also the useful, which is ordered to the end. Evil, however, has a cause by way of an agent. . . .

We must know that evil is caused in the action otherwise than in the effect.

Reply to Objection 1. As Augustine says, "The Lord calls an evil will the evil tree, and a good will the good tree." Now, a good will does not produce a morally bad act, since it is from the good will itself that a moral act is judged to be good. Nevertheless the movement itself of an evil will is caused by the rational creature, which is good. Thus good is the cause of evil.

Second Article, Whether the Supreme Good, God, Is the Cause of Evil?

Objection 1. It would seem that the supreme good, God, is the cause of evil. For it is said (Isa. 45:5, 7), "I am the Lord, and there is no other God, forming the light, and creating darkness, making peace, and creating evil," and (Amos 3:6), "Shall there be evil in a city, which the Lord hath not done? . . . "

On the contrary, Augustine says that "God is not the author of evil because He is not the cause of tending to not-being."

I answer that as appears from what was said, the evil which consists in the defect of action is always caused by the defect of the agent. But in God there is no defect, but the highest perfection.... Hence, the evil which consists in defect of action, or which is caused by defect of the agent, is not reduced to God as to its cause.

But the evil which consists in the corruption of some things is reduced to God as the cause. And this appears as regards both natural things and voluntary things.... For the order of the universe requires ... that there should be some things that can, and do sometimes, fail. And thus God, by causing in things the good of the order of the universe, consequently and as it were by accident, causes the corruption of things.... The order of justice belongs to the order of the universe; and this requires that penalty should be dealt out to sinners. And so God is the author of evil which is penalty, but not the evil which is fault....

Third Article, Whether There Be One Supreme Evil Which Is the Cause of Every Evil?

Objection 1. It would seem that there is one supreme evil which is the cause of every evil. For contrary effects have contrary causes. But contrariety is found in things, according to Sirach 33:15, "good is set against evil, and life against death; so also is the sinner against a just man." Therefore there are two contrary causes: one of good, the other of evil....

Objection 3. Further, as we find good and better things, so we find evil and worse. But good and better are so considered in relation to what is best. Therefore, evil and worse are so considered in relation to some supreme evil....

On the contrary, the supreme good is the cause of every

being, as was shown above. Therefore there cannot be any principle opposed to it as the cause of evils.

I answer that it appears from what precedes that there is no one first principle of evil, as there is one first principle of good.

First, indeed, because the first principle of good is essentially good. But nothing can be essentially bad. For it was shown above that every being, as such, is good. And that evil can exist only in good as in its subject.

Second, because the first principle of good is the highest and perfect good which pre-contains in itself all goodness. But there cannot be a supreme evil, because although evil always lessens good, yet it never wholly consumes it; and thus, while good ever remains, nothing can be wholly and perfectly bad. Therefore, the Philosopher [Aristotle, *Ethics,* 4:5] says that "if the wholly evil could be, it would destroy itself," because all good being destroyed — which it needed to be for something to be wholly evil — evil itself would be taken away, because its subject is good.

Third, because the very nature of evil is against the idea of a first principle, both because every evil is caused by good. . . . and because evil can be only an accidental cause, and thus it cannot be the first cause, for the accidental cause is subsequent to the direct cause.

Those, however, who upheld two first principles, one good and the other evil, fell into this error from the same cause, whence also arose other strange notions of the ancients, because they failed to consider the universal cause of all being and considered only the particular causes of particular effects. . . .

Reply to Objection 5. Evil can only have an accidental cause. . . . Hence reduction to any per se cause of evil is impossible. And to say that evil is in the greater number is simply false. For things which are generated and corrupted, in which alone can there be a natural evil, are the smaller part of the whole universe. And again, in every species the defect of nature is in the smaller number. In man alone does evil appear as in the greater number, because the good of man as regards the senses is not the good of man as man — that is, in regard to reason. More men seek good in regard to the senses than in regard to reason.

7

For Thine Is the Kingdom and the Power and the Glory, Forever. Amen.

Healing and Hope

Divine Mercy at Ground Zero

**Fr. Benedict Groeschel, C.F.R., founder, Franciscan Friars of
the Renewal, and director, Office for Spiritual Development,
Archdiocese of New York, in the *Marian Helper* (Winter 2001)**

Most of us watched the television news with surprise and
horror as the Twin Towers of the World Trade Center
collapsed in flames on September 11. It was only a few
moments later that it dawned on us that there were still
people in the Towers.

How many? Most watching were like myself — we
vastly underestimated the numbers, which were not in the
tens or hundreds, but in the thousands. For those of us
who share a special regard for Divine Mercy through the
private revelations of St. Faustina and through the apostolic teaching of Pope John Paul II, this was another time
for mercy.

Here, in New York City, hundreds of clergy of all denominations turned out to help people cope with their

grief in the aftermath of the tragedy. Many of the victims were Catholic, and priests were especially busy. Our little community of friars from the Bronx was on the site every day from the start, offering spiritual support and first aid to the many rescuers and the few who were rescued. Among the rescuers, so many of the firefighters and police were particularly heroic.

In the midst of the tragedy, everyone was asking, "How could God let this happen?" I was so distressed that I did what I always do when I can't pray — I made the Stations of the Cross. There, at the first station, I found my answer. This station shows wicked and stupid men leading our innocent Savior to torture and death. God can and does permit great evil, even the death of His Only Son, in order to bring out of it a far greater good. All of us know that Jesus suffered and died so we could be saved. "When I am lifted up, I will draw all things to Myself," He tells us (John 12:32).

Yet many questions remain. And in such tragedies, behind the main question "Why?" there is a painful and often unspoken question: "Will they be saved?"

It is in the hearts of parents, wives, husbands, children, and other relatives of those who have died suddenly. Suppose they were not ready. Suppose, like so many, they were lackadaisical Catholics or had fallen away from the Sacraments. There was no chance for them to confess.

There are some answers to these questions. First of all, most of those who died had some time — perhaps several minutes before they left this world — to pray for God's mercy. Some called on cell phones and said goodbye to their dear ones. I am sure that the first priests on hand — like Fr. Mychal Judge, O.F.M., the fire chaplain who lost his life ministering to the dying — gave general absolution as soon as they arrived on the scene. It may have been the biggest general absolution in history. After all, this is exactly the kind of occasion that general absolution was intended for!

A Power Far Greater Than Sin

But, beyond this fact, there is God's unfathomable and inexhaustible mercy, especially for souls in the greatest need of it in just such a tragedy. That is why I am so moved by the beautiful conversations of our Merciful Savior with St. Faustina in which He addresses a sinful soul, a despairing soul, and a suffering soul, as recorded in her diary. These quotations have been collected, along with others, in the booklet *Conversations with the Merciful God*, which I highly recommend.

"My Mercy is greater than your sins and those of the entire world. Who can measure the extent of My goodness?" Jesus says in His conversations with a sinful soul. "For I descended from heaven to earth; for you I allowed Myself to be nailed to the cross; for you I let My Sacred Heart be pierced with a lance, thus opening wide the source of mercy for you. Come, then, with trust to draw graces from this fountain" (*Diary of St. Maria Faustina,* 1485). For those of us who are grieving or sorrowing the loss of a loved one or friend after such a tragedy, these words remind us that Our Savior's mercy is far greater than any sin humans are capable of committing. The fountain of mercy flows from His Sacred Heart pierced on the cross. It flows for our loved ones and friends, as well as for each of us.

Now some people will say, "But, Father, this is private

revelation and does not have the authority of Scripture." True enough. But it is a fact that God has made His mercy and His will known through private revelations any number of times in the history of the Church.

Frequently, these revelations have been given to simple peasant girls, ranging from Joan of Arc, who changed the history of Europe, to St. Bernadette and St. Catherine Labouré. Is it any wonder, then, that God should use a simple peasant girl from Poland, whom we now call St. Faustina, to share His message of mercy in our day?

Final Grace for the Unprepared

Yet, many of us will still wonder about the spiritual fate of those who were not prepared. How far will God go in offering them mercy?

Here, a crucial passage in St. Faustina's diary from Jesus' conversations with a despairing soul — the most unprepared of all — gives us reason to hope:

> Jesus: "O soul steeped in darkness, do not despair. All is not yet lost. Come and confide in your God who is love and mercy."
>
> In the soul arises this reply: "For me there is no mercy," and it falls into greater darkness, a despair which is a foretaste of hell and makes it unable to draw near to God.
>
> Jesus calls to the soul a third time, but the soul remains deaf and blind, hardened and despairing. Then the mercy of God begins to exert itself, and without any cooperation from the soul, God grants it final grace. If this too is spurned, God will leave the soul in this self-chosen disposition for eternity.

The grace emerges from the merciful Heart of Jesus and gives the soul a special light by means of which the soul begins to understand God's effort, but conversion depends on its own will. The soul knows that this, for her, is final grace and, should it show even a flicker of good will, the mercy of God will accomplish the rest." (*Diary of St. Faustina,* 1486)

We see that God in His infinite mercy pursues even a "soul steeped in darkness" that is falling ever deeper into despair. All that is needed for the soul to receive God's mercy is "a flicker of good will" as "final grace" is given. And this passage — admittedly from a private revelation — acquires more force when we see how it echoes Jesus' own powerful words of mercy in the Gospel. I'm thinking here of how Jesus Himself prayed for those who had committed the worst sin of all by crucifying Him, "Father, forgive them; for they know not what they do" (Luke 23:34). We also have the witness of Jesus forgiving the repentant Good Thief, Dismas, who was crucified along with Him. From his own cross, Dismas said to the Savior, " 'Jesus, remember me when you come into Your kingdom.' And He said to him, 'Truly, I say to you, today you will be with Me in paradise' " (Luke 23:42–43).

So, too, the prophet Ezekiel in the Old Testament tells us that God does not will the death of the sinner: "I have no pleasure in the death of the wicked, but that the wicked turn from his way and live" (Ezek. 33:11).

Our God is a God of Mercy in the Old Testament, the New Testament, and now in the Third Millennium — even on days like September 11.

The Final Apostle of Mercy

So, in the millionth of a millionth of a second between life and death, when time stops for the soul, Jesus Himself can certainly be His own apostle. He calls even to the despairing and hopeless soul. I believe that He does. If you place all hope of salvation on a person receiving the Sacraments, you put the salvation of the world in the trembling hands of the clergy. That's not very reassuring. Certainly, we must make every effort to receive the Sacraments as the normal means of salvation. And I do believe that those who died that day received general absolution. But what is far more important is that Jesus comes as His own apostle of Divine Mercy. He comes and offers "final grace" to the souls of those who are unprepared to die. All of us who are devoted to Our Savior and His urgent message of mercy need to spread this good news throughout the Church and among our non-Catholic friends. We need to say that ultimately the salvation of the world is in the hands of Jesus, and there is no place where anyone could be safer.

A Beautiful Day

John Garvey, Orthodox priest and columnist, *Commonweal*, October 12, 2001

On September 11, I heard that a plane had hit one of the World Trade Center towers, and thought it was a terrible accident; within minutes another place sliced through the other tower, and we all knew that it was not.

The light and air on the day of the attack were beautiful. I was reminded of a chilling passage in Endo's *Silence*. During the persecution of Christians in Japan a priest is told that unless he renounces his faith, those he has been serving will be drowned, one by one; and as they are dying, Endo makes a point of the fact that the day was beautiful. The birds sing, a breeze is blowing, the trees are lovely.

I live in eastern Queens. When I looked west down the Long Island Expressway I could see the horizon full of smoke. My wife called to say that she probably couldn't make it home from Manhattan that evening; the subways she needed weren't running. She spent the night in Harlem with friends. It wasn't an easy night to be alone, but I was glade she was safe. When I woke at night I heard an airplane, and knew it was a military plane. I realized that this was an unusual thought for an American to have.

A couple of days later the streets in our neighborhood were filled with the smell of burning and a haze that stung the eyes, blown in from lower Manhattan. I thought of the attention to breath that is important in meditation practice and wondered as I breathed not only what I was breathing in, but who. When I mentioned this to my sister she said, "There's something sacramental about that," and it is a dark truth.

The small Orthodox church I serve as pastor is usually full on Sundays. The Sunday following the horror it was packed. We were lucky, in a way; no one in our congregation was lost. But we do have members who know people who were. Almost any words said in the face of this sort of evil sound pale and trivial. All I could think to say was that while we can't help being obsessed by this mystery of evil, by the hardness of the hearts behind it, there was the heroism of the firefighters and rescue workers; there were the people who lined up to donate blood in such numbers that the system could not accommodate them; there was the fact that so many of those final phone calls, from the towers and from the planes, were not calls for vengeance, but final declarations of love; and while there are nervousness and anxiety on the streets, there is also a tenderness I have never seen before. Gandhi said somewhere that what we usually regard as history is a history of failures, a history of human beings behaving in disastrous ways; but the truer history of the human race is the daily fact of cooperation, help, and even love. That was apparent in many ways after the attack.

The Sunday following the disaster was, on the Orthodox calendar, the Afterfeast of the Elevation of the Cross. It occurred to me that on this side of the grave the cross is the most obvious fact: human beings suffer and die. It is not a small thing that while all the Gospels describe the crucifixion of Jesus, not one describes the Resurrection. This must be understood by faith. We are shown the empty tomb; we do not see him rising in glory. When he appears to the disciples at Emmaus the risen Lord appears as a stranger. There is nothing obvious about the Resurrection, nothing easily seen or grasped; the cross is all too obvious, and we can be stopped by it, we can think that this is all there is to life. Faith in the Resurrection does not cancel out what happens on the cross; the cross is its beginning. Archbishop Anastasios of Albania has said that the Resurrection begins in the cross, and this is where our faith must be, especially in a time when we are confronted with evil and hatred on such a massive level.

It is not, however, a faith that on this side of death everything will be all right. We know more than ever how small and vulnerable we are. And while the vulnerability can make us more tender, it can also make us want to strike out....

As I drove to church toward the end of the week, I saw a few planes in the sky and had two emotions at once: things are returning to some sort of normality; and I felt a deep foreboding, one I feel every time I see an airplane now. One woman in our congregation told me that she found it hard to pray after this horror. I thought of St. Paul's words about the truest prayer: the Holy Spirit prays in us, with groans too deep for utterance. That's how we are praying now.

To Mourn, Reflect, and Hope

Dr. Arthur Caliandro, senior pastor, Marble Collegiate Church, New York, sermon preached September 16, 2001

Stories. Each one of us has stories about Tuesday and what has happened since. We need to tell our stories. We need to hear each other's stories. We, ourselves, are stories.

Tuesday morning at 8:45 a.m., I got out of a taxi here at the corner of Fifth Avenue and 29th Street. I heard the sound of a jet plane flying very low overhead. I looked up. I didn't see the plane, but the sound struck me as odd, because one doesn't hear big jet planes flying low over Manhattan. It doesn't happen, but this day it did. I gave it no further thought and I went to my desk. Moments later, my younger son called me and said, "Dad, get to a television. A plane just hit the World Trade Center." As he was describing the scene, he said, "I see another plane coming. It hit the other building! What's going on? Something's happening?"

And it was. We've seen those pictures a thousand times since. For generations of Americans, things have changed permanently. For you and for me, things will not be the same again. America has changed permanently. Something has happened. For thirty years, as I would walk down Fifth Avenue and look straight ahead toward the very bottom tip of Manhattan Island, I would see those two gigantic buildings. And never did I see them without a feeling of awe and wonder that the human mind could create such mammoth, extraordinary structures. I never paused to calculate the immense human loss if all the people who worked in those towers ever became the victims of some attack or calamity. Even with rescue efforts underway today, we still have no way of comprehending just what the toll will be in human loss and pain. As I look back over the years, I recall that in the first building, building one, there was a restaurant on the 107th floor called Windows on the World. My wife and I would often go there, bringing friends and family members from outside of the city and state. Sometimes we would enjoy special celebrations there. We would look from the south, we would look from the north, we would look from the east, we would look from the west — and see extraordinary views. We felt as if we were seeing the entire world.

Those twin towers were the symbol of American free enterprise. They were a symbol of New York and a symbol for the United States.

They were important symbols, like the *Titanic*. But the *Titanic* has sunk again and with it, thousands of lives have been lost. It's a strange feeling now, coming down Fifth Avenue and not seeing those towers there. I'm still numb.

I'm stunned. Where do we look for meaning and answers when we've lost such an important symbol and when people we knew and loved are never going to return?

Time published a special edition on the attack on America, which arrived yesterday. They called those buildings "America's cathedrals." And now the cathedrals are gone. What do we do? Where do we go?

We can go to the wisdom of the ages, the Scriptures, the wisdom of the universe, the word of God. In the 46th Psalm we read: "God is in the midst of the city. The city will not be moved. God will help it when the morning dawns."

God is. God has been. God will be. Nobody can destroy the city when God is in the midst of it. We depend on the presence of almighty God. We believe in it and have faith in it. It is an unchangeable, immovable presence.

What else do we do? What must we do for ourselves? Primary, and important, and many people are not likely to do this, but it's essential for our mental health, the health of our communities, the health of the nation: we must take time to mourn and express our grief and our anguish. We must get deeply in touch with our feelings — the feelings of sadness, the feelings of terror, the feelings of fear, the feelings of anxiety. We need to get in touch with our anger. It is important that we get in touch with our feelings, and hold them up and honor them. We need to respect them and give them time and space to do their work. It's important to go deep and get in touch with them.

That is why, on Friday morning, I went to see a therapist.

"Arthur, how are you?" he said. "How are you handling yourself?"

"I'm fine," I said. But I knew inside that I wasn't, and he knew that too.

And then I told him how I had built a protective wall around my emotions. I had allowed none of the pain or anguish to get in. I had kept it all outside. I was protecting myself from hurt, from pain, and from feeling.

"Arthur, have you cried?" he asked me.

"No, not really," I said. "There were a couple of times when I started to, but I stopped it right away."

"Tell me about them," he said. "And as you do, cry."

And I said, "I got a call from out of state, from somebody very important to me, in whom I've invested so much of myself. We had become estranged. This person had even refused to take my calls. But that person called after the disaster and then when I heard that voice — 'Arthur, are you all right?' — I started to cry. But I cut it off."

"Cry now," he said. And I did.

"What was the other instance?" he asked.

"This was a strange one for me," I said, "but when I heard that two of the terrorists rented a car in my home-town of Portland, Maine, drove to Boston and came and did that dastardly thing, that got to me. There are two places that I feel that I belong, that I am passionately in love with — New York City and the coast of Maine — and both were involved, and somehow that got to me."

And I cried in his office. I learned years ago that it's one thing to cry by yourself, but it's very healing to cry in the presence of a significant other person. "How are you feeling now?" he asked.

"I feel sad — overwhelming sadness," I answered.

And he began to help me explore the sadness, and the

other avenues and tributaries of my life where sadness exists. I began to discover why these two incidents got to me. And he said, "Arthur, I hope you can stay in this place of sadness." And I have. The sadness is still with me, but identifying the feeling and talking it out have relieved some pressure.

Some of you may be feeling sadness. Others of you may be feeling something different. Many of you are feeling intense anger. You're enraged. That's a legitimate feeling. Let it be, and honor it. Only share it with a thoughtful person so that it doesn't get solidified and eventually become destructive. I have told you a part of my story. You have your story, your journey, your emotions. But please, go down deep, get in touch with the deepest feeling, and let it come out. And give it time. Give it space.

We go again to the Scriptures, to the wisdom of the universe. Jesus said: "Blessed are you who mourn." Better off are you who mourn, who grieve, who express your sense of loss, for you shall be comforted. And what He meant by that is, "You will be made whole again."

And then we know that Jesus, with a great reality check, also said, "In this world there will be tribulation, but take comfort. I have overcome the world."

Then He said: "In this life you will have pain, but your pain will turn into joy." What are we confronting when we deal with this horrific thing that has happened? We're dealing with evil. We're dealing with evil which is expressed with vicious hatred. It is anger gone mad. And when anger goes mad, when anger goes wild, it destroys.

If we were to know the personal histories of each of these terrorists, I'm certain that we would learn that somewhere in their lives, early on, they were rejected, they were hurt, they themselves were terrorized. And rather than work through the mournfulness and the grief of the emotions they, the victims, became the victimizers.

Victims become victimizers. This is a pattern that we all know happens again and again. When something bad happens to us, we go back and inflict the pain and the hurt on somebody else.

We have to stop the cycle. We cannot institutionalize an anger that has been rigidly formed in our hearts with bitterness and vengeance.

One of our deacons, who is present today, is a top executive at American Express, whose building was across the street from the World Trade Center. When the disaster happened, she evacuated her building, left everything there, and walked up to the church. When she entered a room where a group of staff had gathered, she began to sob. Later she and I went out for a sandwich, accompanied by two members of the church's staff. As we talked, we spoke about the dark side of the human being. Some of you remember Dr. Elisabeth Kübler-Ross, who spoke from this chancel a number of years ago. She wrote the seminal work on grief, *Death and Dying*. In her talk, she spoke about the dark side of humanity, and gave a name to it. She said, "Each one of us has a Hitler within," which means that each one of us has within us potential for evil, for hatred and destruction.

Our deacon, that intelligent, balanced, gentle, and sensitive woman, talked with us about the feelings she was dealing with. She told us that a number of years ago, when she lived in the Midwest, her husband had been murdered in an adulterous relationship. Justice had never been served, and she said that whenever she saw someone who slightly resembled the other woman, she was angry enough to kill. Anger can do such things to us. But we must be careful with our anger, and how to express it.

The other night, on CNN, Judith Miller, a writer for the *New York Times,* said, "We must be careful that we do not become the enemy we are fighting." I'm going to repeat that again: We must be careful that we do not become the enemy we are fighting. We must seek justice, but not with vengeance. We go again to the Scriptures, to the wisdom of the universe, to the word of God, which says: " 'Vengeance is mine,' says the Lord."

Our national leaders will be planning some kind of response. Let us pray that the cycle is broken and that the response is finding some way to locate these people and bring them to justice, and not to annihilate people as we have been annihilated. Jesus spoke to just this question in one dramatic moment of his life. He was being arrested the night before He died. As the soldiers were arresting Him, Peter drew his sword and cut off the ear of one of them. And Jesus sternly said, "Enough of this, Peter. Put your sword back. Enough of this." He was pointing to another way. And we have got to find that other way. With all of the darkness, with all of the nastiness and the horror and the sadness of this evil, we still see the greatness of the human spirit. We see extraordinary bigness. We see the wonder, we see the grandeur, we see the excitement, we see the beauty, we see the saintliness of human beings — the best of the human spirit.

The other night I was on a panel with Bill Moyers on public television. In the televised segment before our panel was on, Bill Moyers did a very poignant thing. He showed pictures of scenes of people in stress and pain. In the narrative was a litany: "We were coming down," said a man, "and they were going up. We were running out of the building. We were going for our lives, and they were going up. We were coming down, and they were going up." The ones going up were the firemen, and nearly every one of them went to his death. They responded to the call and became great.

Over the decades of time, when we have been needing greatness, God has lifted up people.... Today, in New York City, we have hundreds, if not thousands, of superheroes. They are ordinary people who, when all the others were coming down, were going up. I have hope, I have tremendous hope.

I saw one beautiful scene, reported on the news. It was tragic, but beautiful. On hearing of the tragedy, a chaplain for the Fire Department changed from his clerical garb into fireman's protective clothing and went down to the disaster area. As he was giving last rites to a dying fireman, he took off his cap. In an instant he was hit by falling debris and was killed. And the firemen around him picked him up, took him to the altar of a nearby church, and left him there as they went out to rescue others.

This is the beauty of the human spirit. The greatness of the human condition.

On Wednesday night, I participated in an interfaith service at Fifth Avenue Presbyterian Church, sponsored by the Partnership of Faith, a partnership of Roman Catholic, Protestant, Jewish, and Muslim clergy. There, at the altar of that church, Rabbi Ronald Sobel and Shaykh Ali, both of whom have been on this chancel and have preached in this church, were speaking together, in a brotherly embrace. They represent very different backgrounds. There has been so much hostility between faith groups, and yet those two men were together. I have hope, because I have witnessed the beauty and the greatness of the human spirit. We will rise again, and we will be a greater people.... And, Lord God, please, please, help us to love. Amen.

A Response to Despair

Lawrence S. Cunningham, John A. O'Brien Professor of Theology at the University of Notre Dame, September 24, 2001

When a colleague alerted me to the tragedy in New York City, I turned on National Public Radio to get some news updates. Late in the morning someone interviewed Billy Collins, the poet laureate of the United States. When asked what kind of poetry is suitable for such occasions, Collins said that one could do worse than going back to the psalms. That answer, I would suggest, is most apposite.

There is something to be said for going back to an old poetic tradition that has a running motif of asking (imploring? demanding?) God why evil falls on people and how people respond to such evil when God seems absent. That questioning in the psalms is never sentimental. After all, in the moment of his greatest desolation, Jesus cries out from the cross: "My God, my God, why have you abandoned me?" Psalm 22 goes on in the same vein:

> Why so far from my call for help
> from my cries of anguish?
> My God, I call by day, but you do not answer,
> by night but I have no relief.

Yet for every cry in the face of evil in the psalms there is always a response, an echo, that keeps the psalmist and his audience on this side of the edge of despair. The great alphabetical Psalm 37 has strophe after strophe in which the tension between the threat of evil and presence of God is always balanced with the assurance that evil never triumphs completely; is never a match for the goodness that wells up from God:

> Trust in the Lord and do good
> that you may dwell in the land and live secure
> Find your delight in the Lord who will give you
>   your heart's desire. (Ps. 37:3–4)

The psalms have the added advantage of having been tested over the millennia by those, Jewish and Christian, who have faced the calamities which evil people can rain down on the world. Those who do evil have their moment, they fade ("like grass they wither quickly / like green plants they wilt away," the same Psalm 37 says) into the memory house of history, but people still turn to the psalms for the assurance of the Good.

William Wordsworth, famously, wrote that poetry is "emotion recollected in tranquillity." When calamities strike we are often too close to the raw reactions they provoke to be able to respond in words; that is why we say that the events are "indescribable" or "beyond description." It is then that we can go back to language that has been tested by time and absorbed by use but still redolent of contemporary application. It is that precise need to express ourselves in that fashion which instinctively compels people to make the most ancient of gestures: create a spot that is sacred, festoon it with flowers, light candles, drape ribbons, scrawl messages, and tape up pictures.

In those moments we also draw on a vocabulary that demands that we hope and seek the sense of things and affirm our will to survive and thrive and resist the dark specter of despair. When I could no longer listen to or watch the news and buoyed by an outdoor Mass on our campus (Holy Communion was given to nine thousand persons) it was to that old Hebrew poetry that I turned. To the many people who e-mailed from various places I sent out snatches and lines as a better substitute for my own paltry attempts at saying what I felt:

> God is our refuge and our strength,
> an ever-present help in distress. (Ps. 46:1)

> Raise me up, set me upon a rock
> for You are my refuge. (Ps. 61:3a)

> All who call upon me I will answer;
> I will be with them in distress. (Ps. 91:15)

One could make a catena of such lines — lines to be repeated and taken to heart. If we could take into our being the sense of such sentiments we would both hold within ourselves the reality of evil and the firm conviction that evil never fully triumphs — that God stands out there in front of us beckoning us away from the night and towards the Light:

> May God be gracious to us and bless us;
> May God's face shine upon us.

> So shall your rule be known upon the earth,
> Your saving power among all the nations.
>
> (Ps 67:1–2)

Notice that the above prayer — some of the most famous lines from the psalter — is a yearning towards the future: "May God be gracious to us..." That sentiment is one that we need always to keep before us, said with the confidence that God will answer. And, God will.

Under Attack; Under God

Dr. M. Craig Barnes, pastor, National Presbyterian Church, Washington, D.C., sermon preached September 16, 2001

On Monday I planned to preach about something else today. On Tuesday I knew that for the first time in twenty years, I would have to change the sermon. A lot of things changed on Tuesday...probably more than we know. Whether or not the nation changes for the better in the days ahead will depend on our ability to see ourselves not only as a nation under attack but also under God.

Lord God, we gather this morning in churches all over the world, all of us more open than ever before to a holy word from you. Do now what only your Spirit can do. Speak into our souls. Amen.

As a pastor who has spent a lot of time in the emergency rooms of life, I am accustomed to the profoundly sad, numb feelings that arise from the soul in a crisis. All week it felt like the whole nation is in an emergency room. There is only one thing that we have been thinking about. Everything else, all other business, seems unimportant and even profane.

Like an anxious family stuck in the waiting room, we have had an insatiable thirst for news about what happened. "Have you heard?" we asked. "How did it happen? How bad is it?" Then, like a family that learns things are very bad, we know that we will never be the same again. We will recover, but the nation will never be the same again.

Sooner or later every individual ends up in the emergency room. Something happens that you were not planning on, something that permanently alters the plans you had. Maybe a loved one dies, a deadly disease is discovered, or a cherished relationship unravels. When that happens, you realize you will not leave the emergency room the same person you were when you entered. That is exactly where our nation is today. Wounded with a broken heart and certain only that things have changed.

As we leave the emergency room and make decisions about how we get on with life, let us remember that the nation is strong. It is strong enough to survive this atrocity. Actually, it is strong enough to do more than survive. It can become a different, better nation than we were on Monday. But that all depends on the choices we make in the days ahead.

The French philosopher Paul Ricoeur has written about the creative possibility of "limit experiences." A limit experience is an experience that is beyond the limits of normal life. It's the one you spent most of life avoiding, dreading, defending yourself against, like death and separation. Beyond the limits of those things, we think there's nothing but emptiness, loss, and anomie. But as Dr. Ricoeur reminds us, there is more. There is also God whose creative love knows no limits.

Watching enormous skyscrapers crumble into dust is beyond the limits of comprehension. It doesn't matter how many times we watch the video, it's still beyond comprehension. As is seeing a gaping wound in the side of the Pentagon. And imagining how men can be so evil as to crash full airplanes into these buildings. And understanding how thousands could so easily die on our own well-protected soil. It's all beyond our limits.

Be clear. None of that was the will of God. It was not a judgment against us, retribution for our sins, or God teaching us a lesson. Rather the will of God is always that evil be redeemed and not given the last word. That is why God can always be found at work beyond the limits of evil's destructive powers, waiting to bring us back to new life.

The greatest catastrophe of history happened not on Tuesday, but two thousand years ago when we crucified the Son of God. That was the ultimate experience beyond humanity's limit. But it was then that history was given the possibility of resurrection. When Jesus Christ defeated death, he did so that we may experience something beyond our limits — to rise with him into a new life. After every cross, the resurrection remains a possibility. The stone that covers the tomb is rolled back, but it is up to us to emerge as a new nation. It all depends on the choices we make.

If our choices arise out of a new vision of service and justice, if we now commit ourselves to something greater than collecting more and more personal wealth, and if we unite around our leaders and stop whining about how small a piece of the American pie they are giving us, then we'll emerge from this tragedy as a nation ready to fulfill its calling in the earth. But if our future choices arise out of fear, we might as well stay in the tomb.

Near the end of the week, I took a break from reading newspapers to look again at Tom Brokaw's popular book, *The Greatest Generation.* As I reviewed all of those wonderful stories of the World War II generation, I was struck by the ordinariness of the lives he was describing. No one in that war was born a hero. But as they were pushed beyond the limits they found something heroic in their souls they did not know was there. It wasn't that the hard times made the hero. Hard times are just hard. Heroes are ordinary people who refuse to be governed by fear when times are hard.

Is this not also what inspired us this week as we heard about ordinary men and women rising above their fear to overtake the hijackers, firemen sacrificing their lives in the line of duty, and rescue workers tirelessly digging through the rubble searching for survivors while buildings fell down around them? When you heard those stories, you couldn't help but ask yourself, "What about me? Could I do that?" It all depends on how you handle fear.

You don't have to wait until you're in a hijacked plane to find out if you can rise above fear. That was their moment. This is ours — the moment that follows the crisis. The moment we leave the emergency room to form a new spirit in this nation. If we are afraid, we will spend all our energy arguing over blame. We will waste this moment by retreating into a national fortress, and we will allow the terrorists to win by terrorizing us. But if we refuse to be afraid, we will unite this great country into a new creation that looks a lot more like the New Kingdom Jesus talked about. The soul of the nation can go either way, depending on how we respond to this moment.

This is not the first great hour of decision our nation has faced about its soul, and we are not the first nation to face it. But historically each generation receives only one opportunity. This is ours, and we dare not miss it.

The Bible reminds us that Jerusalem faced such an hour whenever it was attacked and threatened. Generation after generation struggled to rise above their fear and act like a holy, just people. Some generations succeeded. Some did not. This is what the psalmist was addressing when he wrote, "God is our refuge and strength, a very present help in trouble. Therefore we will not fear, though the earth should change...." Well, the earth has changed. For us, it changed last Tuesday. Whether or not the earth changes for good depends on where we go for refuge and strength.

If we believe as the psalmist says, "God is in the midst of the city; it shall not be moved," then we shall not be moved. "Though the earth change, though the mountains shake in the heart of the sea, though its waters roar and foam," we shall not be moved! Not because we are so strong or invincible, but because we take refuge in the God who is in our midst. When we can see that God is with us, then we know that even when we are pushed beyond the limits, God will be waiting there to lead us into a new risen life together.

"God is in the midst of the city." He is not sitting indifferently above and beyond the horrific destruction we witnessed this week. Perhaps you saw the television interview of the distressed woman who lamented, "Where was God when the planes crashed into those buildings?" I can answer that: in the midst of the city. He was in the offices that collapsed down upon each other as the towers crumbled. He was under the rubble where the dead and wounded lay buried. He was in the planes filled with terrified passengers that called to warn us of what was happening or to say goodbye to their families. God was in the midst of all that pathos. As the cross of Jesus Christ proclaims, God can always be found in the places of suffering. He is there not simply to comfort, but to lead us to resurrected life.

At the end of the fourth century when the city of Rome was being attacked by barbaric tribes from the north, St. Augustine was called upon to provide a theological interpretation of those days. In response he wrote a classic philosophy of history called *The City of God*. Augustine claimed that from the beginning there have always been only two cities in history. The city of self-love, and the city of God's love. One of these cities may be more visible, but they exist in the same place at the same time, and you have to choose to which city you really belong. Since the city of self-love is motivated by greed, it always eventually decays from the inside out. Every empire, every city of earth that prides itself on itself has not survived. But the city of God will always persevere, like the love of God in our midst.

What our society is deciding in the weeks and months ahead is which city we will be. Maybe for too long we have flirted with self-love. Maybe we have deluded ourselves thinking that we could each live for ourselves, or that the nation existed only to serve our individual needs. If this country is to survive, we will have to start looking like the other city. We have to start living for a holy purpose greater than ourselves and demonstrating the love of God to each other.

I can tell you we are off to a good start. Our leaders are weighing carefully the options for how we must proceed. Volunteers have come out of the woodwork, and people are waiting five hours to donate blood. Flags are everywhere, as if we have discovered we belong to a nation. Now it falls to the houses of worship to teach people how to pray again and live out of God's Word. And it falls to each of you to make a critical decision about the sacred purposes of your life. A nation is nothing more than the collective souls of its people, and this nation is counting on you to know how to live all your life under God.

I am not only calling you to nationalism or patriotism. I'm calling you to something even greater. I'm echoing the Bible's call to come out from the tombs, embrace the gift of life, and follow Jesus as he leads us into a future filled with hope.

O God, when we face an evil day that pushes us way beyond the limits of our experience, may we find refuge in your perfect love that casts out all fear, making room for heroes. Amen.

Where Do We Go from Here?

Cardinal Theodore E. McCarrick, archbishop of Washington, address at the Interfaith Prayer Service of Mourning and Unity, Georgetown University, September 13, 2001

The smoke has finally cleared away and the persistent fires, no longer burning. It was not the smoke that brought the tears to our eyes, nor the fires that moved our hearts to fear. It was the awesome, terrible loss of people we love, of neighbors we know, of colleagues with whom we worked, the tragedy of lives never finished, of pain and suffering never imagined.

We wonder about tomorrow. Will our nation change? Will it be a time of fear? Will the awful experiences of 9/11 turn our hearts to hatred and revenge?

This must not be. All that is foreign to the ideals and values of America. We must come back to that motto on which we built this great nation more than two hundred years ago. We must never forget that it is "in God we trust."

All our religions teach us the sanctity and dignity of human life. They all teach us to love God and each other. They do not — and cannot — teach us to hate or teach us to destroy or teach us to kill the innocent.

Then this must be our resolve for tomorrow. This must be the journey on which we all embark together. We will build up our trust in each other, we will teach our children that generosity is better than riches; that love of neighbor is better than power; that care of the poor and the down-trodden and the victims of injustice is the greatest of all pursuits and the one that pleases God the most.

It will not be easy. Those who hurt us must be brought to justice. Those who seek to destroy us must be made to realize that it is a dangerous and impossible adventure. But these lessons we will teach within the boundaries of our system of law and according to the precepts of our values.

We do trust in God as a people and as a nation. We know that He loves us and that He will see us through these dark days. We will overcome even this crisis. We have placed our hope in the Living God.

Bishop Meets Christ during Visit
to Pentagon Disaster Site

Tom McAnally, director of the United Methodist News Service,
September 17, 2001

United Methodist Bishop Joe Pennel saw symbols of all
that's wrong, evil, and sinful as well as symbols of that
which is good, just, and kind when he visited the Pentagon
Sunday, September 16. Most importantly, he said, he met
Christ.

"There aren't words for me to describe what I saw and
heard," the bishop said, "but I met Christ. We believe that
Christ is with the broken in a unique way and that Christ
dwells in suffering in a unique way. I felt the presence of
Christ there."

Pennel resides in Richmond and supervises the church's
Virginia Annual (regional) Conference.

After attending services at nearby Calvary United Methodist Church, Pennel said he spent about two hours at
the Pentagon site visiting with police and fire department
workers, Red Cross and military personnel, and others.
About 188 people are believed dead or missing following a September 11 attack, in which terrorists crashed a
hijacked plane into the Pentagon.

During his visit, Pennel was within fifty yards of the
damage. "The people working there were solemn, intense, almost reverent about what they were doing," he
said.

"I identified myself as being with the United Methodist Church and had prayers with various groups of
people," he said. "I listened and shared their pain. I visited with families on the fence overlooking the site. I was

there when body parts were being removed out of the wreckage."

The value of his visit, Pennel said, was simply that of being present. "They were appreciative that a bishop of the church would come and stand with them."

With emotion in his voice, the bishop said one man told him, "Bishop, I could not pray the Lord's Prayer this morning in church because I could not say that about trespasses." Another person said, "I'll shake your hand, bishop, but I'm mad as hell at God."

Though chaplains and other clergy are providing an important and meaningful ministry at the site, Pennel said he was compelled to visit it himself. "The Pentagon is within the bounds of our conference, and I felt that is where I needed to be."

There Are Children to Raise and Poems to Be Written

Alphonse Vinh, poet and writer, Capitol Hill, Washington, D.C., October 7, 2001

I still cannot speak of the recent horror, not fully anyway. Last week I read an article about the increased loneliness of New York's young singles in the aftermath of September 11. It said that in the week following the horrific attacks on America, people retreated into the womb of home. Pizza deliveries went up 17 percent. New York singles interviewed for this article explained the new desire to belong to someone, someone with whom they could share their feelings of grief, shock, and sense of vulnerability. Now we know how truly fragile the human condition really is, how fragile our own lives are, so easily snuffed out like a small candle by a quick breeze.

At work as a journalist I have dealt with this horror every day since the fateful events in September. Tonight I drank some wine and read from Jane Austen, Krishnamurti, and Ryokan.

Sunday was a glorious gift from God. This weekend I remained close to home and did not leave my beloved neighborhood. I left my home, which I call Mole's End, today and strolled down leafy East Capitol Street. A cool, sunny October day. Passing Capitol Hill Baptist Church, I saw several happy young couples leaving church. A tall middle-aged man jogged earnestly pass me. Little children played on the brick-laden pavement. Jimmy T.'s was filled with people enjoying a late breakfast. The American flag stood proudly inside the front window. I see American flags hanging from windows and from rods outside the handsome front entrances of Victorian houses.

And even as many of us continue to grieve and live in a fog of depression, we move on. Life is precious. There are children to raise and love, acts of mercy to be done, poems to be written, sorrowful people to embrace.

Late tonight I listen to some ancient Middle Eastern Christian hymns by the Lebanese contralto Fadia El-Hage. The sense of awe towards God is deeply ingrained in these long-ago love songs to the Creator of the Universe. It is good for us to retain within our hearts a sense of awe before God. America's war against men poisoned with hate has begun. We need all the awe and love we can muster with God's help.

The autumn roses flourish on the Hill.

I go back to rereading a poem by my fellow recluse Ryokan.

> In this world
> If there were one
> Of a like mind
> We could spend the night
> Talking in my little hut!

Playing for New York's Heroes: What It Means to Communicate Music

William Harvey, Juilliard student, letter to his friends in Indiana,
September 17, 2001, from the World Wide Web

Yesterday I had probably the most incredible and moving experience of my life. Juilliard organized a quartet to go play at the Armory. The Armory is a huge military building where families of people missing from Tuesday's disaster go to wait for news of their loved ones. Entering the building was very difficult emotionally, because the entire building (the size of a city block) was covered with missing posters. Thousands of posters, spread out up to eight feet above the ground, each featuring a different, smiling, face. I made my way into the huge central room and found my Juilliard buddies.

For two hours we sight-read quartets (with only three people!), and I don't think I will soon forget the grief counselor from the Connecticut State Police who listened the entire time, or the woman who listened only to "Memory" from *Cats*, crying the whole time. At 7:00, the other two players had to leave; they had been playing at the Armory since 1:00 and simply couldn't play anymore. I volunteered to stay and play solo, since I had just got there. I soon realized that the evening had just begun for me: a man in fatigues who introduced himself as Sergeant Major asked me if I'd mind playing for his soldiers as they came back from digging through the rubble at Ground Zero.

Masseuses had volunteered to give his men massages, he said, and he didn't think anything would be more soothing than getting a massage and listening to violin music at the same time. So at 9:00 p.m., I headed up to the second floor as the first men were arriving. From then until 11:30, I played everything I could do from memory: Bach *B Minor Partita,* Tchaik. *Concerto,* Dvorak *Concerto,* Paganini "Caprices 1 and 17," Vivaldi *Winter and Spring,* Theme from *Schindler's List,* Tchaik. *Melodie, Meditation* from Thais, "Amazing Grace," " My Country 'Tis of Thee," "Turkey in the Straw." Never have I played for a more grateful audience. Somehow it didn't matter that by the end my intonation was shot and I had no bow control. I would have lost any competition I was playing in, but it didn't matter. The men would come up the stairs in full gear, remove their helmets, look at me, and smile.

At 11:20, I was introduced to Col. Slack, head of the division. After thanking me, he said to his friends, "Boy, today was the toughest day yet. I made the mistake of going back into the pit, and I'll never do that again." Eager to hear a first-hand account, I asked, "What did you see?" He stopped, swallowed hard, and said, "What you'd expect to see." The colonel stood there as I played a lengthy rendition of "Amazing Grace" which he claimed was the best he'd ever heard. By this time it was 11:30, and I didn't think I could play anymore. I asked Sergeant Major if it would be appropriate if I played the National Anthem. He shouted above the chaos of the milling soldiers to call them to attention, and I played the National Anthem as the three hundred men of the Sixty-Ninth Division saluted an invisible flag.

After shaking a few hands and packing up, I was prepared to leave when one of the privates accosted me and told me the colonel wanted to see me again. He took me down to the War Room, but we couldn't find the colonel, so he gave me a tour of the War Room. It turns out that the division I played for is the Famous Fighting Sixty-Ninth, the most decorated division in the U.S. Army. He pointed out a letter from Abraham Lincoln offering his condolences after the Battle of Antietam . . . the Sixty-Ninth suffered the most casualties of any division at that historic battle. Finally, we located the colonel. After thanking me again, he presented me with the coin of the regiment. "We only give these to someone who's done something special for the Sixty-Ninth," he informed me. He called over the division's historian to tell me the significance of all the symbols on the coin.

As I rode the taxi back to Juilliard . . . free, of course, since taxi service is free in New York right now . . . I was numb. Not only was this evening the proudest I've ever felt to be an American, it was my most meaningful as a musician and a person as well. At Juilliard, kids are hypercritical of each other and very competitive. The teachers expect, and in most cases get, technical perfection. But this wasn't about that. The soldiers didn't care that I had so many memory slips I lost count. They didn't care that when I forgot how the second movement of the Tchaik.

went, I had to come up with my own insipid improsation until I somehow (and I still don't know how) got
to a cadence. I've never seen a more appreciative audience, and I've never understood so fully what it means to
communicate music to other people.

And how did it change me as a person? Let's just say
that next time I want to get into a petty argument about
whether Richter or Horowitz was better, I'll remember
that when I asked the colonel to describe the pit formed
by the tumbling of the Towers, he couldn't. Words only
go so far, and even music can only go a little further from
there.

The Arab Brothers
Thomas Zaunschirm, "Joseph Beuys and the World Trade Center,"
in *Neue Zürcher Zeitung,* September 19, 2001

In the face of world-transforming events the arts stay
mute. They neither announce them prophetically, nor
offer appropriate analysis. The fine arts have coped insufficiently with the detonation of the atom bomb, just as
novels have not delivered anything of literary merit on the
division of Germany or the end of the cold war. Nothing
can evoke the terror of September 11 more cogently than
the repeatedly shown, traumatizing TV images of the attacks by civilian planes on the World Trade Center and
the sudden collapse of the Twin Towers.

Yet such a historic catastrophe changes the way we
perceive art. One example is the three multiple variation postcards of the World Trade Center named "Cosmas
and Damian" (1974) by Joseph Beuys. One of the main

art of Joseph Beuys was healing. His
n expansive understanding of art, espe-
famous yet easily misunderstood words:
n artist." For Beuys, the greatest capi-
... asset is creativity. Through the creative process people
contribute their individual performances to society, which
may be seen as a "social sculpture." Viewing society
in those terms requires a series of conceptual changes.
Beuys's constant efforts to transform common materials
into new shapes and uses, seen in this context, take on
added significance.

A cold cubicle of concrete or steel might defy transformation and have to stand as immutable, dead forms.
But other substances, like insulating felt, copper wire, or
fat that melts when heated, are malleable materials that
can represent states of art without becoming symbols with
specific content....

During his first visit to the U.S. in 1974, Beuys performed his piece "I Love America and America Loves
Me" in the shadow of the World Trade Center. For him,
the Trade Center was a prime symbol of a view of capital that needed transforming through art. To do so he
used a familiar act. Pretending to be a magician, he trans-
formed the twin skyscrapers into two towers of fat to
symbolize changing the crystal cold system of "inhumane
capitalism," a "dead form," into the "creative capital of
social warmth." But that was not yet enough to effect
healing. So he decided to give the towers names. Across
the towers he wrote the names of the Arab twins, Cosmas
and Damian.

Legend has it that the two brothers were known for
their poverty and their healing. They went about doing

medical work and never taking a fee. They later were martyred for spreading the Christian faith and became patron saints of pharmacists and doctors.

Joseph Beuys died fifteen years ago, and his image of the healing twins had faded into the memory of his performance art.

The black and white world of fanatic fundamentalists has no room for therapeutic transformation. Because they presumably thought that Allah had been supplanted by money in the cathedral of global commerce, it became a target of their blind, destructive hatred. Suddenly Beuys's work has taken on a tormenting significance.

Music, the Soul, and Tragedy
Very Rev. Robert Giannini, dean, Christ Church Cathedral, Indianapolis, October 6, 2001

On September 11 Christ Church Cathedral filled in the early evening for an interfaith service of prayers in a time of calamity. We discovered again the power of art — specifically music — to move the soul. Cantor Sharon of Temple Beth El-Zedek chanted a Hebrew lament, and the music sunk into our depths. The singing of "My Country 'Tis of Thee" brought tears, and the final descant of the Boys' Choir as we sang "O God Our Help in Ages Past" helped us leave with a new sense of peace. On Friday the cathedral was filled beyond overflowing. The music we heard that stunning hour carried us from an awareness of sin and destruction (Bach) into communion (Frank) and through death to resurrection (Langlais).

Other music is available to us, also, music that may help define the contours of our own souls as we wrestle with the enormity of the shattered world in which we now live. My work in life is to deal with the soul, the deepest dimension of human existence. The following pieces of music, I believe, touch that dimension.

The first place to turn may be the Symphony No. 3 of Henryk Gorecki, the "Symphony of Sorrowful Songs." Perhaps many of you who know the piece already have found it a logical place to turn. Composed in 1976, this expansive symphony — hauntingly mournful — is an elegy for Poland's desecration by the Nazis during World War II. The symphony orchestra is joined by a soprano who sings the work's three songs: a late fifteenth-century lamentation, a folk song in one of the local Polish dialects, and a prayer by an eighteen-year-old woman inscribed on a wall in a Gestapo basement prison. It is the first place I turned in my grief for September 11.

Listen as well to Estonian composer Arvo Part's "Fratres" (Brothers). Here is a simple hymn played first by a string orchestra and percussion, and then repeated by a variety of combinations of instruments, including strings and harp, string quartet, cello and piano, and eight cellos. It is relentless in its increasing depth — "serenely contemplative, ending in a prolonged silence."

My turning to the Cello Concerto of Sir Edward Elgar, especially the adagio, would not surprise those of you who know my interest in the First World War. It is his lament for that absurdly destructive and stupid conflagration. Listening to it I always marvel at the remarkable effect that the war had on this man who, not long before the deadly guns of August 1914, had written a series of Pomp and Circumstance marches, still wildly popular today. If you do not already have a recording of this beautiful concerto I would suggest the one by Jacquelyn DuPre, a sprightly and energetic soul whose outstanding musical talent, and life, was cut short by the ravages of multiple sclerosis.

Charles Ives's masterpiece, the Fourth Symphony, like Elgar's concerto, is about the agonies of the First World War, and its discordant and chaotic textures are frighteningly descriptive in the aftermath of airliners slamming into buildings. It is a marvelous work, and although it asks the right questions — which way, America? — it can be terribly painful to hear. Turn, then, to a much more positive piece, Richard Strauss's "Death and Transfiguration," and in light of the sacrifice of the firefighters and other rescuers in New York, Beethoven's majestic *Eroica* (Heroic) symphony.

Since many of us have felt torn in all of this, at times not knowing what we were thinking or feeling or believing, we have a brother in Robert Schumann. His music, especially his works for solo piano, displays brilliantly the composer's own tendency to be torn apart and to seek resolution between contrary themes and ideas and feelings. One of the greatest musical geniuses of all time, Schumann was plagued with a disorder that ranged somewhere between bi-polarity and schizophrenia. His agonies, so honestly faced, make him a man for our time.

And there is Mozart, silly, light-hearted, wonderful Mozart. I particularly relish the Clarinet Concerto, the Clarinet Quintet, and the Oboe Quartet — but anything of his will do. In times of ugliness, creations of sheer and unabashed beauty will always be welcome. And that is Mozart.

Nailed to the Nexus of the Universe

John Farina, "Simone Weil and Loving a God Who Is Absent,"
October 18, 2001

There are few people in history who understood what violence and destruction could do to the soul more than the citizens of Europe fifty years ago. Millions were killed, ancient cities leveled, art treasures burned, civilians slaughtered and in some cases systematically exterminated by their own governments. In the ashes of World War II were born the seeds of postmodernism in literary criticism and philosophy, and the Death of God school in theology. Those movements were premised on a radical reexamination of meaning that came out of the cataclysm. The very idea of God and of universal values was questioned.

One woman whose life was shaped by that great conflagration was Simone Weil. Born in France in 1909, she died while still a young woman in 1943 while the war raged around her. A Jew, she went through allegiances to radical politics — a cause that drove her to enlist in the Spanish civil war against the fascists — agnosticism, and finally Christianity. She never entered the church and on her deathbed refused baptism. Yet there are few writers of the twentieth century who can match her understanding of how we can approach God in times of anguish.

Her essay "The Love of God and Affliction," written just a few years before her death, is a masterpiece of modern religious thought. The essay's premise is not God's presence, but his absence. Any easy confidence in the loving, protective presence of God that Weil might have known as a child had been obliterated by the thousands of tons of TNT and hundreds of corpses that haunted her memories. In such a world, one did not see God in the book of nature. The sunsets were obscured with smoke from a thousand blown-up buildings. One did not find God in the mind, in magnificent Augustinian schemes of how the Trinity was present in the memory, the intellect, and the will. Nor could one easily talk of ascending to God through his vestiges in nature and his image in the soul, as did Europeans like Bonaventure five centuries before. And any sense that bliss awaited one who would ascend the celestial hierarchy through the intellectual powers, as in the Pseudo-Dionysius, had been lost beneath the Blitzkrieg.

Weil's essay starts with an effort to find a way of talking about anguish beyond what one usually understands by "suffering." She used the French word *malheur*. Her first sentence assures us that *malheur* is distinct from simple psychological suffering. It is also different from physical suffering, although it usually includes physical feelings of discomfort. It is not humiliation, not simply fear or a feeling of powerlessness. The English word used by most translations is "affliction." I do not think it carries enough weight to the contemporary reader. I prefer "depression." Weil describes something very much like what we today call clinical depression. Listen to some of her descriptions of *malheur:*

It is quite a different thing from simple suffering. [All quotations are from *Attente de Dieu* (Paris: La Colombe, 1950).] It takes possession of the soul and marks it through and through with its own particular mark, the mark of slavery.

Malheur is inseparable from physical suffering and yet quite distinct.

Malheur is an uprooting of life, a more or less attenuated equivalent of death, made irresistibly present to the soul by the attack or immediate apprehension of physical pain.

Understandably this all "makes God appear to be absent for a time, more absent than a dead man, more absent than light in the utter darkness of a cell." That absence predictably horrifies a person who fears she is truly alone in the universe, open to evil at every turn. It is all the more frightening because *malheur* is most often brought about by the unjust, criminal acts of others.

But beyond that, *malheur* makes a person complicit in his own destruction. It injects the poison of inertia that impedes all efforts he might make to improve things.

Weil's description of depression thus far is remarkable only in its intensity. Her next description of depression is more noteworthy: "One can accept the existence of depression only by considering it as a distance." She goes on to tell us that God created beings capable of love from all possible distances. God even went so far as to share the experience of alienation from God with us. When on the cross, Jesus, true God of true God, called out: "My God, my God, why have you forsaken me?" at that moment he had taken on fully the human condition of alienation from God. Yet God could love his son even when he was accursed hanging on the cross bearing the culpability of sin, when he was as far as he possibly could be from God. This simultaneous tearing apart and reaching out in love, finding its way through the great distance, like a lone arrow flying into the cloud obscuring the holy mountain, are what characterizes creation at its most fundamental level.

> This tearing apart, over which supreme love places the bond of supreme union, echoes perpetually across the universe in the midst of the silence, like two notes, separate yet melting into one, like pure and heart-rending harmony. This is the Word of God. The whole creation is nothing but its vibration. When human music in its greatest purity pierces our soul, this is what we hear through it. When we learn to hear the silence, this is what we grasp more distinctly through it.

Recasting depression thus, Weil sees it as placing us precisely both at the greatest distance from God and at the nearest point to him. The love of God that the experience of distance creates is the love of lovers who, though desiring perfect union with one another, love one another so that they love the absence of the beloved more than the presence of anyone else.

At that moment of the realization of love in distance, both the pain and the ecstasy of love enter the soul. They penetrate it like the nails penetrated Jesus. If one can stay turned toward God even in the moment of great pain, one can be carried to the center of the mystery of God's presence to his creatures in this imperfect world.

> She whose soul remains turned in the direction of God while the spike enters it finds herself nailed to the nexus of the universe. It is the true center, not just somewhere close to it. It is beyond space and

time. It is God. In a dimension not owned by space or time, a distinct dimension, this spike has pierced a hole though all creation, through the thickness of the screen separating the soul from God.

Sustaining the Moral Surge

John Sexton, dean, New York University School of Law,
and president designate, New York University, October 15, 2001

A month has passed, the first commemoration has been held at ground zero, and Congress is about to declare September 11 a yearly National Day of Remembrance.

Surely it will be another date that will live in infamy; no law is needed to ordain that, and no law could change it. But September 11 was, and should be, something more. And after the devastation is cleared, new buildings raised up, and commerce and finance return — all critical to the prosperity of New York and the nation — the other great test will be whether we sustain the moral power surge which moved across the city and this country in response to the terrorist attack.

On one of the worst of days, we found the best in each other. Instead of being defined by the terrorists, as they had planned, we defined ourselves. I saw this moral surge manifest itself as our students and neighbors gathered for a vigil in Washington Square Park. One first-year law student from rural Georgia told how terrified he was that Tuesday morning, asking himself: "Why am I here?" Now he said, as he stood in front of the great arch that marks the square: "I have seen New York, my classmates, my community. How could I be anywhere else?"

Amid the outpouring of spirit in the days that followed,

we were all rescue workers, saving and affirming our humanity. Tens of thousands contributed their food, their money, their sweat, and their blood. Volunteers in record numbers were frustrated by their inability to do more. We all saw clearly the commitment of our police and firefighters, and we came to view them differently than we ever had before. Confounding past enmities even as he confirmed the strength of his leadership, Mayor Giuliani became a unifier and healer. We all reached out; we comforted; in the face of so much death, we gave a new and unforgettable life to the idea of community.

But the moral surge could recede, just as the good feeling during the blackouts of the past faded after the lights came back on. If so, the commemorations of September 11 would become just rituals of remembrance, the rebuilding just business as usual. So in the end, rebuilding structures is not enough; we have to build a renewed spirit of New York based on our values of freedom and tolerance, our vision of a diverse, open society — the true targets the terrorists were trying to destroy.

Each of us has a part to play. Universities like ours can and will provide scholarships for the children of the victims. We can and will create chronicles of this singular moment, to capture not just the horror, but also the affirmation that rose from the ashes. We can and will send witnesses, teams of students and faculty, into schools and communities across the country, sharing what they saw and felt here, and striving to convert the spirit of the moment into the spirit of an era.

But I also believe that whatever any of us does separately, all of us have to ask what we can do together in this transformative time. We are at a moral crossroads, and universities have a singular responsibility to shape the ideas that matter and to advance the creation of the future. As a first step, we at NYU will ask other universities and institutions to join with us this fall in convening a summit of cultural, financial, political, religious, and educational leaders. The purpose will be to begin an ongoing process, not just to rebuild physically, but to sustain and strengthen the moral surge. It is easy to celebrate the extraordinary response to this crisis. The real challenge is to make the unforgettable sense of community after September 11 more than a memory or a moment in time, but the new ground of our common being. Just as we may have a worldwide architectural competition to rebuild ground zero, so we must build on the moral underpinnings which the people of New York have shown the world since the attack.

We are the world's first city, not just America's. And the world is ready to hear from us, to respond, to join us in renewal. A French newspaper proclaims: "We are all New Yorkers." The Mayor of Rome offers to withdraw that city's bid for the 2012 Olympics in favor of New York, so the Games can open in the sight of the Statue of Liberty as a global expression of solidarity.

Societies live by stories. On September 11, the page turned and now we have to write a new chapter. We must make it the story of a continuing moral surge — and of a New York that truly will be the world's "shining city on a hill."

A Word from the Publisher

In the usual life of a publishing company, we don't ask ourselves the question of whether or not to write. By working in a business that deals in words written on a page, all of us have, in our own way, made a commitment to the value of words in the life of the human community.

Of course, since September 11, life has been anything but usual. Routine life, day to day, has become day-by-day life, where we cannot predict what will happen. In such a climate, speech can become difficult, because with news unfolding so quickly, the very moment words are spoken, they can become obsolete. What's more, because so many people are suffering so intensely, one wonders if speech is fleeting and even cruel — do we really believe that a few well-chosen phrases can describe the suffering or help alleviate the pain in people's hearts?

And yet, in the midst of this suffering, our world has seen a remarkable outpouring of words and, like seeing the familiar sunrise as though for the first time, people realize again how much language matters. In every New York neighborhood, entire sidewalk walls were covered with paper, inviting passers-by to share by writing. At the national level, as print media watchdog Cynthia Cotts observed, the major media maintained a remarkably high standard of coverage and analysis. And countless individuals from all walks of life committed their thoughts and questions to writing — beautiful, inspiring, heartfelt writing. As a people, we have sought to share these public and personal utterances. Most of us have sent or received notes recommending a particular story, reflection, or report. We add our own commentary and invite our friends to do the same. "Have you read...?"; "What do you think?"

And so, in the midst of suffering, when we might have expected words to become abstract and irrelevant, they are more vital than ever — reading has become an act of patriotism and faith. With the added help of the Internet, we passionately mail each other, taping stories to our refrigerators and cubicles and tacking them onto bulletin boards.

This volume is a collection of readings we offer for reflection and sharing. A book, like no other medium, can gather together the voices of the human family like candles of all kinds create the beautiful altars in the streets of Manhattan.

Index of Contributors

Abou El Fadl, Khaled, professor, UCLA Law School, 71

Abuzaakouk, Aly R., American Muslim Council, 208

Albacete, Lorenzo, professor at the Seminary of the Archdiocese of New York, 129

Ali, Muhammad, 40

America magazine, 187

American Baptist Churches USA, 37

American Jewish Committee, 48

American Muslim Council, 177

Anderson, Carl A., supreme knight of the Knights of Columbus, 25

Aquinas, Thomas, 236

Arab News, Jeddah, 8

Ashraf, Syed Ali, 233

Badawi, Dr. Zaki, principal of the Muslim College and Chairman of the Imams and Mosque Council of the United Kingdom, 37

Baig, Naeem, Islamic Circle of North America, 208

Bailie, Gil, president and founder, Florilegia Institute, 224

Barnes, Dr. M. Craig, pastor, National Presbyterian Church, Washington, D.C., 261

Birnbaum, David, author, *God and Evil,* 235

Bonhoeffer, Dietrich, German Lutheran pastor and theologian, 149

Bray, Libba, writer, Presbyterian News Service, 101

Brown, Most Rev. Tod D., bishop of Orange, 208

Buddhist Association (USA), 169

Burnham, Revd. Anthony, Free Churches moderator, 37

Bush, George W., 174

Caldecott, Stratford, co-director of the Centre for Faith & Culture, Oxford, England, 228

Caliandro, Dr. Arthur, senior pastor, Marble Collegiate Church, New York, 250

Canadian Catholic Bishops, 24

Carey, Dr. George, archbishop of Canterbury, 37

Carroll, Vincent, editor, *Rocky Mountain News,* 79

Catholic Bishops, Canadian, 24

Catholic Bishops, U.S., 22, 207

Catholic Family and Human Rights Institute, 198

Christiansen, Drew, S.J., senior fellow, Woodstock Theological Center, 58

Colombani, Jean-Marie, *Le Monde,* 5

Cunningham, Lawrence S., John A. O'Brien Professor of Theology at the University of Notre Dame, 258

Dalai Lama, 168

Dostoevsky, Fyodor, 227

Eaton, Charles le Gai, 209

Edgar, Dr. Robert W., National Council of Churches, 45

Edwards, Revd. Joel, general director of the Evangelical Alliance, 37

Egan, Cardinal Edward, archbishop of New York, 21

Elizabeth II, queen of England, 10

Elshtain, Jean Bethke, Laura Spellman Rockefeller Professor of Social and Political Ethics at the University of Chicago Divinity School, 41

Episcopal Church, USA, 27

Episcopal Diocese of Indianapolis, 199

Evans, Rev. Dr. John Clinton, interim pastor, Madison Avenue Presbyterian Church, New York, 118

Falwell, Jerry, senior pastor, Thomas Road Baptist Church, Lynchburg, Virginia, 126

Farina, John, 280

Ferrara, Peter, professor, George Mason University School of Law, senior fellow, Hudson Institute, 3

Fiorenza, Most Reverend Joseph A., president, United States Council of Catholic Bishops, 24

Florilegia Institute, 224

Garvey, John, Orthodox priest and columnist for *Commonweal,* 247

Giannini, Very Rev. Robert, dean, Christ Church Cathedral, Indianapolis, 277

Giuliani, Rudolph W., mayor of New York, 182

Gomez, Most Rev. Jose, auxiliary bishop of Denver, 110

Granberg-Michaelson, Rev. Wesley, Reformed Church of America;, 45

Griswold, The Most Rev. Frank T., presiding bishop, Episcopal Church, USA, 27

Groeschel, Fr. Benedict, C.F.R., founder of the Franciscan Friars of the Renewal, 242

Harvey, William, Juilliard student, 272

Herder, Hermann, 217

Hijackers' Prayer, 226

Jarjour, Rev. Dr. Riad, general secretary, Middle East Council of Churches, 36

Jensen, Rt. Rev. Dr. Peter, Anglican archbishop of Sydney, Australia, 29

Jerusalem Post, 155

John Paul II, 15, 17, 204

Johnson, Paul, historian and journalist, 158

Jones, John N., 210

Khamenei, Ayatollah, Iranian spiritual leader, 53

Khoury, Dr. Nuha, International Center of Bethlehem, 12

Kook, Abraham Isaac, chief rabbi of Palestine, 234

Krause, Bishop Dr. Christian, president, Lutheran World Federation, 39

Lapin, Rabbi Daniel, president, Toward Tradition, Seattle, Washington, 221

Le Moignan, Revd. Christina, president of the Methodist Conference, 37

Le Monde, 5

Lerner, Rabbi Michael, editor, *Tikkun* magazine, 136

Lutheran World Federation, 39

Maharaji, 48

Marty, Martin E., Fairfax M. Cone Distinguished Service Professor Emeritus, University of Chicago Divinity School, 163

McAnally, Tom, director of United Methodist News Service, 269

McCarrick, Cardinal Theodore E., archbishop of Washington, D.C., 267

Mead, Rev. Andrew C., rector, St. Thomas Church Fifth Avenue in the City of New York, 113

Middle East Council of Churches, 34

Mohammed, Imam W. D., Muslim American Society, 208

Morrow, Lance, staff writer, *Time* magazine, 152

Murphy-O'Connor, Cardinal Cormac, archbishop of Westminster, 37

Nagashima, Daniel, general director, USA Buddhist Association, 169

National Association of Evangelicals, 30

Neuhaus, Rev. Richard John, publisher, *First Things Magazine,* 194

Noko, Rev. Dr. Ishmael, general secretary, Lutheran World Federation, 39

Novak, Michael, George F. Jewett Scholar at the American Enterprise Institute, 63

Observer, The (London), 49

Perry, Pastor Cecil, president, British Union Conference of the Seventh-day Adventist Church, 38

Polish, Rabbi Daniel F., director of the Commission on Social Action of Reform Judaism, 143

Pollard, Miriam, O.C.S.O., Trappistine nun of Santa Rita Abbey, Sonoita, Arizona, 202

Presbyterian News Service, 101

Putin, Vladimir, president of Russia, 11

Raheb, Revd. Dr. Mitri, pastor of Christmas Lutheran Church – Bethlehem, 12

Raiser, Rev. Dr. Ronald, general secretary, World Council of Churches, 170

Reese, Thomas, S.J., editor, *America* magazine, 187

Roberts, Robert H., interim general secretary, American Baptist Churches USA, 37

Robertson, Pat, president, Christian Broadcasting Network, 122

Roth, John K., Russell K. Pitzer Professor of Philosophy at Claremont McKenna College, Claremont, California, 230

Ruse, Austin, president, Catholic Family and Human Rights, 198

Rushdie, Salman, British novelist and author of *The Satanic Verses,* 75

Sabbah, Michel, Latin patriarch of Jerusalem, 31

Sacks, Professor Jonathan, chief rabbi of the United Hebrew Congregations of the Commonwealth, 37

Saghiyeh, Hazem, columnist for the Arabic newspaper *al Hayat,* 55

Said, Edward, *The Observer* (London), 49

Saperstein, Rabbi David, Religious Action Center of Reform Judaism, 46

Schneider, Reinhold, vii

Seventh-day Adventist Church, 38

Sexton, John, dean, New York University School of Law, and president designate, New York University, 284

Siddiqi, Dr. Muzammil H., Islamic Society of North America, 208

Sider, Dr. Ron, Evangelicals for Social Action, 46, 165

Singer, Saul, *Jerusalem Post,* 155

Skillen, James, president, Center for Public Justice, Annapolis, Maryland, 127

Sobhani, S. Rob, adjunct professor, Georgetown University, 178

Sullivan, Andrew, contributing writer, *New York Times Magazine,* 83

Syeed, Dr. Sayyid M., Islamic Society of North America, 208

Thomas Aquinas, 236

Tikkun magazine, 136

Time magazine, 55, 152

Toward Tradition, Seattle, Washington, 221

United Nations, 14

Vatican Council, 204

Vinh, Alphonse, poet and writer, 270

Wallis, Rev. Jim, Call to Renewal and Sojourners, 45

Waynick, Rev. Catherine M., bishop of the Episcopal Diocese of Indianapolis, 199

Weigel, George, senior fellow of the Ethics and Public Policy Center, Washington, D.C., 190

Weil, Simone, French philosopher and mystic, 280

Wiesel, Elie, author, *The Trial of God,* 150

Wiesner, Gerald, O.M.I., president, Canadian Conference of Catholic Bishops, 25

Witham, Larry, *Washington Times,* 98

World Council of Churches, 170

Zaunschirm, Thomas, *Neue Zürcher Zeitung,* 275